THE LIBERTY WE SEEK

THE LIBERTY
WE SEEK

Loyalist Ideology
in
Colonial New York and Massachusetts

JANICE POTTER

HARVARD UNIVERSITY PRESS
Cambridge, Massachusetts
and London, England
1983

Publication of this book has been aided by a grant from the
Andrew W. Mellon Foundation

This book is printed on acid-free paper, and its binding materials have
been chosen for strength and durability.

Library of Congress Cataloging in Publication Data
Potter, Janice, 1947–
    The liberty we seek.

    Includes index.
        1. American loyalists—New York (State)   2. New York
(State)—Politics and government—Revolution, 1775–1783.
3. American loyalists—Massachusetts.   4. Massachusetts
—Politics and government—Revolution, 1775–1783.
I. Title.
E277.P67 1983   973.3'14   82–21165
ISBN 0–674–53026–8

To my husband, Peter MacKinnon

PREFACE

ON MARCH 17, 1776, the British army evacuated Boston. About 170 small but heavily laden sailing vessels protected by three men-of-war sailed out of the harbor in one of the largest fleets ever seen in America. On board the ships destined for Halifax, Nova Scotia, were approximately a thousand Loyalists. Many had fled to Boston to escape the harassments of the Patriots who controlled the Massachusetts countryside. When British authorities had decided that Boston was indefensible, Loyalists in the blockaded city were given less than five days to prepare for their departure, and most took with them only whatever personal property they could carry. Some had abandoned valuable land and magnificent houses; virtually all were leaving behind close friends and relatives.

The British retreat from Boston was dwarfed by the evacuation, seven years later, of New York, which since its capture by the British in late 1776 had served as a haven for Loyalists seeking the protection of the British army. In 1783 about 28,000 Loyalists left the city for various parts of what is now Canada. Refugees and their belongings crowded the docks as the spring fleet was loading for Nova Scotia. Added to those who left on British ships were an unknown number who traveled overland through the wilderness of northern New York to the British colony of Quebec. The exodus ended, in a formal sense at least, on a clear but cold November 23, when the British turned the city over to American authorities. For most Loyalists this last act was merely a formality; they had known for months that the war was over, that the peace had been signed, and that they were the losers.

Loyalists from New York, Massachusetts, and other colonies had been as deeply attached to America as the Patriots, and most who left did so because of necessity, not choice. The American Revolution was a civil war in which Americans were deeply divided over fundamental issues. Loyalist and Patriot writers differed in their views of the British-American empire, in their ideas about contemporary American society, and in their basic intellectual assumptions.

Historians have long accepted the fact that the Patriots provided a logical, coherent, and compelling case to support independence and republicanism. But the same recognition has not been given to Loyalist ideology. Though there have been several recent studies of various aspects of Loyalist thought, none explains fully the complexities and roots of the ideology. Bernard Bailyn's *The Ordeal of Thomas Hutchinson* is a superb study of one very prominent Loyalist, but Bailyn does not make any general conclusions from his study of Hutchinson. Neither does John Ferling in *The Loyalist Mind: Joseph Galloway and the American Revolution*, nor Anne Zimmer in *Jonathan Boucher: Loyalist in Exile*. Leonard Labaree's *Conservatism in Early American History* contains many insights into the conservative mentality of the Loyalists, but it is not a comprehensive analysis of their ideas and the origins of their ideology. The same is true of William Nelson's *The American Tory*, which was written before recent work was done on radical Whig ideology. Moreover, Nelson stresses the irrelevance of Loyalist ideas to mid-eighteenth-century American society, a contention I dispute here. The most comprehensive book about Loyalism is Robert Calhoon's *The Loyalists in Revolutionary America, 1760-1781*. Calhoon examines the writings of Loyalists of all shades of opinion and from all regions; he describes three different kinds of Loyalist thought but does not reconcile them with each other to provide a systematic overview.

My book seeks to fill the need for a clear statement of Loyalist ideas. Its aim is to show that there was an ideology common to Loyalists from different backgrounds and regions. This thought was rooted in the British and colonial past and was also relevant to at least some concerns of contemporary Americans. The term "ideology" is used in two senses. It means, on one level, the argument made by Loyalist writers rejecting American independence and republicanism and supporting the British Empire and British institutions. This argument merits definition as an ideology because it was a comprehensive, logical, and consistent alternative to Patriot proposals. It included a perceptive anti-Patriot interpretation of the Revolution, a critical analysis of contemporary American politics, and a unique vision of the Anglo-American empire. On a less explicit level, ideology consists of an individual's fundamental assumptions about such issues as the nature of liberty or the role of government in a society. In this sense also, Loyalist writers shared a common ideology that distinguished them from Patriot leaders.

The emphasis in this study is on the public appeal of the Loyalists rather than on their private thoughts; I have relied more on widely read sources such as pamphlets, broadsides, and newspapers than on private papers. By singling out writers from two colonies — New York and Massachusetts — I have been able to examine in greater detail local controversies in the 1760s and early 1770s which laid the foundations for Loyalist ideas. But the ideology outlined here was not restricted to a small group; it was part of a more general statement of ideas. I chose to focus on Massachusetts and New York in part because they were so dissimilar and because the Loyalist spokesmen in the two colonies had virtually no contact with each other. It is most significant, then, that a common ideology crystallized in the two colonies at the same time and through the same media, despite the differences in the societies and the lack of any obvious means by which these writers could have worked out a common response to the Revolution. Moreover, many of the ideas expressed by New York and Massachusetts Loyalists were shared by leading Loyalists from other colonies. Evidence of this can be found in recent biographies of Loyalists from other colonies and in more general studies of their ideas, such as Robert Calhoon's work.

One reason for the common ideology was that Loyalists from different parts of America relied on the same reservoir of colonial and British ideas. Prominent eighteenth-century British theorists shared their views about the imperial relationship and their more conservative ideas about the nature of man and the role of government. Moreover, in local disputes in Massachusetts, New York, and other colonies in the 1760s and early 1770s there emerged a critique of colonial society that differed significantly from the one later used by the Patriots. And this analysis of colonial society provided an interpretation of American problems which was fundamentally at odds with that of the Patriots. Thus the ideological division between the two groups was deep, and it was only to be expected that some Loyalists would become refugees after the defeat of their cause and their ideology.

I WOULD LIKE to thank the Canada Council and the Killam Research Program for financial support while I was researching and writing this book. I am indebted to several people for their advice and encouragement. George A. Rawlyk of Queen's University at Kingston has been a conscientious, stimulating, and extremely perceptive adviser as well as a very good friend. Robert M. Calhoon of the University of North Carolina at Greensboro shared ideas with me, pointed me to key sources, and was most helpful and thoughtful. J. Michael Hayden of the University of Saskatchewan displayed a keen editor's eye in recommending revisions; for this, as well as his encouragement and sense of humor, I am very grateful. Patricia U. Bonomi of New York University made a significant contribution to this work through her astute criticisms of its structure and organization and her very valuable ideas about its content. Elizabeth Suttell, senior editor at Harvard University Press, was most helpful and encouraging. The skill of manuscript editor Peg Anderson was greatly appreciated. My greatest debt of gratitude is one that cannot be measured or defined: it is to my husband, Peter MacKinnon.

CONTENTS

Treating all men as mortal foes,
Who dare their high behests oppose.
Stark raving mad, with party rage,
With coward arms, those foes engage,
. . . Dares the poor man impartial be,
He's doom'd to want and infamy . . .
Sees all he loves, a sacrifice,
If he dares publish, ought — but lies.
. . . Alas, vain men, how blind, how weak;
Is this the liberty we seek!
Alas, by nobler motives led
A Hampden fell, a Sydney bled.

Rivington's Gazetteer, December 8, 1774

1

LOYALIST WRITERS, THE MEDIA, AND THE MESSAGE

When I became satisfied, that many innocent, unsuspecting persons were in danger of being seduced to their utter ruin, and the province of Massachusetts Bay in danger of being drenched with blood and carnage, I could restrain my emotions no longer; and having once broke the bands of natural reserve, was determined to probe the sore to the bottom, though I was sure to touch the quick.

—[DANIEL LEONARD], *Massachusettensis*,
JANUARY 9, 1775

THAT LOYALISTS were evacuated from Massachusetts at the beginning of the Revolution and from New York at the end indicates much about the nature of the Revolution in these two colonies. Massachusetts spearheaded the Revolutionary movement by establishing extraconstitutional committees and congresses, by using violence to protest the importation of East India tea, and by advocating resistance to the Coercive Acts. The polarization between supporters and opponents of these actions began earlier in Massachusetts than in other colonies. There were few Loyalists there, and most refugees left before the Declaration of Independence.[1]

New York, in contrast, had more Loyalists than any other colony and was most reluctant in its support of independence. When fighting between British troops and Massachusetts militiamen began in the spring of 1775, the political situation in New York was confused and indefinite. Revolutionary committees functioned alongside the legally established colonial government, and some future Loyalists were still participating in these extralegal committees in the hope that a reconciliation with Britain was possible. External events and pressures were influential in persuading New Yorkers to support independence.[2]

1

These differing responses to the Revolution reflected dissimilarities in the two societies. Massachusetts had been settled in the 1630s by Puritans, who had escaped from religious persecution in England to establish an ideal society in the New World which would be a model for others to follow. Despite changes in the late seventeenth and eighteenth centuries, Massachusetts retained a certain idealism, sense of mission, and moral purpose; by the mid-eighteenth century there was an awareness of its own special provincial identity. Massachusetts' Puritan heritage was also reflected in its political culture. The Puritan ideal of an organic society in which deferential citizens were united in a covenant-like relationship with public-spirited leaders persisted into the eighteenth century, even though the ideal was often at odds with political reality. Another widely accepted belief was that the community should be knit together by the bonds of consensus, achieved at the local level at the town meeting, so that unity, harmony, and order would prevail.[3]

New York, on the other hand, had been Dutch until 1664 and was the most polyglot of all the colonies. It was an ethnic mosaic of Dutch, English, Scottish, Indian, German, French, Swedish, and Jewish communities and was religiously diverse, including Anglicans, Presbyterians, Quakers, Moravians, French Calvinists, and members of the Dutch Reformed Church. While Massachusetts colonists might claim that their ancestors had come to North America to seek refuge from religious persecution in England, New Yorkers of Huguenot or German Palatinate ancestry could point out that their forefathers had fled to England in search of religious freedom. "The destruction of Old England would hurt me," wrote the New York Patriot John Jay, whose ancestry was French and Dutch. "I wish it well. It afforded my ancestors an asylum from persecution."[4] Because of its ethnic and religious diversity as well as its regional and economic divisions, New York had no common, overriding sense of identity comparable to that of Massachusetts. Instead, New Yorkers had worked out a pragmatic tolerance of diversity over the years to meet practical considerations, such as development of the colony's commercial potential. The diversity of interest groups in New York also added a peculiar flavor to its political culture. Rival factions and interest groups vied with each other for political advantage, giving the colony a reputation for factiousness and volatility.[5]

The backgrounds of the most prominent Loyalist writers in New York and Massachusetts also showed significant dissimilarities. In New York the core of Loyalist writers whose identity was known were Anglican clergymen, the most skillful and widely read of whom was Samuel Seabury. Scion of an old New England family, a Yale graduate, and an Anglican rector Seabury was a part-time teacher, physician, and farmer, a man of literary talents and an ardent pamphleteer. In his most popular pamphlet Seabury, posing as a simple but blunt farmer, used a direct and hard-hitting style to lash out at the first Continental Congress and its actions. He wrote in contemptuous terms of "Our Sovereign Lords and Masters, the High and Mighty Delegates, in Grand Continental Congress," and virtually seethed as he spat out the epithet, "Our sovereign Lord the Mob."[6] He alternated satire and wit with practical, commonsensical advice, couching his argument in the earthy and direct language of the farmer.[7]

Seabury's example was followed by other Anglican clergymen. Charles Inglis and Thomas Bradbury Chandler collaborated with Seabury in the 1760s to produce a spirited defense of the Anglican church, and in the mid-1770s both became Loyalist pamphleteers. Author of a very able response to Thomas Paine's *Common Sense*, Inglis was then assistant rector of Trinity Church in New York and later bishop of Novia Scotia.[8] Originally a New England Congregationalist, Chandler was a convert to Anglicanism and a scholar; he held doctorate of divinity degrees from Oxford and from King's College, New York, and he wrote eight books as well as the four Loyalist pamphlets of 1774 and 1775.[9] Chandler's impressive scholarly credentials were matched by those of Myles Cooper, graduate of Queen's College, Oxford, and president of King's College, New York, an institution he saw as an Oxford in the New World, which was renowned for its academic excellence as well as its commitment to loyalty and the established order. Cooper wrote one pamphlet and worked with a professor of King's College, John Vardill, to produce a series of articles on the British-American crisis.[10] Another Anglican associated with these Loyalists was Isaac Wilkins, who was born in Jamaica but educated in New York. Besides writing a Loyalist pamphlet, Wilkins, as an assembly representative for Westchester County, made an impassioned speech, which was published, supporting the unity of the British Empire.[11]

While the core of Loyalist spokesmen in New York were Anglican clergymen, in Massachusetts the inner circle of writers was made up of royal officeholders. Jonathan Sewall was an able courtroom lawyer, attorney general, and member of a distinguished though impoverished Massachusetts family. Sewall, a seasoned polemicist, had defended the administrations of governors Francis Bernard and Thomas Hutchinson in the 1760s and early 1770s, a role that he continued in his extensive writing for the Loyalist side in the mid-1770s.[12] Significant contributions were also made by various members of Massachusetts' most distinguished political families, the Hutchinsons and Olivers, who were linked by ties of marriage and of office. At the time of the Revolution Thomas Hutchinson was governor of Massachusetts, Andrew Oliver was lieutenant governor, and Peter Oliver was chief justice. All were active Loyalist partisans.[13] Two less prominent writers were Harrison Gray, treasurer of Massachusetts, and Brigadier Timothy Ruggles, a delegate to the Stamp Act Congress who opposed some of the Congress's resolutions and later, in the mid-1770s, organized a Loyalist Association.[14] Another royal officeholder, Daniel Leonard, was by far the most widely read Loyalist writer in Massachusetts. He was the author of *Massachusettensis*,[15] seventeen letters published widely in Massachusetts, New York, and London, in 1774, 1775, and 1776.[16] John Adams, the Massachusetts Patriot, recalled returning to Boston in late 1774 to find *Massachusettensis* shining among other anti-Patriot pieces "like the moon among the lesser stars."[17] Since Leonard's aim was to trace the historic origins and contemporary manifestations of the "distemper" which plagued his colony,[18] he provided a comprehensive and sophisticated overview of the Revolution from the Loyalist point of view. He also wrote cogently and even elegantly and often summarized in a concise and compelling way arguments made less skillfully by other writers.

What is significant, then, is the fundamental dissimilarities between the colonies of New York and Massachusetts and in the backgrounds of their key Loyalist spokesmen. Nonetheless, these two groups, along with writers from other colonies, responded to the Revolution in very similar ways. Most important, they used the same kinds of arguments, premised on common assumptions about basic issues like the nature of man and the role of government, to discredit the Revolution and to support the British Empire and its institutions. But the similarities in their response to the Revolution went beyond ideology. The Loyalist writers from different colonies all used the same media to communicate their case to the people. They relied on the same *kind* of ideology and the same nature of appeal. And, despite differences in the course of the Revolution in the various colonies, they published most of their writings at about the same time.

The Timing of the Loyalist Appeal

More Loyalist pamphlets and articles were published in the two years before independence than in any previous or subsequent period, and the writings of these years had an argumentative quality and an urgency not characteristic of later Loyalist literature.[19] These facts can be explained by the events of that period. The time between June 1774, when the last of the Coercive Acts was passed by the British Parliament, and July 1776, when independence was declared, was a watershed in the American Revolutionary movement. The Coercive Acts were Britain's response to the Boston Tea Party. Massachusetts was to be punished for the violent destruction of private property, and royal authority and order were to be restored. The American Patriots retaliated in the first Continental Congress of 1774 by denying Parliament's right to tax and legislate for the colonies, except in the case of trade regulation, and by making plans to oppose British authority. By the fall of 1774 the stage was set for the British-American confrontation. In April 1775 the conflict became more intense with the resort to arms, and in July 1776 the final breach came with the Declaration of Independence.

The worsening of the crisis in 1774–1776 prompted many Loyalists to write tracts in the hope of influencing events, and it dramatically changed the course of some writers' personal lives and loyalties. An excellent example was Daniel Leonard, who had been born into an old and wealthy Congregational family in Bristol County. After graduating from Harvard in 1760 and taking an advanced degree at Yale, Leonard became a lawyer and carried on the family tradition of holding public office. Appointed a justice of the peace in 1767 and king's attorney in Bristol County in 1769, he was elected to the House of Representatives in the early 1770s. As befitted his wealth and station in life, Leonard and his family resided in a magnificent mansion on Taunton Green. Leonard was popular, handsome, and charming and was considered an urbane and widely read individual who enjoyed parties and card playing. Add to this his two marriages to attractive, rich women from distinguished families, and his happiness would seem to have been assured.[20]

In the course of 1774, however, at the age of thirty-three, Leonard's life changed. Earlier in the decade he had been considered an ardent opponent of British measures and had been elected to various Patriot committees. But as the British-American crisis deepened after the Boston Tea Party, so did Leonard's doubts about the Patriot position. Between February and August 1774 he moved farther and farther away from his former allies by voting against the majority on key measures in the House of Representatives. His abandonment of the Patriot cause was completed in August when he was appointed a mandamus councillor. After a mob fired into his house and his life was threatened, Leonard and his family fled to Boston. They were evacuated with the British troops in March 1776, and in 1778 he was formally banished.[21]

Leonard's opponents attributed his fateful political shift in 1774 to self-interest and greed for office; however, his letters reveal that had other reasons for acting as he did. Most revealing in this respect is his letter dealing with the Boston Tea Party, in which he candidly stated his views of the Patriots and of the events of late 1773 and 1774. He described the self-interested motives of the opponents of the Tea Act, the Patriots' clever manipulation of meetings and other events, their unwillingness to compromise and agree to pay for the tea, and the violence of the Tea Party itself, which constituted nothing less than "high treason."[22] What the Boston Tea Party and its aftermath showed him was that his native colony was moving relentlessly toward rebellion, a horrifying prospect to a lawyer, and Leonard discussed in detail the grave legal consequences of being convicted of treason.

The specter of rebellion was especially terrifying, considering his view of its origin. Rather than the product of an unforeseen eventuality, he concluded that the colonial revolt was the result of a plot to tear the colonies from the British Empire. America, in other words, had not drifted into rebellion but had been intentionally steered in that direction by self-interested and unscrupulous Patriot leaders. Spurred to action by this realization, Leonard became a man with a mission.

He took up his pen in 1774 in part to dissociate himself publicly from the treasonous actions of his former political allies. But he also felt a duty to try to stem the tide of rebellion by exposing the Patriots' designs and by dispelling the "thick mist, that hovers over the land and involves in it more than Egyptian darkness" so that he could reveal to his readers the bonds of affection, history, and self-interest which tied them to the mother country.[23]

Although not all Loyalist writers shifted their allegiance as dramatically as Leonard, they did share his feeling that the Boston Tea Party and its aftermath marked a decisive turning point in the British-American controversy, and they shared his sense of duty in trying to influence their fellow colonists' attitudes and actions. Between 1774 and 1776 many colonists were being forced to make irreversible decisions. Many had to decide whether to sign the Association established by the first Continental Congress, whether to abide by decisions of provincial congresses, and whether to swear an oath of allegiance to the Patriot cause. The aim of Leonard and other Loyalist writers was to affect the choices made by Americans. But these writers also feared, as Leonard did, that the Revolutionary ferment had spread beyond Massachusetts to engulf the rest of the thirteen colonies. This conviction was fostered by the calling of the first Continental Congress and by its Resolves. The Congress drew Americans' attention beyond their own provincial boundaries to the broader intercolonial scene. It defined clearly the "American" position and advocated specific actions to protest British measures. The Congress, in other words, provided a concrete set of ideas and proposed actions to which Loyalists from different backgrounds and regions could respond.[24] The Revolution had become by 1774 a continent-wide concern: as a result, it generated not only a systematic body of ideas justifying it, but also an opposition, Loyalist ideology.

The Media

In addition to writing at the same time, Loyalist spokesmen used the same standard media for eighteenth-century polemics—pamphlets, broadsides, and newspapers—to convey their ideas to their readers. Broadsides were single sheets of paper on which were printed notices, proclamations, lists of offenders of the Association, or sometimes political essays crammed into three or four columns of miniscule type. They were quickly and inexpensively produced and widely distributed, often pinned to doors of public buildings or trees during the night to be read by crowds which gathered the following day.[25]

Pamphlets have been hailed as "the chief weapon in the intellectual warfare of the American Revolution," a source in which the "constitutional-political debate" of the 1760s and 1770s can be traced, and a medium in which "everything essential to the discussion of those years appeared if not originally then as reprints."[26] Pamphlets, consisting of a number of pages stitched together and sold unbound for a shilling or two, could be produced easily, quickly, and cheaply. Used widely in England and the colonies to publish commentaries on public issues, they were characterized by long, unwieldy titles and the use of pseudonyms to conceal the authors' identity. Despite variations in their style and approach, pamphleteers were primarily polemicists.

Just as important in popularizing Loyalist ideas were colonial newspapers.[27] Between 1763 and 1775 the number doubled, increasing from twenty-one to forty-two.[28] The growing popularity of the weekly newspapers was related to their cost—a yearly subscription might cost as little as twelve shillings[29]—their wide distribution, and the variety of information in their four to five pages. They had much to offer: news from Britain—including world news, accounts of Parliamentary debates, political gossip about life in London or at court —news and reprinted articles from other colonies, local news, public proclamations, stories about spectacular events, and information about commodity prices, ship departures and arrivals, as well as the inevitable advertising.

Of greatest interest to the student of Loyalist ideology are the political articles which were prominent in many weekly newspapers in the 1760s and 1770s. In the decade before independence, newspapers were at times filled with tracts about local controversies, and the ideas in these pieces foreshadowed the arguments made by Loyalists in the 1774–1776 period. In Massachusetts the *Boston Evening-Post* published articles by Jonathan Sewall and a host of anonymous polemicists as well as a series of letters attacking John Dickinson's "Farmer's Letters" —"Letters in Answer to the Farmer's"—which discussed local political controversies and the Anglo-American dispute in terms very similar to those used by Loyalists in 1774 and 1775.[30] Equally political were the

Boston Chronicle, which was edited by John Mein and printed from December 1767 to June 1770,[31] and the *Censor*, published between November 1771 and May 1772 and edited by Thomas Hutchinson and Andrew Oliver.[32] In New York the ideological foundations for the Loyalist position were laid in the 1760s in articles in the *New-York Gazette and Weekly Mercury*, owned and edited by Hugh Gaine,[33] and to a much lesser extent in the *New-York Chronicle*, published briefly in 1769 and 1770 by future Loyalists James and Alexander Robertson.

In the especially tense times following the Boston Tea Party, it was not uncommon for a newspaper to carry two or three political tracts in one issue. In Massachusetts the two main Loyalist presses—the *Massachusetts Gazette and Boston Weekly News-Letter* and the *Massachusetts Gazette, and the Boston Post-Boy and Advertiser*—carried hundreds of Loyalist pieces. Both papers showed their colors in the 1760s by printing articles defending royal governors; in the 1770s they printed pieces by unknown partisans and prominent Loyalists like Jonathan Sewall and Henry Caner, Anglican rector of King's College Chapel in Boston and author of the series published under the pseudonym Chronus.[34] James Rivington "was by far the most influential Loyalist printer and publisher not only in New York but in North America." *Rivington's New-York Gazetteer, or the Connecticut, New Jersey, Hudson's River and Quebec Weekly Advertiser*, published initially between April 22, 1773, and November 23, 1775, probably had a wider circulation than any other colonial newspaper. It reprinted series like *Massachusettensis* and introduced hundreds of other articles and many testimonials by rank-and-file Loyalists.[35]

To the newspapers, pamphlets, and broadsides one might add other sources, such as the histories of the Revolution written by Judge Thomas Jones of New York and Peter Oliver of Massachusetts.[36] The Loyalist alternative to independence was foreshadowed in the 1760s in "Thoughts upon the Dispute between Great Britain and her Colonies" by William Smith, Jr., Yale graduate, lawyer, New York councillor, historian, and later chief justice of Quebec, who hoped until the very last for a reconciliation between Britain and America.[37] Useful in studying some of the philosophical assumptions of individual Loyalists and their private thoughts are the personal diaries, journals, letters, and other papers of such men as Jacob Bailey, an Anglican missionary in rural Maine; James Murray, a Boston merchant; John

Chandler, a Worcester county judge; Peter Van Schaack, a lawyer from Kinderhook, New York; and four distinguished Salem Loyalists — Benjamin Pickman, a well-to-do merchant; Samuel Curwen, a judge; William Browne, a very wealthy lawyer and landowner; and William Pynchon, another lawyer.[38]

The Nature of Loyalist Ideology

It is significant, then, that Loyalists from various backgrounds and regions took up their pens at the same time and used the same conventional media to communicate their message. Even more important, however, are the similarities in the content of their writings and the nature of their appeal. One outstanding feature of Loyalist literature was that it dwelt upon familiar themes. In defending the British Empire and institutions, these writers used arguments which were conventional wisdom to Britons and Americans in the mid-eighteenth century. Their ideas about the nature of man and the role of government were the same as those popularized by British theorists like Sir William Blackstone. Their critique of colonial society was not original; it had emerged in the 1760s and early 1770s in the course of local controversies in the various colonies. Thus it is vital to analyze the British and colonial sources of Loyalist thought to show that the ideology did not suddenly appear in the 1774–1776 period. The derivative nature of their ideology also helps to explain the similarity of the arguments made by writers from various colonies.

Another important characteristic of the Loyalist appeal was its relevance to contemporary Americans. Although the vast majority of the writers whose identity is known belonged to the educated elite, their message was not aimed only at the educated or even literate segment of the population. Samuel Seabury and his Anglican colleagues in rural New York, for example, traveled extensively delivering speeches on behalf of the Loyalist cause.[39] This is especially noteworthy since one of the largest groups of Loyalists that emigrated to what is now Canada were New York farmers, many of whom were illiterate.[40] The Loyalist argument was not conveyed to such people in written form, but they could have heard it from Seabury and the other New York leaders. Moreover, there is evidence that the Loyalist message influenced at least some rank-and-file Americans. In the two years before independence literally hundreds of Loyalists signed addresses, declarations or associations in which they stated, sometimes in simple language, their view of the Revolution. It is interesting that they supported the basic ideas and aims of the more educated and well-known Loyalist spokesmen.

That Loyalist writings were aimed at a broad cross section of the colonial population can be seen from their ideology. Although some tracts contained visionary theorizing or philosophical arguments about such abstract concepts as the essence of man, most assumptions about such abstractions were implicit and contained in personal papers rather than in public appeals. But ideology can also mean "the integrated assertions, theories, and aims constituting a politico-social program".[41] In this sense, an ideology is an argument on behalf of a cause which is coherent, consistent, and comprehensive, but not necessarily philosophical, abstract, or even complex and subtle. An ideological as opposed to a scientific account provides a "simple and clear-cut" picture which "uses sharp lines and contrasting blacks and whites".[42] It is more subjective than objective, and "draw[s] its power," it has been argued, "from its capacity to grasp, formulate, and communicate social realities that elude the tempered language of science."[43] Its aim is less to convey an accurate perception of reality than to inspire a sense of commitment and to motivate action on behalf of a cause. It was this kind of ideology which was most prevalent in Loyalist articles and pamphlets.

The Loyalist message, though not lacking in sophistication, was one which could be applied to practical realities that affected the day-to-day lives of average Americans. The content, however, would be more meaningful to some, as was also true of Patriot thought. To cite one example, it could be argued that people in Massachusetts, because of their deeply rooted sense of mission, found many aspects of the Revolutionary movement appealing. The zeal for moral reform associated with republicanism[44] or the desire of many Patriots to restore the simplicity and frugality of the Puritan past[45] would probably hold more meaning for Massachusetts colonists than for New Yorkers. Also, Massachusetts' experience with challenges to freehold land titles nurtured fears of excessive taxation as a prelude to a descent into tenantry.[46]

New Yorkers, on the other hand, had their own reasons to be more receptive to Loyalist ideology. The argument that the British tie brought prosperity and unity to the colonies was important to contemporary New Yorkers. The colony had prospered in the British Empire; its economic fortunes were on the rise at the time of the Revolution, while those of Massachusetts were waning; and New York had benefited substantially because of its strategic location, which made it an ideal base for British military operations. Because of the colony's diversity, New Yorkers were more likely to fear dramatic changes which might threaten the fragile accommodation of diverse interests within the colony and to value the unity and stability associated by Loyalist writers with membership in the British Empire.[47]

Other Americans might well have been attracted to Loyalist arguments because they could relate these ideas to their everyday lives. An essential part of the ideology was the vision of an Anglo-American empire: Britain and America, Loyalists believed, were united by history, trade, and a common attachment to the empire and to British institutions. Buttressing this argument was a reasonably sophisticated view of the British Empire and some of the political, constitutional, and economic theories which supported it. Yet the general theme of Loyalists' arguments on behalf of the empire was quite simple. The British tie was a positive historical and contemporary force which was associated with prosperity, liberty, and unity. Some readers could very easily apply such ideas to their own daily existence or the life of their community. Did they have reason to believe, as New Yorkers did, that colonial prosperity was nurtured by the British connection, or did they feel that America's achievements should be credited primarily to the initiative of Americans themselves? What was their view of colonial history? If colonists saw the Puritans as their literal or figurative ancestors, then they might well doubt that Britain upheld freedom in the world and be more open to Patriot thought. On the other hand, some religious minorities, such as the Palatinate Germans and Huguenots in New York, would have reason to equate Britain with religious liberty.

Some religious minorities in Massachusetts also could, on the basis of their own experience, link the British connection with liberty. In Ashfield, for example, many Baptists were Loyalists, and their allegiance was in part related to their resistance in the 1760s to paying taxes to support the local Congregational minister. After this request was rejected by the Massachusetts General Court in 1768, the British government agreed in 1771 to disallow taxation of the Baptists for support of the Congregational minister. Soon after, however, the Baptists were persecuted as enemies of their country by the dominant Congregationalists in the community. Preserved Smith, an Ashfield Baptist who became a Loyalist, wrote this of the local Patriots: "Sons of liberty. . . did not deserve the name, for it was evident all they wanted was liberty from oppression that they might have liberty to oppress!" To Smith and members of other religious minorities in Massachusetts the British government was the "final line of defense against unwanted encroachments by the Massachusetts authorities." To them, the British government represented freedom, and the local colonial elite threatened oppression.[48]

Loyalist writers also argued that the British government played an important supervisory role in America because of its power to regulate the activities of individual colonies, and to some Americans, for example, the Iroquois of northern New York, this would be a strong inducement to support the Loyalist position. The decision by the majority of the Six Nations to remain loyal was influenced by several considerations, including the fur trade, as well as kinship ties between the Mohawks and the Johnson family, who were staunch Loyalists. But another determinant of their loyalty was pointed to by General Thomas Gage: "The Indians," he wrote, "well know that in all their land disputes the Crown has always been their friend." The British government, as the Mohawk leader Joseph Brant realized, was the only power which could intervene, as it had in the 1760s, to curb the encroachments onto Indian lands by often-powerful New York landlords.[49] To groups like the Iroquois the idea that the British government was a positive force which acted paternally to protect subjects — even those who lacked political influence within their own colony — would have some meaning. By the same token the tendency for New York landlords to be Patriots could well have been related to the British government's restrictions on expansion onto Indian lands and its even more menacing moves in the 1760s to challenge the dubiously acquired land titles of the landlords.[50] These Americans would be more receptive to the Patriot view that British intervention into colonial affairs was a negative force which restricted local initiative and freedom to prosper.[51]

Similarly, Loyalist arguments denouncing republicanism and supporting British constitutional principles of government could be related to local circumstances. Loyalist writers associated republicanism with the committees and congresses established to organize colonial protests against British measures. Although their analysis of the threat which such bodies posed to colonial order and freedom was relatively complex, the basic elements of their case against the committees were quite straightforward. The committees were illegal bodies which assumed unlimited powers to dictate the activities of other citizens. Whether readers accepted this interpretation of the committees depended upon their view of the activities, aims, and legitimacy of the local committee. Did they, for instance, regard the Revolutionary committees and congresses as popularly supported, representative agencies created to defend American liberty from British encroachments? Or did they doubt the legitimacy and legality of the committees, question their members' motives, and see committees as coercive combinations which undermined the civil liberties of other community members? Such basic beliefs were not elusive abstractions but products of the experience of the individual or group, and all colonists, educated or illiterate, had opinions on these matters.

THUS a common Loyalist ideology emerged in New York and Massachusetts, as well as in other colonies, despite differences in the backgrounds and societies of the spokesmen. This ideology included a logical, coherent, and even reasonable interpretation of the origins and nature of the Revolution. It rested on certain basic assumptions, which were shared by respected and influential British theorists, about man's nature and government's role. It provided a well-reasoned defense of the imperial status quo at the same time as it outlined ways of improving both the British Empire and British institutions in America. Tying together these various dimensions of Loyalist thought was the pervasive theme that Americans had more to fear from self-interested factions in their midst than from the power of the British government. Loyalists, like Patriots, cautioned their readers about the imminence of oppression, but the tyranny they warned of was, in the words of Jonathan Sewall, a "democratic tyranny."[52]

2

"DEMOCRATIC TYRANNY"

I don't believe there ever was a people in any age or part of the world that enjoyed so much liberty as the people of America did under the mild, indulgent government (God bless it) of England and never was a people under a worse state of tyranny than they are at present. —Dr. Sylvester Gardiner to Oliver Whipple, May 9, 1776 (in Calhoon, *Loyalists in Revolutionary America*)

Such was the view of Dr. Gardiner, a Massachusetts Loyalist who left Boston with the British troops in 1776. A New Yorker who traversed the northern frontier of his native colony the following year to seek his own asylum in Quebec, echoing Gardiner's sentiments, was chagrined that in his "native Country," "all Government was subverted." "Caprice was the only Rule and Measure of usurped Authority," and his fellow countrymen suffered the "Distress" that "Power guided by Malice can produce." "It gave me a sensible Pleasure," Richard Cartwright, Jr., concluded, "to quit a Place where Discord reigned and all the miseries of Anarchy had long prevailed."[1] And Cartwright's feelings were shared by Loyalist refugees from other colonies.[2]

The language used by Cartwright and Gardiner to explain their exile was vivid and emotive: the colonies were not merely going through difficult times, they were laboring under the shackles of nothing less than tyranny. But the dramatic imagery was the same as that used by Loyalist propagandists in the public debate which raged in the colonies between 1774 and 1776. Although there is no evidence that either Cartwright or Gardiner contributed to this debate, their feelings about the Revolution mirrored nicely those of earlier Loyalist spokesmen.

15

Before independence many writers had warned in very stark terms of the dangers confronting America. "Discord and tyranny, in the guise of liberty, stalk forth among us," a New York Loyalist proclaimed in early 1775. Others from the same colony voiced fears of oppression, slavery, or "tumultuous tyranny" and one spoke ominously of a design "to make us worse than slaves."[3] In Massachusetts Gardiner's parting testimonial was foreshadowed in late 1774 by a Loyalist who was disgruntled that his fellow colonists would sacrifice the mild and free administration of the British king for a "state of licentious tumult and the evils of lawless anarchy." And his concerns were shared by others who lamented the fate of their colony, experiencing "lawless anarchy," the "shackles of Anarchy," and the evils of tyranny and oppression.[4]

The Loyalists' highly colorful imagery resembled that employed by the Patriots. Both groups of writers warned of a plot to deprive Americans of their freedom, yet the chasm between the two views of the Revolution was unbridgeable. To Patriots the threat to colonial freedom was an external one, from government. Britain, enervated by luxury, corruption, and tyranny, was conspiring to enslave the colonies: evil or designing ministers, a corrupt Parliament, and by 1776 the king himself were masterminding the insidious plots against American freedom.[5] Loyalists were equally convinced that self-interested men plotted to subvert American liberty, but the threat they pointed to was an internal one, from below rather than above. Loyalist spokesmen outlined the historical origins and contemporary manifestations of an American-based conspiracy to destroy colonial freedom and happiness, and they beseeched their fellow subjects to wake up and realize the real source of their danger.

Warnings that Americans were in danger because they were obsessed with potential external threats to their liberty while being oblivious to the actual and more serious violations of freedom occuring in their midst abounded in the mid-1770s. As early as 1773, the New York Loyalist Myles Cooper cautioned his fellow colonists: "While we are watchful against *external* attacks on our freedom, let us be on our guard, lest we become *enslaved* by tyrants within." "Take heed," another wrote, "that while the words tyranny and oppression are bandied about, and fixed on Britain, you are not unawares enthralled at home."[6] Peter Oliver was amazed that the colonists would, on the one hand, "trample upon the laws of the mildest Government upon earth," and on the other hand, "submit to a tyranny uncontrolled either by the laws of *God* or man."[7] Other Loyalists stressed that while tyranny could be imposed by a few, it could also emanate from the many, or as Samuel Seabury put it, "The *tyranny* of a mob, is the *freedom* of America."[8]

Thus the Patriot rationale for independence did not go unchallenged. An alternative interpretation of the Revolution and it origins was made clearly and forcefully by Loyalist spokesmen just before independence. The fact that Loyalist refugees—not only from New York and Massachusetts but also from other colonies—shared the ideas of these propagandists suggests that Loyalist writers had a significant impact on the views of their readers. What was most distinctive about this widely accepted version of the Revolution was the warning that there was a conspiracy by a self-interested faction to impose a democratic tyranny on America. To understand Loyalist ideology, then, one must begin by examining more closely their argument about the origins and nature of this democratic tyranny.

The Loyalist History of the Revolution

Patriot ideology, it has been pointed out, was so forceful because it made sense of the disturbing events of the 1760s and early 1770s: the various British measures of this period were tied together by Patriot spokesmen to reveal a design against American freedom.[9] What has been overlooked, however, was the skillful way in which Loyalist writers wove together quite different events to fashion their own interpretation. The history of the Revolution, from their point of view, was traced in lengthy accounts, notably Peter Oliver's *Origin and Progress of the American Rebellion* of 1781, a greatly expanded version of his 1776 "Address to the Soldiers," and Judge Thomas Jones's *History of New York During the Revolutionary War*. Less detailed accounts included Daniel Leonard's *Massachusettensis* letters and Thomas Hutchinson's *The History of the Colony and Province of Massachusetts-Bay*.[10] Even more abbreviated histories were contained in the many pamphlets and newspaper articles published in the two years before independence. Although there are some differences in emphasis, what is remarkable are the similarities in the various histories. This common thread makes it possible to outline the basic elements of a Loyalist history of the Revolution.

Ironically, a central theme, as it was in Patriot accounts, was that the Revolution originated with a conspiracy. The "republican party" was of long standing in Massachusetts, Daniel Leonard claimed, and had "long been indulging themselves, in hopes of rearing up an American commonwealth, upon the ruin of the British constitution." [11] Peter Oliver was equally certain that the Patriots had plotted to seek independence for some time. In late 1775 he observed: "I assure you that this independent empire, which you are now assisting those pretended patriots to erect, was formed above seven years ago, though I dare say, that most of you are ignorant of the black design." [12] Though Loyalists stressed that it was a cabal or faction of Patriots who plotted to break the imperial tie, none was as extravagant as the Reverend Henry Caner, who claimed that the flame of "Sedition, Anarchy. . . & Violence [was] kindled & kept alive by about ½ doz. men of bad principles and morals." [13]

Loyalists in New York were just as convinced that the Revolution was a product of the designs of a small faction in the colonies. As early as December of 1774 an anonymous writer affirmed that he had no doubt that the "Republicans of North-America, particularly those of New-England, have long been aiming at independency." [14] Judge Jones also believed that a triumvirate in New York had been intriguing for some time "to pull down Church and State, to raise their own Government and religion upon its ruins, or to throw the whole province into anarchy and confusion." The intrigues of New York conspirators, Jones contended, were abetted by republicans from other colonies. New Yorkers, he felt, looked to the first Continental Congress to reconcile the Anglo-American dispute. However, their hopes were frustrated since the New York delegates were subjected to the "artful cabals of the republicans in Congress" and became "converted into fixed republicans." The outbreak of fighting between the British troops and Patriots in Massachusetts in 1775 was a boon to the republicans in New York, who "had wished for it for a long time" and "received the news with avidity." [15] T. B. Chandler also felt that it was long suspected if not "pretty well known" that a group whose headquarters were at Boston, "have for many years been aiming at, and preparing the way for a government of their own making, independent of Great Britain, to be erected as soon as the disposition of the colonies would be brought to favour the attempt."[16] In short, one basic assumption shared by Loyalists was that the turmoil and sedition in America were produced by the machinations of a small group.

There was consensus as well about the Patriots' motives for conspiring to incite rebellion, and it was again ironic that Loyalists and Patriots agreed that their political foes were motivated by self-interest. The Patriots, according to Loyalist writers, were motivated by envy, ambition, or malice, which made them necessarily turbulent and rebellious. The association among the three character defects was frequently made in the following manner. Since the Patriots were ambitious or avaricious, they were not content with their lot in life but were anxious to advance themselves. They often found their way blocked by respected and successful colonists, presumably Loyalists, who already held the positions to which Patriots aspired. The Patriots, envious of the power and status enjoyed by their more successful fellow colonists, were determined to gain vengeance on those who had unjustly curtailed their aspirations. Being consumed by envy or malice, the Patriots became of necessity turbulent and finally seditious. In order to make their way to the top of the ladder, they played upon or even created popular discontent with the colonial status quo, because only through major changes in personnel and ultimately in institutions and allegiances could the Patriots realize their most basic aim — to seize for themselves power and status.

Daniel Leonard asserted, "I confess myself to be one of those that think our present calamity is in a great measure to be attributed to the bad policy of a popular party in this province." On the one hand he portrayed the "friends of the English constitution," who upheld both British constitutional principles of government and loyalty to Britain, and who, as capable and dedicated public servants, had earned "popularity" and the "confidence of the people." On the other hand he depicted the republican party who opposed the first group because they envied its "principles, firmness and popularity" and because they were at heart republicans — determined to subvert both the British constitutional system of government and allegiance to the mother country. Although of long standing, the republican party had been dormant for several years. The Anglo-American crisis was of the utmost importance, according to Leonard, because it gave the Patriots "scope for action." The Patriots managed to associate "adherents to the constitution" with unpopular British legislation like the Stamp Act. This was essential to their purposes since it undermined the popularity and prestige of established colonial leaders. Unscrupulous enough to publish complete falsehoods and fabricate character assassinations, the Patriots finally succeeded, so that "many of the ancient, trusty and skillful pilots, who had steered the community safely in the most perilous times, were driven from the helm, and their places occupied by different persons, some of whom, bankrupts in fortune, business and fame, are now striving to run the ship on the rocks, that they may have an opportunity of plundering the wreck."[17] To Leonard, then, the Revolution was begun by the Patriots. They were ambitious republicans who attacked established leaders and institutions—most successfully by linking them with unpopular British measures—not because of any sincere belief in their shortcomings but as a way to discredit them. Their aim was to establish an independent republic in which they, rather than their Loyalist opponents, would enjoy the prestigious and powerful positions.

Peter Oliver also believed that the envy and malice which consumed the Patriot leaders were the sparks which led to the Revolution. Concerted opposition to government began, he claimed, when James Otis's father was bypassed for a judgeship when Thomas Hutchinson became chief justice. The patriot demogogues, like Otis, Samuel Adams, and Joseph Hawley, envied Hutchinson's prestige and popularity and resented his success. Thus, they were "determined to ruin him, tho' they plunged their Country & theirselves too, into absolute Destruction." This group of conspirators found natural allies in the smugglers, whose motives were equally sordid. Through the practice of smuggling they had lost any sense of honor or virtue and were quite willing to plot with the junto of Patriots to undermine the authority of the legally established government. For Oliver, as for Leonard, the Anglo-American dispute "gave a Stimulus to the Passions & Designs of the Factious." The Patriots' triumph in defying the authority of the British government by successfully opposing the Stamp Act merely whetted their appetite for power. After 1765, the popular faction gained control of the lower house, then purged dissidents from the council and effectively isolated the governor so that the legal government was replaced by a democracy. Thus, the Patriots saw their ambitions satisfied and their malice avenged when they "broke down the Barriers of Government to let in the *Hydra* of Rebellion."[18]

Thomas Hutchinson and Jonathan Sewall also believed that the Revolution originated with a conspiracy. Hutchinson, too, contended that opposition to government in Massachusetts began when James Otis, Sr., was not appointed a judge. "From so small a spark," he wrote of the incident, "a great fire seems to have been kindled."[19] Sewall asserted that the "present unhappy situation" was due principally to the "smuggling merchants," who "finding themselves too closely watched" determined to oppose the authority of the British government in America. More generally he claimed that the opposition to government was directed by scheming men whose interest it was to "keep alive the coals of sedition" to promote their own popularity and power.[20]

Loyalists in New York also described the Patriots as being motivated by ambition, envy, and spite. Judge Jones pointed to a triumvirate of conspirators he described as a " discontented, turbulent, presbyterian republican faction." As early as the 1750s this triumvirate, Jones claimed, had plotted to establish the Presbyterian religion and republican form of government in New York. Jones believed that one of the three, William Smith, Jr., had a personal motive for his opposition to government. Smith's father, like Otis's, had been bypassed for a judicial appointment, for which Smith blamed Cadwallader Colden, who was in charge of the administration at the time. It was this incident, Jones contended, that "originated all that abuse, scandal, infamy, billingsgate, and blackguard stuff, that was shortly afterwards so liberally bestowed in pamphlets, newspapers, and handbills upon that venerable old gentleman [Colden]."[21] Other New Yorkers agreed about the Patriots' self-interested motives. Charles Inglis shared Jones's view that the New York Patriots sought to advance Presbyterianism at the expense of Anglicanism. Their ambitions could only be realized if the Anglican church were destroyed in America; "it is now past all Doubt," Inglis wrote, "that an Abolition of the Church of England was one of the principal Springs of the Dissenting Leaders' Conduct." Again, the British-American crisis was a godsend to the Patriot faction since "emancipating themselves from the Jurisdiction of Great Britain, & becoming Independent, was a neces-

sary Step towards this grand Object."[22] More generally it was assumed that the republicans in New York as in Massachusetts were interested men who could only better themselves through far-reaching
changes in the status quo.[23] Perhaps Anti-Licentiousness summarized
best the feelings of his fellow Loyalists when he declared, " Sensible
that in a calm they [Patriots] must grovel in the dirt, they have tried to
raise a storm, by which they hope to be elevated into notice."[24]

Thus from Loyalist tracts the Patriots emerge as an aspiring and self-
interested faction. That they sought their own betterment at the expense of the well-being of their country was illustrated, Loyalists contended, in their motives for criticizing public leaders and institutions.
Honest criticism would have been public spirited. But the Patriots attacked established institutions and leaders because this suited their purposes, as was pointed out in an open letter to General Thomas Gage,
governor of Massachusetts. The author consoled Gage with the
thought that although he was being mercilessly attacked by Patriot
leaders, he had to remember that "it is not Mr. Gage, but the Governor, who is to be the object of abuse." It was, the author lamented,
"the established rule" to criticize governors—"some Governors have
been too short, others too tall"—as a way to discredit the office. And
discrediting symbols of authority was essential to their purpose of replacing the old order with a new one headed by the aspiring Patriots.[25]

The charge that they were aspiring reflected The Loyalists' prejudicial assumptions about the characters of the Patriots and in some
cases about their socioeconomic status. Loyalists suggested that some
leaders—presumably Patriots like Alexander McDougall in New York
or Ebenezer McIntosh in Massachusetts—were from humble or disreputable backgrounds. They were described as being "ignorant men,
bred to the lowest occupations" or as people "either having nothing to
loose; or having wasted their own substance, would gladly become the
masters of yours."[26] As one Loyalist explained, the Patriots had "not a
shilling to lose in the contest" and were "taking advantage of the present *dispute* [with Britain], and forcing themselves into public notice."
The Patriots welcomed "Every change in the affairs of government,"
since "the more confusion they can create, and the nearer they can
drive us into a state of perdition, the greater chance have they of
enriching themselves by the spoils of their country."[27] They were not
"industrious artizans," "honest farmers," or "frugal tradesmen"; they

either had never been successful in their callings or had squandered whatever good fortune they had had.[28]

Especially galling to many Loyalists was that such men aspired to become leaders of the community, replacing what Leonard called "the ancient, trusty and skilful pilots," and were thrusting themselves — "bankrupts in fortune, business and fame" — into public prominence.[29] The Loyalists' elitist view of political leadership showed through in their sense of outrage that men so ill-suited to guide the community were rising at the expense of those who were the natural leaders of society. "I feel indignation and shame mingling in my Bosom," Myles Cooper declared, "when I reflect that a few men (whom only the political storm could cast up from the bottom into notice) have presumed to act in the character of *representatives and substitutes of the Province*."[30] The Patriots' failings as leaders were summarized aptly by an unknown poet who described his foes as being

> Overstock'd with Ambition and high mettled spirit;
> Without either Wisdom, or Prudence or Merit.[31]

Despite the disreputable ambitions, backgrounds, and motives of the Patriot leaders, there was no doubt that by the mid-1770s they were accomplishing their designs to create confusion and to thrust themselves into leadership roles. How could such undeserved success be explained? The answer most commonly given by Loyalist writers was that the Patriots were crafty, hypocritical and manipulative. Loyalist sketches frequently described them as designing, crafty, artful, unprincipled, or cunning.[32] Some of the villians in Judge Jones's account included William Livingston, a "sensible, cunning, shrewd fellow", William Smith, Jr., who "enjoyed a smooth, glib, oily tongue", Peter R. Livingston, "Jew Peter," who was "well known in New York from his art, low cunning, avarice and hypocrisy"; and John Morin Scott, an innocent dupe of some of his more manipulative colleagues.[33] The cast in Peter Oliver's drama included Samuel Cooper — "His Tongue was Butter & Oil, but under it was the Poison of Asps"; Benjamin Franklin and James Otis, both of whom were "devoid of all Principle"; Samuel Adams, a Machiavellian who was "all serpentine Cunning"; and, as in Jones's account, a victim who was deceived by these intriguers — John Hancock, whose mind was "a meer *Tabula Rasa*."[34] Oliver's literary genius was revealed in his magnificent description of Samuel Adams, the epitome of the cunning Patriot, duping the highly esteemed President of the United Colonies, John Hancock, whose gullibility was not a product of innocence but of stupidity: "With his oily tongue he duped a man whose brains were shallow and pockets deep, and ushered him to the public as a patriot too: He filled his head with importance and emptied his pockets, and as a reward hath kicked him up the ladder, where he now presides over the twelve united provinces, and where they both are at present plunging you, my countrymen, into the depths of distress."[35]

The Patriots' manipulative abilities were used with greatest effect on people whom they deftly maneuvered to achieve their self-interested aims. According to Daniel Leonard, they "applied themselves to work upon the imagination, and to inflame the passions; for this work they possessed great talents; I will do justice to their ingenuity; they were intimately acquainted with the feelings of man, and knew all the avenues to the human heart."[36] Peter Oliver wrote of Samuel Adams: "He understood human Nature, in low life, so well, that he could turn the Minds of the great Vulgar as well as the small into any Course that he might chuse."[37]

The populace was easily deceived, it was argued, because the avenue to the human heart chosen by the Patriots was so effective. Playing upon fears of oppression kindled by British actions in the decade before independence, they fabricated the specter of imminent enslavement and deviously wormed their way into public confidence by posing as the saviors of their country's freedom. The Patriots, it was charged, wore the "mask of patriotism" and used civil liberty as the bait that was "flung out to catch the Populace at large, & engage them in the Rebellion."[38] Peter Oliver and Samuel Seabury agreed that the merchants who had accumulated large inventories stood to benefit by the nonimportation schemes, but they had hypocritically masked their "selfish Designs" by, in Oliver's words, "mouthing it for Liberty."[39] Probably an unknown Loyalist captured the essence of the attitude toward the Patriots' manipulation of the populace when he declared that they conjured up the "bugbear" of slavery to "usher in the demon of sedition."[40]

Thus, Loyalist spokesmen provided a comprehensive, consistent, and compelling explanation of the origins of the Revolution. Ironically, they countered the Patriot version of a British design against colonial liberty with their own conspiracy theory of an American-based plot against freedom.[41] While the villains in the Patriot piece were Loyalists and their allies in the British government, the conspirators in the Loyalist interpretation were self-interested, aspiring Patriot leaders who manipulated the people by playing upon fears of oppression to undermine popular support for the status quo. The British-American dispute fostered anxieties about oppression and gave the Patriots an excellent opportunity to set their design in motion. The aim of the conspirators, according to the Loyalist version of the Revolution, was the same as the goal of the plotters in the Patriot view of events—to oppress Americans. With the colonies reduced to chaos, the Patriots would take advantage of the confusion to erect their own regime—a democratic or popular tyranny—on the ruins of their country.

The Nature of Democratic Tyranny

The aim of Loyalists writing in the mid-1770s was not only to trace the origins of American problems, but also to warn colonists of the dangers they confronted. Ringing through their tracts was the message that while Patriot leaders diverted colonists by pointing out oppression in British actions, Patriot-dominated bodies were imposing a far more substantive and dangerous tyranny on the colonies. The second step, then, in coming to grips with Loyalist ideology is to understand exactly what was meant by the evils of a democratic tyranny.

Anarchy, or a breakdown in the rule of law and in the order of the community, was the first step on the road to popular tyranny. But for many Loyalists it was the Patriot success in manipulating the populace and in undermining public esteem for traditional institutions and leaders that paved the way for chaos. Several writers were alarmed by a discernible and all-important shift in public attitudes toward authority, by the blurring of social distinctions and the lack of deference accorded to social and political leaders. A Suffolk Yeoman denounced the license of the press which "made odious" people of wealth, merit, and virtue and was "reducing to a *level* the necessary distinctions of rank and fortune." Philo Patria was distressed that the veneration formerly felt for governors was being eroded because of the constant criticism and defamation of public leaders to "make them odious" to the people so that "all distinction and subordination to government are set at defiance." [42] Several others agreed that the intemperate and unfounded attacks by Patriots on the virtue and integrity of public leaders and institutions was undermining respect for them. The prevalence of "rude and indecent language" by government critics was leading to the "dissolution of all order and government." [43] The press was blamed for publishing "blasphemy, perjury, treason and personal slander." Mercator, for example, lashed out at the *New-York Journal* for publishing "inflammatory piece[s]" which tended "to inflame the minds of the people against government, and by means thereof to introduce anarchy and confusion." [44]

Loyalists assumed that deference and respect for authority were vital to the long-term health of the body politic. As J. G. A. Pocock has argued, "deference," as used in the eighteenth century, rested on two key assumptions. One was that there was a natural aristocracy of men of superior merit whose role it was to guide the community. The second and more important premise was that in a postfeudal society, deference involved the *voluntary* acceptance by the majority of the minority's right or superior merit to lead or govern. That is, in a deferential society, especially in one like the American colonies where law enforcement agencies were weak, the authority of leaders and institutions rested very heavily on popular acceptance of their right to lead or govern. [45] If the masses ever came to question seriously the power of traditional leaders or institutions, then the essential mortar of the body politic would begin to crumble. That is, once people were taught to distrust rather than trust authority, leaders and government would be deprived of a vital ingredient of their power, and the door would be open to anarchy. And chipping away at the legitimacy of symbols of authority was exactly what the Patriots were accused of doing.

This point was made very effectively by an anonymous Loyalist who lashed out at John Hancock for declaring in his oration on the anniversary of the Boston Massacre that the British soldiers who had been acquitted of murder were in fact guilty of the crime. What was so dangerous about Hancock's charge was that it "lessen[ed] the consequence and authority of the superior court . . . and [brought] into contempt, trials by juries." If the soldiers were indeed guilty of murder but were acquitted by the courts, either the court and jury were "invincibly ignorant and stupid, or incorrigibly vicious and wicked." Either conclusion, if generally accepted, would be dangerous since the "characters of both judges and jurors ought to be held in veneration"; otherwise their authority would not be respected or obeyed, they would no longer be able to uphold the law and maintain order, and soon "the strongest arm and longest sword will triumph over justice."[46]

Fears that a decline in deference and respect for authority would lead to anarchy were reinforced by concrete evidence. By the mid-1770s Loyalists had no difficulty finding manifestations of chaos in their midst. Mobs pressured judges to close courts or prevented the courts from sitting, and magistrates lacked either courage or virtue to enforce the law. Grand juries were packed with Patriot partisans who regularly acquitted their cohorts. The legally constituted colonial governments were either ineffective or greatly weakened. "Libertinism," riot, and robbery were everyday occurrences for Loyalists such as Peter Oliver, who decried the fact that "houses were plundered and demolished, persons were beat, abused, tarred and feathered."[47]

To some Loyalists, anarchy was immoral and oppressive. As several writers pointed out in different ways, once legally constituted authority became ineffective, the door was open for private groups to pursue uncontrolled their own interests. This meant that the stronger—in the mid-1770s the more organized Patriot-led committees or congresses —imposed their will on the weaker—the unorganized, the dissenters, the Loyalists. Force prevailed rather than any definition of morality legally arrived at. Consequently, loyal subjects who were "violators of no law" suffered personal abuse and "invasions and demolitions of [their] dwelling houses and other property." These innocent victims were mistreated, sometimes cruelly, by Patriot mobs whose members were unknown and whose powers were unlimited.[48] Anarchy, then, was oppressive because it was so insecure. Under legally constituted authority, individuals knew the laws and knew what they could and could not do. This was part of the feeling of security. But also, subjects were secure in the knowledge that if they obeyed the law, then government and the courts would protect their lives, liberties, and property. Once robbed of that certainty and exposed instead to the "discretionary violence of any part of the community," mankind, in the view of Myles Cooper, was in the most "abject state of bondage."[49] The oppressive psychological effects of living in a state of constant insecurity and fear were portrayed in a poem entitled "A Poor Man":

> Alas, 'twas all an idle dream,
> These tyrants to oppose,
> In vain we strive against the stream,
> They have us by the nose.
> . . . Tar, feathers, haunt him day and night,
> And check his bold career.
> He's not afraid of human wight
> But loves his wife full dear.[50]

To the insecurity of anarchy was added the outright tyranny of Patriot committees, congresses, and mobs. Crucial to their case that the committees and congresses were the agents of the democratic tyranny were the Loyalists' assumptions about the role and power of these bodies. For Patriots their power and actions were legitimized since they were believed to be acting on behalf of the people to protect American liberty and to maintain order.[51] For Loyalists, however, these bodies did not represent the people, and they dismissed the meetings at which committees or congress delegates were elected on various grounds. Some Loyalists argued that only a small percentage of the electorate, not a majority, went to such meetings; others said only partisans or Patriots with their own interests to further attended; for still others, the Patriot-dominated groups consisted of the least respectable members of the community.[52] For all, there was no sense in which the committees and congresses upheld the public interest; they were nothing more than unrepresentative, illegal combinations which usurped the functions of the legally established colonial governments.

In their warnings about the committees and congresses, Loyalist writers returned again and again to one theme—that by British standards their actions were nothing less than tyrannical. In Patriot committees, Loyalists argued, power was not balanced among three branches as in the British and colonial governments, where this dispersal of power was generally accepted as a bulwark against tyranny. Instead, one Patriot tribunal often assumed all of the authority exercised formerly by three different branches of government. Patriot bodies at times performed not only the legislative and executive functions of government, but also the judicial role of the courts. Myles Cooper

wrote forebodingly about the "arbitrary encroachments" of such con-
centrations of power, and Daniel Leonard charged that the committees
"frequently erect themselves into a tribunal, where the same persons
are at once legislators, accusers, witnesses, judges and jurors, and the
mob the executioners."[53] Samuel Seabury contrasted the arbitrary way
in which the Continental Congress unilaterally levied taxes to help the
Boston poor with the "greater security" under the British system,
where taxes were initiated by the House of Commons but required as
well the approval of the House of Lords and the king.[54] Other
Loyalists were alarmed and angered that long-cherished British institutions, like trial by jury, were being flagrantly violated. One likened
the committees established to enforce the Association to the inquisition since they were "clothed with power to revenge themselves upon
their neighbours without controul, and the poor victim of their mad
zeal, malice or wrath, is to be exposed to infamy and disgrace,
unheard, without the form of trial, and against the laws of his country."[55] The sanctity of the home, it was alleged, was another target
for Patriot excesses, since audacious committees presumed to search
homes without warrants to discover imports proscribed by the Association. In a hard-hitting diatribe against this practice, Seabury expressed the outrage that he and other Loyalists felt:

> Do as you please: If you like it better, choose your Committee, or suf-
> fer it to be chosen by half a dozen Fools in your neighbourhood—open
> your doors to them,—let them examine your tea-cannisters, and
> molasses-jugs, and your wives and daughters pettycoats—bow, and
> cringe, and tremble, and quake,—fall down and worship our sovereign
> Lord the Mob.—But I repeat it, by H....n, I will not.—No, my house
> is my castle: as such I will consider it, as such I will defend it, while I
> have breath. No *King's* officer shall enter it without my permission,
> unless supported by a warrant from a magistrate.—And shall my house
> be entered and my mode of living enquired into, by a domineering
> Committee-man? Before *I* submit I will die: live *you* and be slaves.[56]

The Loyalists' most vehement denunciations, however, were reserved for Patriot suppression of the most basic and cherished freedom
of a British subject—freedom of expression. They accused the Patriots
of denying individuals the liberty to express opinions which did not
coincide with their own and of punishing dissenters for exercising
their rights as British subjects to speak and write freely so long as they

did not transgress the laws. Peter Oliver denounced the Patriots, as
"Christian *Liberty Men*," for "thinking they did *God* good Service in
persecuting & destroying all those who dared to be of different Opinions from them." Another Loyalist proclaimed that Britain "was as
averse to every species of injustice and slavery as your political leaders
are to your freely exercising the right of private judgement."[57]
Jonathan Sewall wondered how the Patriots could justify such oppression and then provided the answer:

> They will say, you are one of the minor party, and don't think as the
> majority do, you are a tory, and enemy to your country & c. But has
> not a man a right to speak his sentiments tho' they should differ from
> the majority? Does it necessarily follow that he must be an enemy to
> his country because he cannot adopt the measures that the greater part
> have gone into, in order to obtain a redress of grievances?

The Patriot intolerance of minority views was particularly galling
when contrasted with the freedom of expression afforded such views
in Britain - the nation Patriots claimed was corrupt and tyrannical. It
was especially ironic to Sewall that Patriots would try to silence the
Loyalists when the minority which supported the American cause in
the British Parliament was free to express dissenting views and was
even applauded by Americans for the sentiments it so freely
espoused.[58]
Even more outrageous was that Patriot committees and mobs
abused those who presumed to express freely their own views. "The
old farce is being played over again," one wrote sarcastically, "and we
are once more required to support our liberties by dealing out terrors
and threats amongst our fellow citizens."[59] One of the many Loyalists
who suffered for publicizing his anti-Patriot thoughts was Samuel
Seabury. His trouble with the Patriots stemmed from the popularity of
his pamphlets and the fact that his identity as the author was known
or suspected. His pamphlets were publicly burned, and on November
22, 1775, he was the victim of the wrath of a group of Patriots. Forty
Connecticut horsemen surrounded his parsonage, slashed to ribbons
the quilt his daughters were working on, and demanded Seabury.
After being seized from his classroom, he was taken to Connecticut
and imprisoned for seven weeks, until his captors allowed him to
escape. Once in Westchester again he enjoyed the support of his
parishioners, but he and his family were harrassed constantly by

Patriot troops en route to New York City. Shortly after the Declaration of Independence was adopted, and as Patriot troops prepared to move into the Westchester area, the Seaburys had no choice but to flee to New York City and seek the protection of the British army.[60]

Experiences like Seabury's provided concrete evidence to back up Loyalist charges about the intolerant, arbitarary, and oppressive actions of Patriot bodies. Daniel Leonard stated very eloquently his own indignation about the persecution of Loyalists:

> It is chiefly owing to these committees, that so many respectable persons have been abused, and forced to sign recantations and resignations; that so many persons, to avoid such reiterated insults, as are more to be deprecated by a man of sentiment than death itself, have been obliged to quit their houses, families, and business, and fly to the army for protection; that husband has been separated from wife, father from son, brother from brother, the sweet intercourse of conjugal and natural affection interrupted, and the unfortunate refugee forced to abandon all the comforts of domestic life.

Patriots would have countered this touching narrative by pointing out that Leonard's "victims" were Loyalists who supported the British government, which was conspiring to enslave America. Surely, then, niceties need not be observed in dealing with such people, especially after April 1775, when fighting had begun, Americans had been killed, and the Revolution was under way; then Loyalists could rightly be seen as potential traitors. Leonard and other Loyalists saw at stake quite a different principle. Leonard continued:

> My countrymen, I beg you to pause and reflect on this conduct. Have not these people, that are thus insulted, as good a right to think and act for themselves in matters of the last importance, as the whigs? Are they not as closely connected with the interest of their country as the whigs? Do not their former lives and conversations appear to have been regulated by principle, as much as those of the whigs? You must answer, yes. Why, then, do you suffer them to be cruelly treated for differing in sentiment from you? Is it consistent with that liberty you profess? . . . It is astonishing, my friends, that those who are in pursuit of liberty, should ever suffer arbitrary power, in such an hideous form and squalid hue, to get a footing among them.[61]

The Loyalists saw no British plot against American freedom. Instead, they were most concerned about what was happening in America, which they believed was divided into two camps. Each side had its own interpretation of the British-American crisis, although Loyalists were certain that their interpretation, unlike the Patriots', was rooted in conviction not self-interest. In the 1774–1776 period, then, an absolutely crucial debate was taking place over the future of the colonies. Since colonists were facing awesome and irreversible decisions it was essential to have all viewpoints represented. The resort to arms, as Charles Inglis argued, only raised the stakes and made it more imperative that Americans examine carefully all of their options and try to avoid a bloody civil war.[62] Seen from this perspective, it was oppressive for the upholders of one view—the Patriots—to use their power to silence their opponents and thereby stifle the all-important debate about the future of their country.

The Patriot design to end all freedom of debate was symbolized for many by their attempts to silence Loyalist presses. "A free press has been the honour and glory of Englishmen, by it our most excellent constitution has been raised to greater perfection, than any in the world," an unknown Loyalist proclaimed. "But we [Americans]", he wrote sadly, "are become the degenerate plants of a new and strange vine; and now it seems, ignorance must be the mother of both devotion and politics." He was referring to the Patriot endeavors to "starve and murder our virtuous [Loyalist] printers." "Are none," he asked of the Patriots, "to speak, write or print, but by your permission?"[63]

Again, concrete examples were not hard to find. There was the experience in the 1760s of John Mein, editor of the *Boston Chronicle*. As an opponent of the nonimportation scheme adopted in 1769 to oppose the Townshend Duties, Mein used his newspaper to criticize the scheme and its supporters. Most spectacular and devastating were his reprints of ship manifests which seemed to prove that prominent leaders of nonimportation, like John Hancock, were importing goods themselves. Such revelations or allegations were too much for the Patriot populace of Boston to bear. Mein was beaten up by a mob, and when Governor Thomas Hutchinson admitted that he could not guarantee his safety, Mein was virtually forced to leave the colony. Mein's paper, of course, was closed, as were other Loyalist presses in the 1770s, like James Rivington's widely distributed *Gazetteer*. On November 25, 1775, members of the same Patriot group that seized Seabury entered Rivington's printing shop in New York City, smashed his press, and carried off the type to Connecticut, where it was melted into bullets.[64]

The destruction of a free press, however, was associated with more than just such spectacular actions. The Patriots used other, more subtle means of preventing colonists from reading Loyalist presses. The Worcester Resolves, Loyalists alleged, pressured citizens not to subscribe to Loyalist newspapers.[65] Loyalist tracts were stigmatized as inimical to American freedom or treasonous, a practice ridiculed in a clever Loyalist satire of Patriot committee resolutions. After condemning obviously seditious works like the Anglican Book of Common Prayer, a fictitious Patriot committee chaired by "William Wormwood" went on to outlaw the Bible on the grounds that the "present translation" was "the work of some high flying priests, the tools of despotism in the arbitrary reign of James I." The Bible was also dangerous because it "contains a severer condemnation of our present glorious struggles, than was ever disgorged from the diabolical press of the Parracide, Rivington." The other part of the Patriot design to muzzle a free press involved drilling into the populace the one-sided propaganda of the Patriot organs. A typical Patriot printer was "Mr. Solomon Sapscull" who had "laboured more abundantly" in the "common cause" than even the editors of the Patriot *Boston Gazette*. He had "not only, in every periodical publication, abused Kings, Lords, Commons, and all tories, in general, but [he] has also . . . [practiced] defamation of private characters, and . . . he has worn himself to a perfect skeleton by devising lies on his bed in order to keep up the spirits of the party." Such "extraordinary merit" deserved a reward. Thus, the committee resolved to force every citizen to take or at least pay for a subscription to Mr. Sapscull's "Mercuries," and "Tories" were to be obliged to pay double.[66] A free press, then, was assumed to be an open or impartial one which printed more than one point of view, and on these grounds as well the Patriots were accused of undermining the liberty of the press.

Freedom of the press was regarded as an essential part of the whole fabric of British constitutional liberty. It was, as one Loyalist put it, the "boast of Englishmen" and "an essential palladium of the constitution." "Can that then be the cause of true liberty, which requires the destruction of this noble privilege? . . . Can the venerable fabric be supported, when its many pillars are pulled down?"[67] A poem, which began by announcing that the Patriots "tremble at an equal press," summarized nicely Loyalist objections to the coercive actions of the Patriots, who seemed incapable of appreciating the true nature of liberty in the British tradition.

> Treating all men as mortal foes,
> Who dare their high behests oppose.
> Stark raving mad, with party rage,
> With coward arms, those foes engage,
> And lurk in print, a nameless crew,
> Intent to slander, rob, undo.
> Conscious of guilt, they hide their shame,
> And stab conceal'd the printer's fame.
> Dares the poor man impartial be,
> He's doom'd to want and infamy.
> Condemn'd by their imperial ire
> To poison, daggers, pillage, fire;
> Precarious lives in constant dread,
> Tar, feathers, murder, haunt his bed;
> Sees all he loves, a sacrifice,
> If he dares publish, ought—but lies.
> . . . Alas, vain men, how blind, how weak;
> Is this the liberty we seek!
> Alas, by nobler motives led
> A Hampden fell, a Sydney bled.[68]

Democratic Tyranny on a Continent-Wide Scale

Besides fears about an oppression imposed by Patriot committees and congresses, Loyalists were concerned that the whole American continent would suffer from a tyranny rooted in anarchy. Britain, for most Loyalists, was the cohesive bond which united the colonies and upheld the interests of the empire. However, as the Patriots challenged the authority of Britain to legislate for America and undermined public respect for British power, this vital tie joining the colonies would be broken. Instead, the self-interest of each colony would prevail, resulting in disunity, chaos, and eventually civil war. Jonathan Sewall predicted that "intestine jars and jealousies" would result from the difficulty of deciding on a form of government. "You will," he declared, "soon have as many forms of Government contended for, as there are men who have ambition, resolution, and ability sufficient to conduct their cause." Ultimately, he believed, either "a set of petty tyrants" would rule with "a rod of iron," or the colonists would "live in a state of perpetual war with your neighbours, and suffer all the calamities and misfortunes incident to anarchy, confusion, and bloodshed".[69]

But just as anarchy was seen as being a stepping stone for tyranny within each colony, chaos on a continent-wide scale, it was warned, would be a prelude to oppression. The general argument was that once the central power in a political unit was emasculated and no longer able to regulate its members, then powerful, self-interested groups would have free rein to impose their will on others in the unit. This argument was applied to the collapse of the British Empire in North America by T. B. Chandler. He cautioned that once deprived of British protection, religious minorities would be vulnerable to the "republican zealots and bigots of New-England," who had a history of persecuting those who "presumed to differ from them in matters either of religion or government."[70] Alternatively, Loyalists warned that after America was reduced to utter confusion, there would be a power vacuum into which would step either an internal or more probably an external tyrant. Isaac Wilkins thought it ironic that independence in the quest of liberty would only lead to anarchy and violence. He wrote:

> But if she [Britain] should think proper to decline the contest; if in her wrath she should give us up to our own direction, and leave us to cut and shuffle for ourselves, and to settle our boundaries, and to appoint our own forms of government, deeper and more terrible scenes of distress will present themselves to our view . . . Factions and animosities will lay waste our country, provinces will rise against provinces, and no umpire to determine the contest, but the sword. This once flourishing and happy land will smile no more; it will become a field of blood, and a scene of terror and desolation.[71]

A most frightening picture of an independent America was painted by Peter Oliver. America, he wrote, would be "cantoned out into petty states," plagued by perpetual wars; fertile fields would be "deluged with blood"; wives and children would be "involved in the horrid scene" and the crowning blow would be that "foreign powers will step in and share in the plunder that remains, and those who are left to tell the story will be reduced to a more abject slavery than that which you now dread."[72]

The Relevance of the Loyalist Argument

The essential Loyalist warning was that Americans had to wake up and realize, before it was too late, the real source of their danger. Much of the impact of the argument about a democratic tyranny lay in its clear, logical, and forceful explanation of the confusing events and disorienting experiences of the mid-1770s. Loyalist propagandists, it is true, never really addressed the substantive issues raised by the Patriots. Loyalist histories of the Revolution stress the style, methods, and dubious motives of the Patriots, not the content of their writings. Assuming that the Revolution was a conspiracy, the Loyalists devoted their efforts to uncovering the crimes of the conspirators. But the Patriots, too, virtually ignored the Loyalists' substantive objections to the Revolutionary movement and stressed instead their opponents' dishonorable motives and questionable aims.[73] By not addressing what truth there was in their opponents' argument, both Loyalists and Patriots sacrificed accuracy but provided a systematic overview of the Revolution in which there was good and evil, black and white. Loyalists, like Patriots, fashioned an arresting ideology designed to generate commitment to their cause and to spur people to action. The Loyalist message was simple, painted in bold colors and easy to grasp for those who wanted an alternative explanation to that offered by Patriots.

To point out the simplicity and emotional appeal of Loyalist ideology is not to downplay its accuracy, sophistication, and contemporary significance. Although the failure of the Loyalists to carry popular opinion suggests that their case was not as appealing to Americans as the Patriot one, still parts of their argument were relevant to mid-eighteenth-century American problems and played upon deeply rooted colonial fears. To cite one example, when Loyalists conjured up visions of a divided and warring American continent being victimized by imperialistic European powers, they were appealing to past anxieties about European encirclement. From the 1690s until the British victory over the French in 1760, the frontiers of the colonies had been subjected to periodic raids by Indians and French Canadians.

In the early part of the Seven Years' War the colonies had found the French and their Indian allies to be formidable adversaries, and the eventual defeat of the French was due primarily to the British troops and navy.[74] Hence, with a history of fearing conquest by an aggressive and alien European foe, colonists would be sensitive to the Loyalist warning that once reduced to anarchy, the colonies would be vulnerable to a tyranny imposed by foreign powers.

Moreover, the contention that the Revolution originated with an American-based conspiracy was no more fantastic than the Patriot claim of a British plot to enslave America. In both positions there was an essential core of truth which lent credibility to their assertions. The Loyalist idea that the Revolution involved a struggle between the "ins" — those who held prestigious and powerful positions — and the "outs" — those who aspired to such places — has some merit. Mid-eighteenth-century American politics increasingly involved just such a struggle for power and status between competing factions and interests.[75] Loyalists were also correct in saying that the British-American dispute was used for partisan political purposes. In New York and Massachusetts, as in other colonies, opposition factions did identify ruling cliques with unpopular British legislation, like the Stamp Act, to discredit and defeat their political foes.[76] Some historians even argue, as the Loyalists implied, that an underlying cause of the Revolution was the restricted opportunities for young, ambitious Americans who found their political aspirations blocked, so the rise to power of one group necessarily had to be achieved at the expense of the other. Within this framework the Patriots, as the "outs," indeed had to discredit the Loyalist "ins" to advance their own fortunes.[77] There was also at least some truth to accusations about the self-interested motives of the Revolutionary leaders. One example was the charge that merchants who advocated nonimportation in high-minded, patriotic language stood to gain substantially by the scheme. Large merchants, it has been proven, did profit by nonimportation, which allowed them to liquidate their large inventories at handsome prices.[78]

Similarly, the Loyalist argument that the power of the Patriot committees and congresses was excessive and used arbitrarily was at least partly true. The Association, for instance, gave the committees broad powers to regulate what individuals bought, sold, and consumed and even urged the regulation of popular pastimes.[79] Heart-rending descriptions of the plight of Loyalist women and children who were dispossessed by local committees and forced to seek asylum in Canada lent some substance to the claims that committees acted arbitrarily and even cruelly.[80] And perhaps most important, there was, on the surface at least, a most blatant contradiction between Patriot rhetoric about liberty and their intolerance of opposing views and willingness to violate others' freedom of conscience.[81]

THUS the Loyalist argument about a democratic tyranny was central to their ideology because it imposed some order on the events of the mid-1770s and explained them in terms which meant something to Americans at that time. To embrace this Loyalist ideology, however, colonists had to accept as well its most basic assumptions. A vital one was that what might be called the "republicanism" of the Revolution — the dramatic changes in attitudes and political practices taking place in the colonies — posed greater dangers to America than did British actions. Loyalists were less afraid of the power wielded by the British government than of the effects of the squabbling and self-interested wrangling of colonial politics. But to understand fully these views which distinguished Loyalists from Patriots, it is necessary to look more closely at the Loyalists' world view — their basic beliefs about the nature of man, liberty, and government — and at some aspects of contemporary American society which molded Loyalist ideas and anxieties.

3

THE LOYALISTS' CONSERVATISM

May supreme laws, by subjects be disputed?
Then say they're wrong, the Sovereign is refuted.
If so, could laws restrain and make them budge,
When they themselves in their own case must judge?
Confused Anarchy is most exerted,
When Order, Rule and Laws are thus inverted.

— *Massachusetts Gazette*
and Boston Weekly News-Letter,
FEBRUARY 25, 1773

ALTHOUGH LOYALIST WRITERS were addressing problems of immediate concern and were trying to persuade readers, not philosophize, their arguments were based on a number of key assumptions—often only implied—which distinguished them from Patriots. This did not mean, of course, that there were not some ideological differences among the Loyalists. However, the similarities overshadowed the differences, and just as it is possible for historians to write confidently about Patriot ideology despite the obvious differences among John Adams, Thomas Paine, and Thomas Jefferson, it is feasible to do the same with Loyalist spokesmen. The case for a common ideology becomes even more compelling when one realizes that the ideas of New York and Massachusetts Loyalists about fundamental issues like the nature of man or the role of government were shared by leading Loyalists from other colonies.[1]

It is not surprising that the general outlines of a common ideology existed in the colonies. Views about basic concepts like the nature of man mold an individual's response to events, but they also flow from the world in which the ideology functions. In other words, the Loyalists' sharing of certain basic beliefs in part reflected the fact that they were all living in the same society, experiencing the same changes, and reacting in similar ways to the social and political realities they confronted. Thus Loyalist ideas and anxieties can only be fully appreciated if they are related to contemporary changes in the colonies.

Reason and Passion

A hallmark of postmedieval thought is the belief that much about the functioning of a society can be explained by the nature of man. Differing ideologies, or prescriptions for a society, are premised on quite dissimilar assumptions about man's nature. If man is presumed to be basically good, for example, then removing restraints on his behavior is possible and even desirable. If, however, man is seen to be essentially evil or unpredictable, then the emphasis will be on restraining his natural impulses. Often the differences between Loyalists and Patriots seem to be a matter of emphasis or nuance, which is understandable since they lived in the same society, yet if one looks more closely, the world views of the two groups emerge as being quite distinctive.

Patriots were more likely to view man in universal terms and to stress the equality, potential, and features common to all. The universalism of Thomas Paine's approach was revealed in his remark that Americans were championing "the natural rights of all mankind" and that the "cause of America" was "the cause of all mankind." Similarly, Philip Livingston explained that the Patriots justified their resistance to British taxation not just on the grounds that taxation threatened their rights as Englishmen, but also because it infringed on their rights as men, a point made in almost exactly the same language by James Otis. A tendency to see man in abstract terms led Alexander Hamilton to write, "All men have one common original . . . one common nature . . . one common right." And Hamilton, along with other Patriots like John Adams, were more inclined than were Loyalists to emphasize man's potential rather than the discrepancies between human capabilities and his actual behavior.[2]

The Loyalists' view of man was more historical. They tended to look to the past for truths about fundamental concepts like man's nature. History, for Peter Van Schaack, was the "grand fountain of instruction." To Jonathan Sewall and other Loyalists, knowledge about human nature was to be found in the "experience of former ages and Nations."[3]

One lesson gleaned from history was that men were unequal creatures. Although there was no general consensus about the nature or cause of these inequalities, Loyalists placed less emphasis than did Patriots on the features common to all men and more on their differences and inequalities. Societies were usually depicted as incorporating diverging classes or interests. Some writers described a hierarchical, corporate, and organic society, reminiscent of seventeenth-century Puritan ideals, where each person existed as part of a larger social body and had a duty to contribute to the well-being of the whole in accord with his own abilities and station in the hierarchy. Others merely described pluralistic societies comprising disparate social, economic, or religious interest groups. Most recognized the necessity or inevitability of disparities amongst men in socioeconomic condition, talents, or potential for good or evil. Some stressed that society was divided into leaders—those whose merit and accomplishments fitted them to guide the community—and followers, whose role it was to defer to the superior wisdom of their leaders. Virtually all Loyalist spokesmen included in society the weak and the strong, the wise and the less prudent, and the relatively good and evil.[4]

The other vital lesson taught by history was that man was imperfect. This belief was part and parcel of Loyalist attitudes toward passion and reason. Though to most eighteenth-century Americans passion usually had pejorative connotations, some Patriots exalted it. "Powerful and sublime passion," wrote a New York Patriot, "by depriving man in some measure of his natural feelings prompts him to love his country independently of himself." Thomas Paine also praised feelings as the "guardians of his [God's] image in our hearts." "The social compact," he proclaimed, "would dissolve, and justice be extirpated from the earth . . . were we callous to the touches of affection."[5] Other Patriots, however, would have been as critical of passion as were Loyalists, the crucial difference being one of emphasis. Loyalists were more acutely conscious of the tension between man's potential for good—to use his reason and act morally and wisely—and for evil — to succumb to the pull of passion — and the fear of passion was more central to Loyalist ideology.

Loyalists who described reason as "that grand and most valuable prerogative of our Being" were reiterating a commonplace of their time. Reason was so highly prized because, among other things, it was associated with the ability to order one's thoughts and arrive at a logical conclusion or the truth. This idea was expressed concisely by an unknown Loyalist poet: "In reason's scale every action weigh/And Truth's bright beams will shine upon thy Mind." Reason to another involved "the harmony and order of our faculties" and was valuable because it "represents things to us, not only as they are at present, but as they are in their whole nature and tendency." Passion, on the other hand, "only regards them in their former light; when this governs us, we are regardless of the future, and are only affected with the present."[6] Another aspect of reason, then, was the ability to reflect clearly and dispassionately on the nature and implications of one's actions.

Since reason involved mental order, calm reflection, and measured judgments, it was associated with prudent, sober, and restrained behavior. Loyalist spokesmen expressed their approbation of sober reason, "zeal and fortitude" that was tempered with wisdom and moderation, and "the most *prudent* course" as opposed to the course with the "most *old Oliverian* glory in it."[7] There is even evidence of an elusive, yet interesting, dissimilarity in personal aesthetic preferences. Whereas Patriots tended to admire zeal, audacity, and commitment, Loyalists preferred moderation, propriety, and prudent detachment.[8]

Because reason was man's highest potential, it was considered to be the source of his freedom and morality. This belief flowed from the assumption that freedom or independence consisted in utilizing the rational faculties that God endowed man with to perceive the truth of a situation and then to act on the basis of this reasoned judgment. Making decisions in this way was considered to be acting in accord with one's conscience. As Daniel Leonard explained, important decisions could not be taken "without first settling with . . . [one's] conscience, in the retired moments of reflection, the important question respecting the justice of . . . [one's] cause." To do this, one had to "hear and weigh every thing that is fairly adduced, on either side of the question, with equal care and attention" and avoid the "disposition to drink in with avidity, what favours our hypothesis, and to reject with disgust whatever contravenes it." Acting on the basis of conscience was inextricably linked to freedom and peace of mind; when Daniel Oliver, lieutenant governor of Massachusetts, allowed himself to be coerced by a mob to resign his office and act against his own judgment, he admitted to Lord Dartmouth that his conscience plagued him: "I am sensible by the common rules laid down on this subject, I may be acquitted in breaking this promise. But in every man's mind there is a certain standard by which he must try his actions. In some, the rule or standard is more vague than in others. Common rules of rectitude are sufficient to satisfy some; while others must, for self approbation, consider the subject more nicely." Dartmouth had acquitted Oliver, yet Oliver could not acquit himself, for he had sacrificed what the Massachusetts councillors described as "that humble satisfaction which arises from conscious integrity" that provided so many of his fellow Loyalists with an invaluable inner peace in trying times.[9]

Perhaps the Loyalist who wrestled most earnestly with the claims of individual conscience was Peter Van Schaack. In 1777 at the age of thirty, Van Schaack could look back on a career which began auspiciously enough when he graduated first in his class from King's College and went on to become a lawyer. Although an active supporter of the Patriot side until 1776, he refused to support independence because he sincerely believed that the Lockean compact theory of government did not justify it. In defending his views to the Provincial Convention he argued that because ot the seriousness of deciding whether or not government had abrogated its trust and could legitimately be overthrown, each person had to make the decision for himself since "every individual must one day answer for the part he now acts"; he then went on to state that "if he must *answer* for the part he acts, which certainly presupposes the right of private judgment, he can never be justifiable in the sight of God or man, if he acts against the light of his own conviction. In such a case no majority, however respectable, can decide for him."[10] The concept of conscience, as defined by Van Schaack and others, helps to explain more fully why Loyalist spokesmen were so outraged at Patriot repression of dissent. The Patriots were guilty of nothing less than depriving them of their right to use their noblest faculty, reason, to decide the merits of the British-American dispute, and to act according to their own consciences.

Although Van Schaack's arguments did not convince the convention, his efforts were not entirely wasted. In 1778 Van Schaack had good cause to despair: he had recently buried his wife, he was going blind, and his refusal to take an oath of allegiance to the state of New York resulted in his banishment. Yet as he departed from his native land, he found consolation in his feeling that he had been true to his own conscience. He wrote:

> Torn from the nearest and dearest of all human connections, by the visitation of Almighty God, and by means of the public troubles of my country, I am now going into the wide world, without friends, without fortune, with the sad remembrance of past happiness, and the gloomy prospect of future adversity, having no other compass to direct me than my own frail understanding, and no other consolation than that consciousness of my own integrity, which, as far as relates to the immediate cause of my now leaving my country, I possess in the fullest manner.[11]

Loyalists who believed that reason was the source of man's freedom, morality, and peace of mind were equally certain that passion—a weakness that all men were susceptible to—undermined freedom and morality. An unmanly weakness,[12] passion was equated with many undesirable emotions or baser instincts, like malice, envy, the desire for revenge, or prejudice.[13] When men were gripped by the malevolent appeal of passion, it was contended, their reason was disturbed and their judgment distorted.[14] "Under the undue influence of prejudice and passion," a "dark and misty medium," Thomas Bradbury Chandler claimed, "every object appears to them under a violent distortion."[15] Men who were "Dupes to their Prejudices" were incapable of perceiving clearly all sides of an issue; according to Censor, the "fatal Deceiver . . . outweigh[s] the most ponderous considerations in the opposite scale," and "obscures the Distinction between Truth and Falsehood, moral Beauty and Deformity."[16] Passion was so dangerous because it divested man of both his freedom and morality. It made man a slave because it disordered his mind and prevented him from using his reason to perceive independently the truth of a situation.[17] It led to immoral conduct because men, blinded by their passions, were incapable of exercising their God-given ability to arrive at a rational and independent judgment by which to guide their behavior.[18]

Passion, it was stressed, also led to unruly, impetuous, and uncontrollable behavior, which was aesthetically abhorrent to many Loyalists. Patriot promoters of passion were denigrated as "wild enthusiasts," "furious sons of Liberty," and "turbulent spirits,"[19] and their behavior was castigated for the same reasons. They were accused of improper conduct, "indecent railing," impropriety, "undignified, violent oppposition," and "rude and indecent language."[20] As a result of the impassioned conduct of irrational creatures, the colonies had sacrificed the contentment and order, the "mutual support and affection,"[21] which many Loyalists prized highly, for what was variously described as a state of "enthusiastic frenzy," libertinism, and "Tumult, Disorder and confusion."[22] Thus, behavior guided by passion upset the order of the universe and introduced in its place ugly, ungainly and uncontrollable anarchy and confusion.

Basic to Loyalist ideology, then, was a keen awareness that man was equally capable of noble and rational conduct, dictated by reason, which allowed man to act freely and morally; and of ignoble behavior, determined by passion, which undermined both freedom and morality. And while behavior based on reason was wise, moderate, and restrained, impassioned conduct was unruly, uncontrollable, and senseless.

This acute sensitivity to passion and reason helps to clarify the Loyalists' perception of the people. One ambiguity in the Loyalist argument was their assumption on the one hand that the people were rational, and on the other hand, that the Revolution occurred because the people were deluded. Some explicitly acknowledged the rational potential of the populace,[23] and the very fact that writers were trying desperately to reason with the people and persuade them to accept the Loyalist view of events meant that they assumed the people to be capable of reasoning and of responding rationally to facts and logic. But the Loyalists also believed that there was no widespread, spontaneous discontent and no legitimate grievances of a magnitude to justify revolution. The Revolution came about because the masses, easily swayed and vulnerable to appeals to their passions or baser instincts, were duped by a crafty and unscrupulous cabal.

This apparent contradiction can be explained by the Loyalist assumption that the people were volatile and malleable. Like individuals, the people as a body could guide their actions by reason and act in a rational, noble, and public-spirited way, so there was some point in trying to penetrate to this rational potential through writing. But, it was equally likely that the people would allow their passions to dictate their behavior, as one Loyalist very aptly wrote. "As a great part of Mankind have, in all ages, been less under the influence of reason than of other things, so they have frequently, under the guidance of those who have carried their brains, persecuted their best friends — opposed their real interests — and directly assisted to their own ruin."[24] Because the people were so malleable, they might well act on the basis of passion rather than reason if the most powerful appeals to them were to their baser rather than their nobler instincts. If man's weaknesses predominated, one could find solace by looking once again to the past. History recorded instances in which men had succumbed to the pull of passion and descended, often for a generation, into a state of tumult and irrationality. Writers who looked for such instances compared the Revolutionary era in America to other disoriented periods of history, like the Salem witchcraft trials in the seventeenth-century or, more commonly, the English civil war.[25] The republicanism, utopianism, and intolerance of the Revolution reminded several Loyalists of similar traits in the Cromwellian period. New York Presbyterians were likened to Cromwellian Independents, and New England Patriots were compared to leaders in the British republican experiment.[26] Like the Cromwellian regime, the Revolution was seen to be characterized by tyranny, bigotry, and fanaticism. There was little consolation in Daniel Leonard's prediction that this generation, gripped by the weakness of its nature, would end up, like its predecessors, subjugated to "a more tyrannical government than that they rebelled against."[27]

Self-Interest and Faction

Along with man's vulnerability to passion, Loyalist spokesmen were also bothered by man's tendency to pursue his own self-interest. An underlying theme in Loyalist literature was that American society was approaching a crisis because of the growth of personal ambition and the all-consuming desire of individuals to advance their own interests rather than promote the public good. Some Loyalists explicitly acknowledged ambition and selfishness as undesirable but irrepressible human traits. Mankind, according to Jonathan Sewall, "are naturally inclined to usurp authority over their fellow-men"; they possessed an irresistible "itch for superiority." This almost animalistic urge to advance oneself, another believed, drove people to extremes. Avarice and ambition, it was asserted, were the two main contemporary evils which sprang from the quest for wealth and power.[28] Other Loyalists merely noted with uneasiness the prevalence of the pursuit of private goals and ambitions at the expense of the public welfare.[29] An important theme in the Loyalist history of the Revolution was that the Patriots had no concern for the public good and were motivated instead by their own ambitions and desire to advance their interests.[30]

For some Loyalists self-interested behavior was a source of anxiety because it conflicted with their social ideals, which were more holistic than those of the Patriots. A society in which it was acceptable for individuals to pursue their own interests would be an individualistic community in which the public interest would be synonymous with the sum of individual interests. Some Loyalists decried such a community and advanced the opposing ideal that when men united to form a society, certain claims of the social whole were established which transcended the aspirations of its individual members. Man in society, according to Sewall, "no longer considers himself as an *individual*, absolutely unaccountable and uncontroulable, but as one of a community, every member of which is bound to consult and promote the general good." Myles Cooper upheld the need for man to look beyond his own individual self-interest and contribute to the welfare of the community; one of the many deficiencies of a state of nature was that instead of a common interest, every part of the community would have a "distinct interest in view." But, he explained in another article, "when men unite in civil society, a common interest of the whole is formed, and each member obliges himself to act jointly with the rest for this common interest." "The good of the whole society," he continued, "must then also be the leading object, and an attention to this greater good, is the criterion by which the patriot is distinguished."[31] Some also rejected what has been called "possessive individualism," the idea that the individual possessed certain abilities or talents which he could use exclusively for his own betterment. Instead, they stressed the belief that man has a duty to use his talents in a public-spirited way to promote the general, as well as his own individual, welfare.[32]

Many Loyalists were also concerned because self-interest was spreading into public life in the form of factionalism. Several expressed alarm
about party faction and the excesses of party spirit, zeal or "designs."[33]
Factions were worrisome because their sole *raison d'être* was self-interest
without any strong commitment to shared political ideals or beliefs.
What bound together members of a faction was the aim to seek power
or influence for the purpose of advancing their own interests. This
point was made explicitly by the Reverend Henry Caner. "Disputes
there always have been, and always will be in a state," he wrote
bluntly, "between those who have the chief management of affairs,
and those who are desirous of being in their places." Leonard expanded upon Caner's argument; the main cause of political conflict, he
believed, was the "competition of individuals for preferment in the
state." This produced party divisions, and each party, he continued,
"professes disinterested patriotism, though some cynical writers have
ventured to assert, that self-love is the ruling passion of the whole."
The only significant difference between the two factions in Massachusetts was that the tories pursued "their private interest through the
medium of court favor," and the whigs pursued "their private interest
by the means of popularity."[34]

What exactly was it that bothered Loyalists most about the growth
of faction—or the pursuit of self-interest—in politics? Undoubtedly,
some denigrated faction because of a nostalgic desire to return to
the Puritan ideal of a corporate society united by Christian brotherly
love and the unanimous commitment of the community to the good
of the whole. But this was not true of the Loyalists generally.
Leonard's bald statement that "party is inseparable from a free state"
would have shocked his Puritan ancestors.[35] What is, in fact, most
striking about the Loyalists' view of political conflict is its modernity.
Conventional eighteenth-century political theory allowed for conflict
between branches of the constitution—between the appointed governor or executive, whose duty it was to uphold the prerogative powers
of the crown, and the elected lower house, charged with preserving
the rights and liberties of the people. There was no provision,
however, within this theoretical framework for factional conflict
within the legislative branch of government, among organized
members of the elite, even though this kind of conflict was very common by the mid-eighteenth century.[36] Although in the course of that

century some colonists, especially in the middle colonies, came to see advantages in party divisions,[37] this was not generally true of Patriot thinkers. The people, in Patriot political theory, were assumed for public purposes to be a united, homogeneous body whose freedom was proportional to the power of elected institutions. Rather than seeing divisions among the people as being an inescapable political reality, the Patriots embraced republicanism in the hope of reforming and uniting the people.[38] Relative to the Patriots, then, Loyalist writers who saw that politics was becoming a struggle among various self-interested factions were going beyond generally accepted political theory and foreshadowing late eighteenth- and nineteenth-century ideas about the inevitability of party divisions.[39] What is most vital, however, is that in denigrating factionalism Loyalists were not merely longing to return to some bygone era of peace and unanimity, nor were they hoping to eradicate either self-interest or faction. Indeed, their view of society as made up of diverse, unequal, frail creatures, activated as often by passion as by reason, would prompt Loyalists to see political conflict and factional divisions as inevitable and unalterable.

Their concern, instead, was with the *effects* of factional politics. One alarming byproduct of faction for many Loyalists was a lessening of private and public morality. By their very nature, factions were amoral in that they were formed solely to acquire power and to advance special interests, and this was reflected, it was argued, in their members' behavior. Political leaders who sought gain at the expense of their country and blatantly "set up their particular interests in opposition to the true interests of their country" were not only acting immorally themselves, they were also setting a bad example for others.[40] Moreover, factions were believed to encourage unprincipled behavior. "There is not anything more astonishing than the unblushing face of party," one Loyalist wrote sadly; "without the smallest confusion she paints the most notorious falsehoods and without the least remorse, attempts to darken the brightest of characters." Party leaders, in other words, only took public positions because of the perceived political advantage of doing so; truth or "national virtue" were irrelevant considerations.[41] Partisanship, or party spirit, and party presses "wholly employed in prosecuting party designs" were intrinsic parts of factional politics, leading to an abandonment of reason in favor of appeals to popular passions and prejudices.[42]

Equally, if not more devastating, were the squabbling and rancor produced by factions. A "partial, vindictive, virulence of spirit," one Loyalist lamented, replaced the "generous warmth and sober firmness of an honest love for our country," as communities were divided along party lines. Animosities and mutual distrusts resulted, another regretted, from the prejudice and partisanship promoted by factions. Several Loyalists feared that if not restrained, factions could reduce communities to virtual anarchy. One, for example, proclaimed that "societies have often been thrown into confusion and disorder, by the turbulence of factious demagogues, who have abused the licence of the press, and credulity of the people, to serve their own interested or ambitious purposes".[43] Also lacking was a sense of common meaning and purpose, as implied in a superb dialogue between a pupil and a teacher of practical politics: "All men, my dear pupil, pursue riches or power, and as some stand in the way of others, parties are formed," all professing "to aim at public good". "Bitter animosity, rancour and enemity" divided the society, and the political behavior of the successful was totally cynical and self-centered. "Your business," the teacher advised the aspiring pupil, "is to keep well with all parties and let the church and state defend themselves."[44]

Thus many Loyalist spokesmen were alarmed about the ways in which self-interested behavior affected their society, political practices, and attitudes. They were seriously concerned with the prospect of social fragmentation. Many writers feared that as individuals increasingly pursued their own self-interest with no regard for the common good or for previously accepted standards of morality, there would be no social cohesion, no bonds to unite the community, no moral guidelines to regulate the behavior of its members. Society would fragment and consist of nothing more than a number of isolated, amoral, self-seeking, and purposeless individuals. Self-interested behavior was also perceived as a major threat to colonial politics. Underlying Loyalist critiques of faction, which to them virtually institutionalized self-interest, was the fear that politics or public life was degenerating into nothing more than an immoral scramble by a myriad of interest groups for place and power. In wondering who was to defend the church and state in a society torn apart by party divisions, the unknown teacher of practical politics was really asking, who was going to define the public interest, promote public morality, and give to the society a sense of common meaning and purpose? Loyalists feared that a society based on self-interest would lack a central focus, a common bond. It would be an unstable and potentially anarchic community.

How legitimate were these Loyalist anxieties? How relevant were their ideas to contemporary colonial society? It would be controversial at best to claim that the Loyalist critique of colonial society and politics reflected exactly the contemporary social and political reality. Mid-eighteenth-century America obviously was not a totally individualistic society characterized only by social disunity and political uncertainty. It is possible, however, to show that many of their concerns were consistent with at least *some* of the changes occurring at the time of the Revolution. In the first place, their perception that ambition and self-interested behavior were becoming more common and accepted was accurate. The North American environment, it could be argued, had always fostered ambition, because the widespread availbility of land meant greater opportunities for advancement in the colonies than in Europe. But ambition and the pursuit of self-interest were especially nurtured by the economic conditions of the time. Between 1720 and 1760 the colonies experienced rapid population growth, economic expansion, and diversification. Colonial society became more individualistic and competitive, and there was greater economic and geographic mobility.[45] Enhanced opportunities to prosper heightened people's ambitions, whetted appetites for a growing array of consumer goods, and encouraged them to act in unabashedly self-interested ways. Americans might still talk about the desirability of subordinating private interests to the general good, but their actions showed that their primary concern was with "the protection and facilitation of group interests and individual enterprise."[46]

Economic behavior also began to affect attitudes about self-interest. Previously considered a weakness or vice which was at odds with public spirit, self-interest came, as early as the seventeenth century in England, to take on more positive connotations. The generally accepted right of the individual to be secure in his property gradually came to encompass as well the right to prosper and advance himself. Moreover, the pursuit of self-interest was increasingly seen as being not only legitimate but also beneficial. Allowing individuals from all walks of life the economic freedom to advance themselves was upheld in some circles as an incentive to individual industry and creativity, which produced economic growth and expansion. Releasing the individual from past restraints could, it seemed, benefit all: ambitions to rise in the economic ladder could be satisfied at the same time as the economy expanded and society prospered. Such views of self-interest laid the foundations for Adam Smith's justification of the market economy. Assuming that profit-seeking was a basic and irreversible part of human nature, Smith argued that there was a natural order which regulated economic activity so that the "actions of self-seeking individuals balanced one another to produce a natural harmony and a momentum toward the maximization of productivity."[47]

There were grounds for the Loyalist view that self-interested conduct was growing and there was also some justification for their concern about social fragmentation and political instability. One of the most significant changes occurring in Britain and America at the time of the Revolution was the emergence of what has been called the market economy. The medieval idea that the economy should be regulated in the interests of the society was gradually being eroded, as economic decision-making passed more and more into the hands of individuals or groups avowedly pursuing their own special interests. The legitimization of this pursuit complemented this significant economic change. One effect of the emergence of the market economy, it has been argued, was the atomization of society.[48] The focus in economic theory and in practice was increasingly on the individual, on his right to use his abilities for his own betterment, and on the benefits to society of allowing him to make economic decisions. Of secondary importance at best was the ideal that the individual had a duty or responsibility to society. If one did not share Adam Smith's belief in a natural balancing mechanism which ensured that economic decisions made by individuals served the public interest, then it was legitimate to ask what would bind together members of the community and prevent it from fragmenting into hundreds of competing interest groups.

The question is especially pertinent when it is considered that other changes were taking place at the time which could be seen as threats to the cohesion and stability of colonial communities. In the generation before the Revolution there were serious challenges to the authority of institutions which had defined the public interest and promoted social harmony and political order. Factional infighting and acrimonious political disputes undermined to some degree the deference, expected of the electorate, toward government as well as toward traditional elites. The church as an institution which upheld the public good and promoted order suffered a setback because of the divisions among the clergy during the Great Awakening and the individualistic religious beliefs of the revival. And as children became more mobile and independent of parents at an earlier age, the family, it has been contended, acted less and less effectively as a stabilizing social institution. Despite the lessening influence of church and family, no alternative agencies to achieve social cohesion or political order or to define the public interest had gained general acceptance.[49]

Certain characteristics of contemporary American politics also fostered uncertainty and volatility. Colonial political institutions, though modeled on those of the mother country, lacked the solid grounding of their English counterparts.[50] Political practices of the eighteenth century merely accentuated the instability. Political factions developed in almost all of the colonies in the course of the century, and very much as Loyalists described them, they were based not on differing political philosophies, but represented various economic and sectional interests.[51] As competing factions curried favor with the electorate, there was greater popular involvement in politics, which in turn added a volatile dimension to public life. Moreover, the press, used increasingly for partisan political purposes, became a powerful propaganda tool that could be used to sway public opinion. And the mob — an accepted part of the political process — presumed to mete out justice often in defiance of the law, and increasingly the lower classes used it to vent their grievances and achieve their goals.[52]

Thus, when Loyalists worried openly about self-interested behavior, instability, and the lack of cohesion in the community, they were reflecting some very real changes occurring in their midst, and this fact sheds new light on their ideology. In the first place, it sets their response to the Revolution in a broader context. In light of the challenges to social unity and political order posed by the development of the market economy and the lessening of influence of the church and family, it is not surprising that Loyalists were deeply concerned when government, the final bastion of order in colonial society, also came under attack. Seen from this vantage point, the Revolution, which swept away the last vestiges of government power, represented the final blow to social unity and political order in America.

Secondly, the fact that there was some substance to Loyalist anxieties about instability affects any assessment of the relevance of their ideology to contemporary Americans, which has been largely overlooked. The Patriots, it has been pointed out, in warning of the dangers of British tyranny, were striking a responsive chord with their readers who had deeply rooted fears about the threat power posed to liberty.[53] But the whole thrust of the Loyalist argument was that anarchy and popular tyranny were more imminent threats to America than was the arbitrary power of British or colonial governments. The Loyalist appeal was to anxieties about instability—the absence of a sense of unity, cohesion, order, and continuity in colonial life. The immediate circumstances of the mid-1770s, when lawlessness, violence, and mob activity were common, fed such fears, as did the more general changes taking place at the time. The growth of individualism and the prominence, even acceptance, of self-interested behavior challenged long-established norms about desirable behavior and fostered concerns about the effects of such conduct on community order. Factions fostered acrimony in public life, and their very existence was at odds with the traditional belief that leaders should act in public-spirited ways to promote social harmony. In the Revolutionary period, then, when there were some signs of instability, uncertainty, and confusion about basic values, Americans were just as likely to be apprehensive about social fragmentation and political instability and their attendant evils as they were to fear tyranny.

Patriots, it should be pointed out, did not share these Loyalist concerns because their ideology was more consistent with self-interested behavior. Loyalists did not believe there were, or could ever be, natural bonds uniting a society of individuals pursuing their own self-interest. Patriots, on the other hand, embraced the ideal of an individualistic society whose members joined together voluntarily and were united by a consensus about basic values.[54] Loyalists could not share this ideal because it was so inconsistent with their beliefs about man and the people. Assuming men were unequal, diverse creatures ruled as easily by passion as by reason, a society that allowed individuals the greatest possible freedom, and left it up to them to find a common basis for their union would be a nightmare, as was the hypothetical state of nature to many Loyalists.[55] Conflict would rage uncontrolled; the stronger members of society would victimize the weaker. And rather than consensus, only disagreement and disorder would result. Underlying Loyalist ideology, then, was the implicit premise that man was too imperfect and the people too unpredictable to be left entirely to their own devices. Loyalists lacked the Patriots' faith in the individual and the people; they had, instead, confidence in the unifying and stabilizing influence of institutions generally and of governments specifically.

Liberty and Government

Loyalist attitudes toward government and other institutions must be studied in relation to Patriot ideology. The American Revolution was premised on a liberal vision of society, and part of this vision was what might be called a positive view of liberty. Associated with freedom from restraint or control over one's destiny, liberty was highly prized by Patriots, who assumed that there was perpetual tension between it and power. To ensure that liberty was not overwhelmed by power required vigilance. Government, from this perspective, was best described by Thomas Paine as a "necessary evil" or a "badge of lost innocence".[56] Government was necessary as an impartial arbiter, to *guarantee* to individuals their natural rights; but because government power posed a potential threat to individual liberty, its authority had to be limited, defined, and regulated. "Supreme, or unlimited authority, can with fitness, belong only to the Sovereign of the universe," the Massachusetts Council declared. "The supreme authority of every government is limited."[57]

The Loyalists' view of liberty, on the other hand, could be called negative in that the stress was not on maximizing individual freedom but on controlling or setting bounds to freedom. This emphasis on restraining rather than liberating the individual was expressed aptly by an unknown writer. "As much liberty as is consistent with good order and government, is the right of subjects in common," he began. "But more liberty," he asserted, "is destructive: and [breeds] a spirit of licentiousness and insolence, in the lower classes of the people, to say nothing of the higher, [it] is in every view criminal and most commonly proves fatal."[58] While Patriots worried that power would be transformed into tyranny, Loyalists feared that liberty would degenerate into licentiousness. "Liberty and licentiousness are nearly

allied to each other; like wit and madness," Isaac Wilkins declared.
"There is but a thin partition between them; and licentiousness in-
variably leads to slavery." Americans had to be especially vigilant that
liberty did not degenerate into licentiousness because "The Americans
love liberty; 'tis their grand, their darling object." "But that love of
liberty," he warned, "if not carefully watched and attended to, will
. . . prove a dreadful source of misfortunes to us, if not of ruin."[59]

Other writers advocated more specific limits on individual freedom.
Several granted that criticisms of government were legitimate or even
beneficial, but effectively limited the freedom to criticize authority by
insisting that critics could not "advance anything in dimunition of the
peace and good order of society."[60] Restraints on individual freedom
were related directly to man's nature by an early defender of Thomas
Hutchinson: "Human Nature is so constituted, that without a restraint from many things, we can enjoy nothing . . . Felicity will not
blossom on the boughs of unbridled freedom; on the contrary the soul
unrestrained runs wild, and like a vine unpruned, shoots into fruitless
branches and leaves, and becomes sterile."[61] The belief that individual
freedom had to be controlled was consistent with the idea that man
was an imperfect being vulnerable to the pull of passion as well as the
higher call of reason; to allow unrestrained freedom to such creatures
would be to invite disorder, instability, and irrationality.

The other side of a limited view of liberty was a more positive view,
based on two main ideas, of institutions generally and of government
specifically. One idea was that institutions were essential to the happiness and freedom of individuals; the other was that institutions and
their authority were seen not as potentially threatening but as benign
or salutary.

Relative to the Patriots, the Loyalist approach to institutions was
historical. Patriots were more likely to posit the law of nature as a
universal principle that should be applied to all institutions, regardless
of considerations like the nature of the population or its stage of
development.[62] Loyalists like Charles Inglis, however, saw institutions less as the creations of a single generation and more as traditions
and practices which unfolded over time to meet the peculiar "genius,
manners, disposition and other circumstances of the people." Leonard
justified the Quebec Act on the grounds that it was "adapted to the
genius and manners of the Canadians." Institutions which evolved

gradually over the course of many generations preserved the "wisdom of ages," as Inglis put it, and at the same time had the flexibility to change in response to new circumstances.[63] This latter point was made very effectively by Thomas Hutchinson, who disputed the Patriot idea of certain fundamental principles of the constitution that, like a bill of rights, could not be changed. He preferred the concept of parliamentary supremacy—the idea that "no act can be made or passed in any Parliament which it shall not be in the power of a subsequent Parliament to alter and repeal"—because customs and institutions which were outdated and no longer served the needs of a generation could be altered in accord with new circumstances.[64] From this perspective, institutions were almost like a mirror of a society; ideally, they retained the wisdom of the past and adjusted to meet the needs of the future. They had for this reason continuity and an enduring quality. For many Loyalists, institutions were unifying and stabilizing forces which embodied the shared experiences of a people, had been tested by time, and were to be esteemed at least as highly as the reasoning of one generation of imperfect individuals.

A common assumption in Loyalist tributes to church and family was that these institutions should use their moral authority to bring out man's potential to act rationally and unselfishly and to discourage or even repress man's baser instincts. The standard belief that the family should "train them [children] to become useful members of society" was upheld by one writer. Achieving this required that the passions be "properly directed." Indulgent mothers were criticized because their children learned "petulance and obstinancy," which led to "an habitual disregard to their authority." Mothers should stress the importance of authority, obedience, and awe and reverence for authority.[65] The church also had the responsibility for encouraging virtue and discouraging vice and more specifically, for inculcating the importance of deference and respect for authority. A defender of T. B. Chandler quoted St. Paul—"The powers that be, are ordained of God"—to prove that "government in general is the ordinance of God and that obedience in general is the duty of Christians, in such a way and measure as the *Constitution* of each country has pointed out."[66]

More common than tributes to the family or church was praise for government, whose positive role was supported for a wide variety of reasons. For many Loyalists the necessity for government was rooted firmly in man's nature. As Charles Inglis explained, the state of nature was a fiction, and "a state of society is the *natural state of man*." Man's wants and weakness as well as his "noblest faculties" made him by nature sociable, so that "whatever *happiness* or *perfection* we are capable of, can only be attained in society." But society could not exist without government; as Inglis put it, man "is born in *society*, whose ends cannot be obtained, but by *subordination, order*, and *the regulation of laws*, and where these are, there is government." [67]

Loyalist writers also saw government as essential to man's well-being because it was a unifying and even paternalistic force which regulated conflict and maintained order. An important function of any central authority, according to Peter Van Schaack, was to balance and harmonize the differing and self-interested claims of the various parts of a political unit. He stressed the importance within the empire of accommodating disparate and potentially conflicting interests within one political framework. The task was to find the point — which for him certainly did exist — "in which the general good of the whole, with the least possible disadvantage to every part, does centre." [68] The task of harmonizing disparate interests was part and parcel of government's broader function of preserving order. Loyalists frequently associated government and laws with peace, order, and security. Government was to secure to individuals their rights and freedoms, foster a peaceful, stable society, and promote order.

Such views of government and law were remarkably secular and modern. Laws were not seen as tools to punish sin and nurture good Christians but as instruments to maintain social and political order and make good citizens. [69] Some Loyalists went so far as to argue that laws need not be consistent with "natural justice." In other words, the law was to be obeyed not because it was consistent with universal moral principles, but because it was the means by which government regulated society and preserved order. [70] Government also played a paternal role in protecting the weaker and more vulnerable members of society. According to Samuel Seabury, "Government was intended for the security of those who live under it; — to protect the weak against the strong; — the good against the bad; — to preserve order and decency among men, preventing every one from injuring his neighbour." For these reasons, "Every person, then, owes obedience to the laws of the government under which he lives and is obliged in honour and duty to support them." [71]

The Significance of the Loyalists' Conservatism

Thus a fundamental ideological division between Loyalists and Patriots lay in their differing views of liberty and government. Whereas a Patriot like Josiah Quincy Junior might assert that "it is much easier to restrain liberty from running into licentiousness than power from swelling into tyranny and oppression," Loyalist writers assumed exactly the opposite.[72] For them liberty was constantly in danger of degenerating into licentiousness, and anarchy loomed as a much more ominous and imminent evil than did government tyranny. Neither side condoned anarchy or tyranny, but their disagreement about which evil was more serious was fundamental. Patriot thought was premised on an almost obsessive fear of tyranny and a pervasive distrust of power. Patriots placed a high priority on individual freedom and assumed an inherent tension between liberty and power. Government authority, therefore, had to be restricted and controlled so that it could not endanger individual liberty.

Loyalist ideas about liberty and government were more conservative. The duty of the state was to protect the lives, liberties, and property of the individual. But because man was happiest, most secure, and freest in a society under government and law, it was also the duty of individuals to uphold the authority of government. In other words, while Patriots believed that individual liberty had to be protected from government power, Loyalists felt that it was government that ensured the security and freedom of the individual.

The Loyalists' more positive attitude toward government and other institutions has to be seen in relation to their views of man generally and of his self-interested behavior specifically. Assuming, as Loyalists did, that society comprised unequal, diverse, and imperfect beings, conflict was seen as virtually unavoidable. This was especially true, for many Loyalists, in mid-eighteenth-century America, where self-interested behavior and its political manifestation in the form of factions threatened to undermine public morality, fragment society, and throw the political order into disarray. Yet, because such behavior was almost to be expected in light of man's weaknesses, Loyalists could not look to some utopian solution, like the ending of political conflict. But they could see in institutions and especially in government countervailing forces that unified and stabilized society and fostered public morality. Families and churches could impress upon their members the virtues of restrained, rational conduct and the vital importance of deference and respect for authority. Government, as an institution which presided over the society, could not obliterate conflict and self-interest—such aims would be utopian—but it could regulate and channel them within legal and institutional bounds. Government could impose order and impart a sense of common purpose to a society of increasingly isolated and contentious individuals. Thus, institutions like government were regarded as being vital to an increasingly individualistic society like that of colonial America because they counteracted what were seen to be undesirable effects of self-interested behavior.

Loyalist ideas about government were neither backward-looking nor totally ill-suited to contemporary American society. The liberal ideology of the Patriots, it is true, was more compatible with the individualistic behavior that was an intrinsic part of the emerging market economy.[73] The Loyalists' more conservative ideology, however, was in tune with other contemporary changes. Their attitudes toward political conflict and the law were remarkably modern and well suited to a pluralistic society, characterized increasingly by conflict among differing individuals or interest groups. Their political ideas were more elitist and antidemocratic than those of the Patriots, but they reflected the social structure and distribution of wealth that was becoming more common in the colonies. By the 1770s colonial society resembled its British counterpart in that it was a stratified structure topped by affluent and politically powerful elites. In New York, especially, the foundations for a hierarchical and deferential society were in the making as the growing demand for land enhanced the profitability of the huge manorial estates.[74] Even in the political sphere, the trend was not entirely in the direction of greater democratization—a larger role for the people or their representatives in the political process. In Massachusetts, for example, evidence suggests that power was in fact gravitating away from popularly elected officials and in the direction of royal appointees like justices of the peace.[75]

The point quite simply is that although the Patriot ideal of a liberal society—stressing individualism and a limited government—triumphed, this was not inevitable. Loyalists offered Americans a more conservative ideology based on a positive view of the state and a distrust of the masses that was also consistent with some aspects of colonial society. The importance of this ideology as an alternative to Patriot ideas is accentuated when it is considered that neither their world view nor their critique of American society were new to their readers; both were rooted in British political theory and in the previous decade of colonial experience.

4

COLONIAL ORIGINS
OF LOYALIST IDEOLOGY

It always seemed strange to me that People who contend so much for
civil and religious Liberty, should bo so ready to deprive others of
their natural Liberty. — THEOPHILUS LILLIE,
Boston Chronicle, JANUARY 15, 1770

LOYALIST WARNINGS about attitudes and practices fostering anarchy
and popular tyranny were not new to colonial readers. In the 1760s
in the course of local controversies, writers in New York and Massachusetts had warned in almost identical terms of the danger posed by
unscrupulous factions which challenged traditional symbols of authority. In other colonies, as well, these ideas were foreshadowed in local
controversies, including the issue of salaries for Anglican clerics in
Maryland, disputes in South Carolina between the upper and lower
houses over control of the purse and about plural officeholding, and
the exchange between pro- and anti-Anglican writers in Connecticut
and other New England colonies.[1] Some of the tracts of the 1760s
were written by future Loyalists who apparently did not become partisans just because of the Anglo-American crisis; they had been critical
for some time of contemporary political practices and changes. More
generally, the resemblance shows that the Loyalist argument did not
suddenly emerge in the 1774–1776 period, but was deeply rooted in a
critique of colonial society which had developed well before independence became an issue. In the two or three years before independence,
then, Loyalists were simply crystallizing and expanding upon ideas
which had been for some time an integral part of colonial political

culture. Thus, the colonial origins of Loyalist ideology lie in various political disputes which raged in the 1760s and early 1770s.

These political squabbles were symptomatic of the problems of the mid-eighteenth-century in America. Rapid changes produced instability, tension, conflict, and uncertainties about basic values. As a result, many colonists felt—and voiced their feelings of—disorientation and anxiety. They expressed fear that their communities were declining from the virtue of some pristine bygone era and longed for the certainties associated with an often mythical past.

What was required at a time like this, when so many colonists were disillusioned, confused, and anxious, was some common thread or central focus to tie together all of these disparate ideas and fears, to isolate the causes and nature of the malady afflicting colonial America, to pinpoint the villains in the piece and to alleviate anxieties by pointing the way to ultimate solutions. These needs were satisfied in the 1760s as two quite different interpretations of the nature and root causes of colonial troubles appeared. One became part of the Patriot rationale for the Revolution, and the other— so far virtually ignored by historians[2]—prepared the way for the Loyalist argument and history.

Exponents of the Patriot view saw the growing concentration of economic and political power in New York and Massachusetts in the hands of elites supported by the patronage of the British crown as the main source of colonial troubles. In the 1760s, for example, concern about economic problems—trade contractions, indebtedness, high food prices, unemployment, and the scarcity of circulating medium[3] —was voiced by writers of all shades of opinion. Some, however, foreshadowing Patriot views, went beyond general lamenting of the troubled economic times to look more closely at economic distress. The poor, facing long winters without work, firewood, or money, were portrayed being carted off to jail for debt or reduced to begging. The destitution of the poor was particularly alarming because of the disparaties between the impoverished and the well-to-do, who wallowed in "luxury and pleasure."[4] The stratification in Boston—"glittering with new and pompous equipages" while many were declaring bankruptcy—was disturbing to one writer, while another bemoaned the general indifference to the dire straits of the less fortunate.[5]

In their view stratification, like many other colonial problems, was related to the British influence on American life. The honors and dignities bestowed by the crown, they contended, fostered the emergence of an intercolonial elite which was entrenching itself, consolidating its economic and political power, and jeopardizing the freedom and even the morality of Americans.[6] It was argued that the rising American demand for sumptuous and frivolous foreign fineries —luxuries made fashionable by members of the colonial elite who aped the manners, customs, and in some cases even the religion of the British upper classes—was enervating the spirit of the American people and the simplicity, frugality, and virtue of the first settlers. A writer in the *New York Gazette* described the "moral decay" produced by the increase in foreign luxuries: The "simplicity, frugality and ancient plainness of that nation [America], were changed for foreign fopperies and luxuries, which all tended to render the morals of men effeminate, and at the same time inclined them to sell everything, to obtain the objects of their desire."[7] Crown patronage was deemed to corrupt political leaders, who abandoned their principles and commitment to the public interest in their scramble for royal favors and places.[8] This group of colonists, then, was convinced that liberty and morality were threatened from above—by an economic and political elite whose virtual monopoly of power threatened popular freedom— and from external forces—the crown's ability to influence American affairs through its distribution of patronage and favors.

This interpretation was countered by another which focused on the growing instability of colonial politics as the most pressing problem. To these observers, the intellectual predecessors of the Loyalists, the unruly behavior and antiauthoritarian attitudes of colonial subjects were the root cause of instability, contention, and immorality. "Tumultuous assemblies, licentious publications, disregard to acts of trade and others" were sources of anxiety to some writers, while others were alarmed by "illegal combinations" and "bullying, Riots, treasons and rebellions."[9] Still other observers were aghast at the "eternal clamor," "Seditions, Factions," "rampant Licentiousness," and "Mob Principles," which it was feared would lead to the breakdown of society.[10] The excesses of the decade, such as the demolition of Thomas Hutchinson's Boston mansion by the mob in 1765, merely fed these fears of disorder.

Such behavior, it was contended, was encouraged by factions and by opponents of government who, in their single-minded and self-interested quest for popularity and power, used the most deplorable tactics to inflame popular passions against public leaders and institutions. These writers were dismayed that public spirit was at a low ebb, as factious interest groups competed with each other for popularity or royal favor and subordinated their principles and concern for the public welfare to the desire for personal power and wealth. "Persons of ability and freedom of thought," exclaimed a New Yorker, "will be considered 'heterodox' in the Present System of Politicks."[11] The prevalence of self-interest, craft, and cunning[12] in political leaders was deplored, as was the increase in electoral corruption[13] and the tendency for politicians to pose as patriots or upholders of popular liberty in order to acquire power, which they used to advance their own private interests.[14] The factionalism and loss of public virtue characteristic of political leaders had also, it appeared, infected the electorate itself, which seemed to be growing more contentious and materialistic and less deferential and public-spirited. A New York author depicted the corrupt and volatile electorate in his colony in the following manner:

> Would it not anger any true born *Roman*,
> To see the giddy multitude together;
> Never consulting who 'tis best deserves,
> But who feasts highest, to obtain their suffrage?
> . . . To-day the drunken rabble reel to one;
> To-morrow they were mad again, for th'other,
> Changing their voices with their entertainment,
> And none could guess on whom the choice would settle.

The New Yorkers, he concluded, were like the Romans who "had far degenerated from the rough virtues of their ancestors . . . [and] they did not long maintain their *greatness*, or their *liberties*."[15] If not restrained, these writers warned, factions and demagogues would corrupt the morality of the citizenry, undermine completely the authority of government and law, and reduce the colonies to a state of lawless anarchy. From this perspective, the greatest threat to freedom and morality in America came from within the colonies and from below— from the self-interested factions which were both undermining the authority of legally established institutions and misappropriating government power to illegal and unconstitutional combinations.

The Defense of the Bernard and Hutchinson Administrations

One of the earliest engagements between the two opposing interpretations of colonial troubles occurred in Massachusetts in the 1760s.
James Otis, Jr., egged on by other government critics and future
Patriots, raised a political storm by his vituperative attacks on the administration of Governor Francis Bernard and, more specifically, by
his devastating criticism of the plural officeholding of Thomas
Hutchinson, who was at once chief justice, a lower court judge, and
lieutenant governor. Hutchinson, along with his associates the
Olivers, had been so successful in courting crown favors, it was alleged, that he and his friends and relatives were appointed to various
judicial and executive positions which were incompatible with each
other. The concentration of so much power in the hands of this elite,
government critics warned, was inconsistent with the theory of the
separation of powers and was therefore a serious threat to the freedom
of Massachusetts.[16]

Alarmed by the implications of the charges leveled by Otis and his
supporters and disturbed by the tone of their opposition to government, Jonathan Sewall and an array of anonymous authors responded.
They called Otis a "disturber of the public peace," "Bluster," or
"Jemmy"[17] and his backers the Junto[18] or conspirators, and they
warned about the cabal's motives and methods as well as the threat
"Juntocracy"[19] posed to the peace, order, and freedom of Massachusetts.[20]

At the heart of the case made by Sewall and his cohorts against the
Junto was the perception of their antagonists' motives for attacking
Bernard and Hutchinson. To Sewall, Otis was undoubtedly motivated
by "a desire of popularity; from a restless turbulency of spirit, from
ambitious views, from envy, revenge or other the like execrable
springs, tho' disguised under the enchanting cloak of patriotism and
public spirit."[21] Another writer offered a more specific explanation:
"The real cause of most of the troubles and madness" was James Otis,
Jr.'s, disappointment over his father's failure to be appointed to the
bench. Otis possessed "a strong inclination to rise in life which urges
most men of parts." When such ambitions were thwarted, "how
poorly our feeble frame supports grievous disappointments, and [how]
wrong and indirect [are the] measures we often pursue to get relief."[22]

Though in truth spurred on by desires to cancel their debts or be highly esteemed as Patriots, opponents of government "must have something plausible to guild over their designs," another antagonist of the Junto asserted, and therefore were compelled to conjure up visions of slavery in order to arouse the people.[23]

Sewall and company were not condemning criticisms of government actions in themselves, but were attacking the perceived motives of the critics. Instead of public-spirited men dedicated to serving the best interests of the colony, Otis and his associates were perceived to be self-interested individuals, whose attacks on government sprang from ambition, envy, or malice. They craved power for its own sake. This assumption about the self-interested and even sordid motives of government critics was crucial since it led to the further premise that there were no deeply rooted ideological differences between Bernard, Hutchinson, and their supporters, on the one hand, and Otis and his followers, on the other hand. The Junto were not criticizing the Bernard and Hutchinson governments because they sincerely believed that measures adopted by these regimes were not in the best interests of the colony or because of fundamental differences in political views. Rather it was the quest for popularity and power or a perverse desire for vengeance which led to the attacks on government. This very important assumption allowed Sewall and other writers to proceed as the Loyalist would and to dismiss rather offhandedly the substance of their opponents' arguments and to focus instead on their methods and aims.

One charge directed again and again at Otis and other government critics, who usually published in the *Boston Gazette*, was that they were perverting the liberty of speech and of the press. Although criticisms of government actions and differing views on public issues were accepted as being inevitable or even beneficial,[24] certain limits to these activities were considered necessary to maintain public peace, order, and decorum. These limits were, it was argued, being flagrantly violated by Otis and his friends. Instead of merely criticizing specific government measures, the *Boston Gazette* writers were accused of vilifying the characters and maligning the integrity of public figures. Otis, according to Sewall, was "abusing every man who has any share in the administration of government" and "traiterously insulting even the Majesty of his Sovereign." "Some of the best and most respectable characters"[25] were supposedly the victims of Otis' barbs. "Indecent and illiberal" charges against the governor, Sewall explained, would only "raise in the minds of the people, discontent, jealousies and contempt of all government."[26]

The Junto had as well transgressed the boundary line between restrained, circumspect criticism and rude, insolent harangues. They relied on character assassination, "poisonous suggestions," "guilded falsehoods," "Billingsgate," reproach, scandal, and "Artful Insinuations." "Bad must that cause be," an ally of Sewall's chided, "which needs Slander and Defamation to keep it from sinking."[27] Moreover, the Patriot demagogues were accused of displaying a total disregard for truth. They used false charges and completely unfounded allegations to arouse fears of slavery and thereby incite popular passions against the government and its supporters. An unknown versifier described the "Plot" as follows:

> The people now Jealous from what's been of late,
> As sure as a Gudgeon will swallow the bait,
> Then quick let us strike while the iron is hot,
> For if once they grow cool, it will blow up our plot,
> Why didn't I tell you we wanted no proof?
> That we'd swear 'twas all true; and pray, aint that enough?[28]

Thus, by attacking traditional figures and institutions of authority in an insolent, unrestrained way, government critics were inflaming the people's passions, undermining public peace, order and decency, and thereby prostituting liberty itself. A New England Man declared, "A Set of Partisans . . . under Pretences of Liberty and Freedom are become a mere licentious Rabble."[29]

The Junto members were also accused of subverting freedom in another way. Their intense and blind partisanship, it was claimed, led them to exhibit an aggressive intolerance of dissenting views. In 1766, A By-stander criticized "*some* men, which are carried to such an extravagant pitch," that they had denounced or questioned the motives of anyone who disagreed with their view of the Stamp Act. In doing this, the "zealous partisans" were "tyrannizing over the consciences and judgements of the people."[30] According to Z. T., an incident in 1768 revealed the persecuting temperament of some members of the General Court. A circular Letter composed by the House of Representatives, summarizing Massachusetts' opposition to British measures, was sent to other colonies to seek their cooperation in gaining redress. When Lord Hillsborough, the secretary in charge of American affairs, threatened to dissolve the House of Representatives if the letter was not rescinded, seventeen Representatives voted in favor of rescinding the letter. Z. T. believed that many had "acted with fidelity." Yet, they were

> in a most scandalous manner proscribed by the art and cunning of some persons, who promoted and published a catalogue of their names, called the black list . . . which had such influence as to exclude a considerable number of them (who had been esteemed worthy members) from being chosen representatives afterwards. Which also served to raise a panic and intimidate many others, and . . . to cause them to be influenced by fear, lest they should not secure their future elections. And did not those popular and zealous partisans in the house of representatives seem fully determined at all events to brow beat every fair reasoner, and to overbear all opposition.[31]

The licentiousness and intolerant partisanship of the opposition faction was not confined merely to the Junto, it was argued, but was being drilled into the body politic as a whole. More than one Massachusetts commentator in the late 1760s and early 1770s interpreted the actions of the Junto as a sign that traditional norms regulating political and even moral behavior were being overturned and replaced by a whole new set of ideas which were gradually contaminating the political culture of the colony. A True Patriot claimed he was writing his articles in the *Boston Evening-Post* "to put a stop to the very prejudicial system of politicks, so long fed and grown under the auspices of the Junto."[32] The notion that some sort of disease, whose symptoms included irrationality and extremism, was plaguing the body politic of Massachusetts was conveyed by a writer who counseled his readers to become more restrained and moderate.[33] A defender of Governor Hutchinson espoused the view that "a kind of confused political Orthodoxy seems gradually substituting [itself] in the place of the very Principles and Maxims, which hitherto have been esteemed . . . tenets of the Constitution."[34]

More specifically, certain of the Junto's political tactics were believed to be fostering an antiauthoritarian attitude among the badly misinformed electorate. "People, Sir, grow factious or submissive to government from habit and custom," one polemicist asserted. Encouraged by the indiscriminate and intemperate attacks on government by the Junto, the people themselves, he feared, were displaying a disturbing libertinism.[35] Philander, who called himself a reader of history, feared that the wantonness and antiauthoritarianism of the masses would prove dangerous to the freedom of Massachusetts: "The Propensity of a State, depends more on the Manners and Principles of the People in general, than on those of their Governors in particular; and that the Liberties of a Commonwealth are more endangered from a prevailing Licentiousness and Debauchery, than they can be from the ambitious Designs, joined with the greatest Abilities, and most enterprising Disposition of any one in Power."[36] To ABC it was symptomatic of the temper of the times that "leaders of a party use sophistry instead of logick . . . [and] traduce the characters of their opposers instead of reasoning with them."[37] Z. Z. complained that the true merits of an issue were never really discussed, since rhetoric and unsubstantiated charges passed for truth and reasoned argument. As to the role of the press and slogans in molding public opinion: "The whole issue of any dispute . . . is now turned upon this single point, who shall first obtain the cry of the papers? No matter by what means, the merits of the question are seldom enquired after. Wilkes and Liberty! are sufficient to satisfy every understanding and stand superior to every argument and reason which can afterwards be brought against it."[38]

When an aroused public opinion and popular esteem were the standards by which leaders were chosen, one author argued, men's qualifications and public spirit were ignored. "Insolvents and bankrupts raise their heads, their hopes and tongues, and cry and pronounce Liberty & c. very loud and distinct. In such a state of things men rise not by merit, but because they make a great noise and use many bold words and threaten to do great things which they can never perform."[39] Several others argued that by forcing leaders to curry popular favor and bow to public opinion, the integrity and independence of judgment of public figures were being undermined. A friend to Peace and good Order applauded an unpopular decision of the council on the grounds that the councillors' aim was to "serve the people rather than please them" and to decide on the basis of conviction what was advantageous to the community.[40] "It is a most infallible symptom of the dangerous state of liberty," another writer argued ominously, "when the chief men of a free country shew a greater regard to popularity than to their own judgement."[41]

Thus to a number of Massachusetts observers writing in the decade before independence, the turmoil, instability, and rancor plaguing their colony could be traced to a faction which had fabricated sensational allegations to arouse popular passions against political leaders as a means of having them overthrown. And such factious behavior was assumed to be spreading. The populace, it was argued, displayed an alarming antiauthoritarianism, a distressing disinterest in discovering the true merits of an issue, and a dangerous proclivity to choose their leaders on the basis of popular appeal rather than merit or commitment to the general good. In the long term, several writers predicted that the debilitating effects of faction would plunge Massachusetts into a state of lawless anarchy or popular tyranny.

Anarchy and Democratic Tyranny in Massachusetts

Warnings that the opposition faction was leading Massachusetts to the brink of anarchy and even tyranny were common in the 1760s and early 1770s. A scathing denunciation of Governor Hutchinson's opponents ended with this description: "Faction is as pernicious as power overstrained, and has undone almost every free government mentioned by antiquity . . . Venice . . . the wisest and most lasting free government . . . has been obliged to make a tyrannic jurisdiction a part of its Constitution in order to crush faction in its bud, and put off the first sparks of party e'er can they kindle the fire of sedition."[42] Jonathan Sewall specifically charged the Junto with subverting "one of the grand bulwarks of English liberty," trial by jury, a "safeguard . . . against tyranny, on the one hand, & the *sudden premature* judgment of the multitude on the other." The incident which prompted Sewall's charge was the condemnation by Sam Adams, the future Patriot, of the acquittal of Captain Preston and the soldiers responsible for the Boston Massacre. Sewall alleged that in criticizing the court's decision Adams was trying to pressure the judge and jurors and was thereby undermining the "perfect uncontrouled *freedom* of mind in the determinations both of judges and jurors," which was basic to the integrity of the judicial system.[43]

Other writers warned that the balance among the three branches of the English constitutional form of government—the assembly, council, and governor—was being seriously undermined in Massachusetts, as was the independence of individual representatives. As the *Censor* argued, in the House of Representatives the dominant faction, through such practices as blacklisting had succeeded in preventing able men from being reelected and in coercing the minority to follow the majority. This was regarded as a blow to liberty in the colony, "for our liberties depend as much upon freedom of speech and a free vote within the house, as upon a Free Press without."[44] At the same time, it was contended, the cabal which controlled the House of Representatives employed its power to exclude those whose views did not coincide with its own. As a result, "the two houses [have] been subjugated to the imperious dictates of the then ruling despots." The final step in the scheme to overturn "the very constitution of our civil government," was represented by the attempts to destroy the power and independence of the governor by insisting that he remain dependent on the House of Representatives for his salary or by disputing his right to follow instructions from the British government.[45] As Henry Caner explained, since the Representatives already controlled the council, their attempts to make the governor—the representative of the king and upholder of the prerogative—dependent also on them "is giving that branch of the Legislature such weight, as would render it absolute and uncontroullable." "From hence it seems evident," he concluded, "that if our constitution is in any danger, that danger is at present most likely to arise, not from the too great freedom or independence of the Governor, but from the too powerful influence of the third branch, or House of Representatives."[46]

According to these writers, opponents of government in Massachusetts were aiming to undermine the British constitutional form of government, thereby threatening stability and freedom. Basic to this theoretical approach to government was the belief that the independence of judgment of individual representatives and the independence of each branch of the constitution guaranteed freedom and order. The alternative—popular control of government and the judiciary—was associated with instability and insecurity. To cite one example, A Quaker expressed horror at the possibility that judges, rather than being independent or accountable only to the king, would be dependent on "a fickle inconstant multitude, who will cry Hosanna to day and crucify to morrow."[47]

Besides evidence of anarchy, there were also signs to some observers in the 1760s that Massachusetts was experiencing popular tyranny. "Tyranny and oppression for the most part spring out of anarchy introduced by slackening the reins of government," one wrote.[48] John Mein and other writers in the *Boston Chronicle* lambasted the arbitrary and oppressive nature of the nonimportation scheme. Because of the weakness of government in Massachusetts, they argued, illegal and unrepresentative committees—"Demi-Pope[s]"[49]—established to institute and enforce nonimportation, assumed the power, which according to the law and constitution was reserved exclusively to government and the judiciary, to pass laws and punish violations of them. In so doing, the "ruling power in this country" relegated nonsupporters of the scheme to the status of outlaws and violated the independence of their fellow colonists.[50]

Some of the most incisive criticisms of the committees were penned by Theophilus Lillie, a future Loyalist who had himself been coerced into joining the nonimportation scheme. He contrasted committee shibboleths about liberty with committee actions. It was ironic, he pointed out "that men who are guarding against being subject to Laws [to] which they never gave their consent . . . at the same time make Laws and in the most effectual manner execute them upon me and others, to which Laws I am sure I never gave my consent, either in person or by my representative." Such behavior was inconsistent with "my poor notion of Government," the role of which was to prevent "one set of private subjects" from punishing at their whim "another set of private subjects. . . I own I had rather be a slave under one master; for if I know who he is, I may perhaps, be able to please him, than a slave to an hundred or more, who I don't know where to find, nor what they will expect of me."[51]

A bitter and impassioned harangue about the tyranny of illegal committees and mobs expressed so well the indignation of other *Boston Chronicle* writers that it merits quoting at length:

> Shall a number of pretended patriots, or even mad enthusiasts, be they merchant, mechanicks, hucksters, or mariners . . . form themselves into a detached body and presume to make laws for the rest, in direct violation of the established laws of the country, and to make a more formidable appearance, constitute sub-agents with delegated authority to ravage the city like a lawless banditti, and have the effrontery not only to demand but menace the destruction of the property and even

the lives of their fellow subjects, if they dare dispute their mandates. And shall we tamely behold every natural, civil, religious and national right thus horribly invaded, and usurped by one subject over another and still pretend to talk of LIBERTY, PROPERTY and RIGHTS without a blush? Have we not by this weak, absurd conduct and indulgence, established courts of inquisition in the colonies unparalleled in any age or nation? Where but in this unhappy, and misled country, was there ever an instance of men, free men, being summoned by illegal & mock-authority, to answer for actions as offences, which are warranted by the laws of the land, the laws of nations, the law of nature and the law of GOD!

Martyr, in his portrayal of some actions of the committeemen, concluded sadly, "Such are the characters of those on whom you depend for the salvation of your country," and asked, "What then, O! My Countrymen, have you to hope? What have you not to fear?"[52]

There was, then, a remarkable similarity between the ideas of some Massachusetts writers in the 1760s and early 1770s and of leading Loyalists in the 1774–1776 period. Both groups warned that a cabal motivated by envy, malice, or ambition was undermining the authority of established institutions and leaders. The result was anarchy and confusion in the colony and the beginnings of a popular tyranny imposed by illegal bodies on the ruins of their country. The resemblance between the two critiques becomes even more compelling when it is considered that the same kinds of themes were also being expounded in New York in the late 1760s and early 1770s.

The Anglican Episcopal Controversy in New York

One of the many issues which evoked strong differences of opinion in New York in the 1760s was the Anglican proposal to establish an American episcopate. Newspaper articles, such as the "American Whig" series written by the Presbyterians William Livingston, William Smith, Jr., and John Morin Scott, associated the episcopal plan with the Stamp Act and other British attempts to undermine American freedom and warned that an episcopate would pose a basic threat to American religious liberty. The Anglican clergymen and later Loyalists Samuel Seabury, Thomas Bradbury Chandler, and Charles Inglis responded in a series of articles entitled "A Whip for the

American Whig" by Timothy Tickle. They formulated a critique of the motives and aims of their opponents and cautioned their readers about the Presbyterians' own designs on American freedom. The argument fashioned by Seabury and his friends in New York was so much like the one outlined by Sewall and his associates in Massachusetts that they even pinned the same name, Junto, on their opponents.[53]

As with Sewall and company, the Anglican clergymen emphasized the motives of their foes, describing the "American Whig" authors as an "ambitious, disappointed Faction" who were "well known to have been always Enemies to the Church of England."[54] Their disappointment, it was claimed, stemmed from their defeat in the last election, their failure to obtain a charter for a Presbyterian missionary society, and the increase in the number and reputation of the Anglicans. The stampede to Anglicanism, it was asserted, would be furthered by an American bishop, and this explained the Presbyterians' opposition to the idea.[55] Their ambition sprang generally from "a lust for Power" which was "one of their predominant Passions." More specifically, the Anglican writers charged, "They continually grasp at Power; are always striving to be the greatest in the kingdom of England."[56] As the "Whip" and another defender of the Anglican Church, the Anatomist, explained, the "American Whig" authors inherited the frailties of their Presbyterian brethren in England and New England, including an intolerance of other religious sects and an ambition to be the dominant or even the only church in America.[57] They possessed "a desire of crushing the church wholly on this continent, for the sake of erecting an exclusive dominion of their own."[58] At times their motives appeared to be even more sordid, not only to alienate Americans from the government and constitution of England but also to "disunite the colonies from Great Britain."[59]

The methods supposedly employed by the New York Junto to achieve its sordid aims were similar, it seems, to those used in Massachusetts. They included the frequent use of slander, invective, and "Billingsgate," a reliance on unfair abuse which "pays not the least attention to Truth or Decency" and defamation of respectable characters.[60] In addition, Livingston and his fellow writers were accused of "ridicule[ing] . . . Truths" held sacred by members of the Anglican Church and raising a "spirit of animosity against the Government . . . by fomenting the prejudices of the ignorant."[61] The

most effective means to arouse popular passions, it appeared, was to
instill into the populace apprehensions about their freedom by fabricat-
ing the "bugbear" of spiritual courts or visions of "spiritual
bondage."[62]

In vilifying the established Church of England—"the only Bastion
of the Protestant Interest"—the "American Whig" was accused of attacking the Protestant religion, morality, and the very Constitution of
Great Britain. Incessant and vociferous attacks on the Anglicans
seemed to the "Whip" to be nurturing a spirit of rancor, distrust,
"mutual Hatred," and a narrow-minded sectarianism which was contrary to Christian benevolence, charity, and brotherly love.[63]

Moreover, the church was seen as a basic institution in society
which worked with the state to promote morality and order. Its "settled doctrines," traditions, and prestige lent stability to the state.[64]
More generally, religion promoted order and harmony by restraining
the "Sallies of Ambition" or "the unrestricted Desire of unlimited
Freedom"—presumably common to mankind—by the promise of
"future Rewards . . . of Virtue" and "Punishments of Vice."[65] Part
of "Wollaston's Religion of Nature delineated" quoted by the
"Whip" portrayed the animalistic urges of man which would be
unleashed without the restraints on human passion imposed by church
and state: "Were it not for that Sense of Virtue which is principally
preserved, as far as it is preserved, by NATIONAL FORMS and Habits of
Religion, men would soon lose it all, run wild, prey upon one
another, and do what else the worst of Savages do."[66] Thus, the
church was a "Branch of the Constitution" and "so interwoven with
it [the state] that the one must be bent and torn to pieces with the
other."[67]

The aim of the New York Presbyterians was considered to be precisely this—to subvert the civil and religious constitution of their
country.[68] As "Ringleaders of Sedition," they subscribed to republican
principles and the democracy and mob principles of the Cromwellians
and were therefore plotting "the downfall of the Queen's religion"
and the erection of a "Commonwealth" on the ruins of the English
Monarchy. The end product, it was predicted, would be a democracy
that led to tyranny, as had been the case under Cromwell.[69]

The tyranny was believed to be rooted in the intolerance of the
Presbyterians, who were depicted as being "furious persecutors" with

"intolerant principles" and who harbored designs "to enslave others" despite their "clamourous outcries for Liberty."[70] At the heart of this accusation was the Anglican definition of religious liberty. Religious freedom, as the "Whip" pointed out, was equated with religious toleration, or "liberty of conscience," which allowed each individual "The free, open, undisturbed profession of our Faith."[71] This meant, more specifically, that each sect should be allowed to follow the ordination, doctrines, and polity peculiar to their particular brand of Protestantism.[72] The nonconformists, however, were perceived to be denying this kind of religious freedom to the Anglicans by attacking "the whole body of her church, her doctrines and discipline and the principles of her clergy and members."[73] In other words, the Anglicans accepted that individuals differed in their religious views, and they regarded it as a sign of a bigoted persecuting disposition to disparage others' religious principles. Since a basic part of the Anglican polity was the episcopacy, the non-Anglicans, by waging such an incessant campaign against the establishment of bishops in America, were infringing on Anglicans' "Liberty of having the Institutions of our church."[74] The persecuting tendencies were only held in check, it was stressed, by the British government, which could overturn any prejudicial colonial legislation and ensure that all Protestant denominations were free to practice their religion. If, however, British superintendence were removed and the Presbyterians left unchallenged, the prospects for other denominations were bleak. "No one religious Denomination would enjoy the least *Toleration*," it was predicted, "but like the poor, harmless, inoffensive Quakers in Massachusetts, must be content to be HANGED for their Religion."[75]

Alexander McDougall and "The Dougliad"

Just as the debate over the episcopacy began to subside, another controversy captured New Yorkers' attention. The event which raised the storm was the New York Assembly's approval in 1770 of the Quartering Act, which allowed the crown to provision troops in the colony. In return for this concession the British ministry agreed to continue allowing paper currency to be issued in New York. According to critics of the maneuver, the popularly elected assembly, lured by the favors of the crown, had allied itself with the executive, thereby concentrating the power of the various branches of government in the hands of one group. When Alexander McDougall, a future Patriot, wrote an article — "To the Betrayed Inhabitants of the City and Colony of New York" — charging that the assembly representatives in approving the unpopular Quartering Act and allying with the crown had betrayed their trust to uphold popular liberty and to check executive power, he was charged with libel by the outraged assembly majority. After his arrest, McDougall became, like John Wilkes, a popular hero in the cause of freedom of the press. The assembly's libel charge was defended in a series of articles, called "The Dougliad," which also warned New Yorkers about the "deformity of principles" and the dangerous "practices" of government critics like McDougall.[76]

In the first of the twelve "Dougliad" articles, the necessity of distinguishing the Patriot from the mock patriot, and social from natural liberty, was emphasized. McDougall, it stressed, was a mock patriot or demagogue to whom liberty was a "hypocritical cloak, to the dirty designs of faction." He beguiled people by "defaming all people's integrity" and "encourage[ing] disaffection to government." His aim was to "blind and seduce, to distract and disunite, to foment discontents, tumult, and sedition; and in short to trample down all legal authority and shake government to the foundation." The aims ascribed to McDougall should have been familiar to colonial readers. They were the same as those imputed to Otis and his friends and to the authors of the "American Whig." The same was true of the methods supposedly used by McDougall. People, aroused by fears for their rights, were an easy prey to demagogues, who took advantage of their fears and shifted the public animus from an "arbitrary ministry" to the "members of our internal government."[77]

By acting in such an unprincipled, unrestrained, and irresponsible way, McDougall was said to be transforming liberty into licentiousness. There was an important difference, one article stated, between John Locke's definitions of social and natural liberty. Social liberty was freedom controlled in the interests of the "peace and happiness of Society," while natural liberty was freedom restrained only by the law of nature, which was tantamount to the rule of force. Natural freedom led inevitably to anarchy, or in the words of the "Dougliad," "From these examples we may learn, how necessary it is, that the bans of society should be dissolved, government *unhinged*, and

the sword of justice *broken*, before *True* liberty can flourish in trium-
phant security." [78]

The writer had no doubt that McDougall, though claiming to be
upholding the invaluable freedom of the press, was in fact contending
for licentiousness. After discussing the importance of the freedom of
the press, the "Dougliad" continued "But if he abuses his independence to the hurt of society, or of individuals, he ought not to be
defended, for this would place him above the Laws, which intends a
general Security; and not to give to any a Dispensation to be mischievious with Impunity. If there was no check to Malice and Falsehood, Government must soon sink into contempt, and the subject be
stript of protection." [79]

In short, the freedom of the individual to act and write as he pleased
had to be restrained by law and by the need to preserve public peace
and order. To countenance a less circumscribed kind of freedom would
lead to anarchy or the dissolution of government. This was a terrible
prospect to the "Dougliad," whose author assumed that government
and law should be somewhat independent of popular control to provide to all citizens security, protection, and defense "against the Encroachment of Lawless Power." [80]

To allow individuals like McDougall to publish wanton and unwarranted attacks on the Assembly of New York would encourage
disrespect for all authority and lead to anarchy. "When the Body of
the people becomes tainted by Error and Corruption, a dissolution of
the Establishment will be unavoidable," one issue warned. Since the
assemblymen were the "guardians of . . . people's liberty," they
should be respected; otherwise, "the Idea of subjection will be lost,
and we shall learn to think all authority despotic; every punish-
ment oppressive." In addition to nurturing antiauthoritarianism,
McDougall and others who posed as patriots and upholders of liberty
encouraged all aspiring politicians to compete with each other for
popular favor and to try to outdo their opponents as upholders of
freedom. The end result was an intense partisanship and an excessive
emphasis on popularity, or as the "Dougliad" put it, New York "is a
popular city, whose inhabitants have too long been the dupes of party
rage." [81]

The case against McDougall included the time-worn charge that his
attack on the assembly was a threat to "the fundamental principles of

our most excellent constitution." In the first place, it was argued, representatives must be free to speak their minds; to destroy this independence, as McDougall was accused of doing, would end their "usefulness" as a "check . . . for our protection." In addition, by accusing the assembly of corruption, perfidy, and treason, McDougall had disgraced the "whole body of the people" by attacking "their immediate representatives." He had "set at open Defiance" the power of the assembly and "flagrantly invaded" that bulwark of people's freedom, "a participation in the councils of their country."[82]

McDougall and his associates were believed to have subverted British institutions in other ways as well. One article satirized McDougall's alleged contempt for the institution of trial by jury in stating that it "was insufficient to protect natural liberty," which was what he was contending for. Another criticized his use of extraconstitutional means to express his grievances and advocated that if he was distressed by some measure adopted by the assembly, "the constitution has pointed out a remedy" which consisted of instructing representatives or petitioning those in authority. By calling public assemblies which passed resolves, McDougall, it was claimed, was inculcating the idea that public decisions should be made not in the assembly but at some illegal or extraconstitutional forum, such as a mass rally. The "Dougliad" series concluded with a tribute to the British Constitution and an often repeated warning about the danger of popular tyranny:

> We love our most excellent constitution, however mangled by arbitrary ministers, or a licentious people, with the most ardent affection . . . we shall ever distinguish between freedom and licentiousness, liberty and faction, a manly and vigorous support of our constitutional rights and the subversion of law and government . . . [we] abhor despotism . . . the worst kind [being] the despotism of our fellow subjects and our equals.[83]

When Loyalists like Daniel Leonard in Massachusetts or Samuel Seabury in New York warned that the political practices and ideas of the Patriots were leading America into the abyss of anarchy and popular tyranny, they were reiterating and expanding upon a critique of colonial politics that was an established and fundamental dimension of American political culture. In fact, the Loyalists' arguments, assumptions, and rhetoric were so similar to those employed by Otis's opponents in Massachusetts or McDougall's in New York that the Loyalist analysis of the Revolution and its origins emerges as an almost stylized view of American problems. When Leonard asserted that "disappointed, ambitious and envious men, instil the poison of disaffection into the minds of the lower classes" by raising false alarms or "bugbears" about imminent enslavement, he was merely repeating the charges leveled in the 1760s and early 1770s at the Massachusetts Junto. Seabury's claim that the Patriots relied on "positive assertions without proof . . . declamatory harangues without argument" to lead the people "into rebellion against the supreme authority of the nation" resembled markedly earlier polemicists' accusations about the methods employed by government critics. The idea expounded in the 1760s that the narrow-minded and blind partisanship of the Junto had made an open and dispassionate discussion of public issues impossible was reiterated in December 1774 by Leonard: "In this temper of the times, it was enough to know who voted with Cassius and who with Lucius, to determine who was a friend and who an enemy to the country."[84]

More generally, Loyalists echoed earlier writers' views about their antagonists' long-term aims. Leonard associated the Patriots with Cromwell, and Seabury depicted the Patriot machinations in the following manner: "Republicans smile at the confusion that they themselves have, in a great measure made, and are exerting all their influence, by sedition and rebellion, to shake the British empire to its very basis, that they may have an opportunity of erecting their beloved commonwealth on its ruins." As earlier writers had predicted, the Patriots were reducing the colonies to anarchy by undermining basic institutions of the British Constitution, according to the Loyalists. The Massachusett's *Censor's* account in 1771 of the plot of a cabal in the General Court to upset the balance of the Constitution, by undermining the independence of dissenting representatives, councillors, and the governor, was reiterated by Leonard, the only major difference being that by late 1774 he was proclaiming it a *fait accompli*. Moreover, while Sewall and others writing in the decade before independence alleged that the institutions of the British Constitution, such as trial by jury, were being undermined, Seabury pronounced that by May 1775 the process would be completed. At that date, Seabury contended, the Continental Congress planned "to take the management of the courts of justice." "*Then* our whole constitution is to be finally destroyed; our trials by jury taken away; our courts of justice shut; our legislature rendered useless; our laws overturned; — in order to make room for an American republic, on a true democratical plan; and then you [Patriots] will laugh at those simple people who believed you ever intended to do otherwise." [85] And when Loyalists writing in the 1774–1776 period argued that the colonies were on the brink of anarchy and were being subjected to a popular or democratic tyranny, they were merely expanding upon ideas expressed by writers in the two colonies in the previous decade.

A final similarity between the Loyalists and their intellectual forerunners was their conviction that they had to write to enlighten a deluded populace. It was considered essential to expose demagogues like McDougall for what they were — "misleader[s] of the people," — and to wake the people from a "fatal security" before they found themselves in "irrecoverable ruin." [86] Samuel Seabury contended in a similar vein that his business was "to detect and expose the false, arbitrary and tyrannical PRINCIPLES upon which the Congress acted," and to reveal the fatal tendency of such action. [87] The Loyalists and their intellectual predecessors assumed that if they could expose their opponents' rhetoric, unfounded allegations, and appeals to popular passions, which clouded the people's judgment, they would rouse the populace to action. One Massachusetts author expressed his hope that "some of these hints may be a means of exciting the good people, in general, among us, to throw off their leading strings, and soberly think for themselves." [88] The "Dougliad" believed that when his "upright and well meaning countryman" realized the dangers of his situation, he would "strip the Factions of their pretended patriotism, and discover the deformity of their principles, and the danger of their practices, and both he will hold in utter Abhorrence." [89] And Daniel Leonard beseeched his readers: "I appeal to your good sense; I know you have it, and hope to penetrate to it, before I have finished my publications, notwithstanding the thick atmosphere that now envelopes it." [90]

Loyalist writers displayed an unduly optimistic faith in their ability to reason with the populace and in the public's willingness or ability to act. Perhaps their appreciation of the dilemmas facing Americans at that time would have been enhanced by a close scrutiny of the confessions of an anonymous poet who believed that it was necessary to counteract the Massachusetts Junto but admitted shamefully that he lacked the courage of his convictions:

> To see the Sufferings of my Fellow creatures,
> And own myself a Man: to see our Senators
> Cheat the deluded People with a Shew
> Of Liberty, which yet they Ne'er must taste of.
> They say, by them our Hands are free from Fetters,
> Yet whom they please they lay in basest Bonds;
> Bring whom they please to Infamy and Sorrow;
> Drive us like Wrecks down the rough Tide of Power,
> Whilst no Hold is to save us from Destruction.
> All that bear this are Villains: And I one,
> Not to rouze up at the great war Call of Nature,
> And check the Growth of these domestic Spoilers,
> That make us Slaves, and tell us 'tis our Charter.[91]

Rather than considering that people like the poet might weaken under the pressure of coercion or intimidation, Loyalist writers and their predecessors were content to find solace in Leonard's maxim, "Magnus est veritas et prevalebit."[92] They believed—and this point must be stressed—in the justice of their cause and that they were upholding and protecting all that was of value in Anglo-American life.

5

BRITISH ROOTS
OF LOYALIST IDEOLOGY

Ye Middlesex Freeholders, what is the Reason
That none you'll elect but the Arch-fiend of Treason,
In Virtue's fair footsteps who never yet trod;
Reviler of KINGS, and Blasphemer of GOD!
Was not in the County, the Suburb, or City,
An Highwayman, cut purse, or Thief, that would fit ye?

—From *Liverpool Mercury,*
REPRINTED IN *New York Chronicle,*
JULY 20, 1769

As HIGHLY LITERATE and increasingly sophisticated societies with economic and cultural contacts with other parts of the world, the thirteen colonies were affected by the main intellectual trends of eighteenth-century Europe. Major concepts associated with the Enlightenment, such as the emphasis on reason and the view of the universe as orderly, harmonious, and rational, were taken for granted by informed Americans.[1] However, the strong political, economic, and religious bonds to the mother country meant that Enlightenment ideas were transmitted to the colonies primarily by British writers.[2] England was the single most important reservoir for colonial ideas. Excerpts from British newspapers and pamphlets were reprinted in American newspapers; British books and pamphlets were sold in bookstores; and colonial lawyers and politicians cited British precedents and authorities to justify their viewpoints. In other words, American political culture was derivative: the standards by which colonials judged their institutions and ideas about basic issues like the nature of liberty or the role of government were derived largely from seventeenth- and eighteenth-century English political theorists and commentators.[3]

One of the ironies of the Revolution was that the ideas used to justify independence came originally from British opposition theorists, and the pamphleteer most responsible for "desacralizing" the old order and popularizing independence was a recently arrived British immigrant.[4] Moreover, the liberal ideology which imbued such landmarks of the Revolution as the Declaration of Independence has been traced to a variety of English and Scottish thinkers.[5] Tracing the British roots of Patriot ideology has for some time interested historians and sparked debates among them.

The search for British sources of Loyalist thought, on the other hand, has been relatively neglected, and there has even been a tendency to assume that Loyalists lacked relevant and dynamic British intellectual models.[6] This assumption is unfounded. Loyalists in search of intellectual kindred spirits or of authoritative references to bolster their arguments could look to well-known theorists such as Judge William Blackstone, Baron de Montesquieu, or Viscount Bolingbroke. These writers provided sympathetic analyses of British institutions and a more conservative ideology than that of the Patriots. Furthermore, Loyalists could glean ideas from British pamphleteers. On both sides of the Atlantic, pamphlet debates, especially in the 1760s and 1770s, were more often than not heated exchanges between two well-defined sides. In Britain country party writers attacked the ministries and their practices, while court party polemicists defended the actions of the government and launched their own assaults on government critics.

In the 1760s British radicals like John Wilkes were popular in America, and British antiministerial articles were reprinted in the colonies.[7] But the other side of this British debate also filtered through. Defenses of extremely unpopular British ministries, notably that of the Earl of Bute, were reprinted in America, as were negative commentaries on popular politicians like Wilkes. Thus, there were varied and rich British intellectual models for Loyalist ideology.

Another problem with discussions of British influences on Loyalist thought has been the tendency to blur important distinctions.[8] It has been argued quite rightly that like the Patriots, Loyalists were Whigs, or Lockeans:[9] they embraced the main political assumptions associated with John Locke and his *Two Treatises of Government* and, like most

eighteenth-century Englishmen, they accepted the principles of the
1688 Revolution.[10] Within these confines, however, there was still
room for fundamental differences. Eighteenth-century theorists of all
shades of opinion worked from Lockean premises but branched out
from the political spectrum to the right and left. Thus, any study of
the British roots of Loyalist ideas has to begin with Locke,[11] then proceed on to Bolingbroke, Trenchard and Gordon, Montesqieu, Burke,
and Blackstone.

John Locke

A number of key concepts in John Locke's *Two Treatises of Government* significantly influenced eighteenth-century political thought.[12]
One was the idea of government by compact or contract. Governors
had a duty to protect the rights—life, liberty, and property—of their
subjects, and if governors abrogated this trust, subjects could legitimately withdraw their allegiance and combine to form a new government. Another idea, which originated with classical writers, was that
of mixed government. Since the simple forms of government, monarchy, aristocracy, and democracy, would inevitably degenerate into
tyranny, oligarchy, and anarchy respectively, the best polity was one
which combined all three simple forms; the resulting counterpoise
would guarantee liberty as well as stability. In the British Constitution
the king represented monarchy, the House of Lords aristocracy, and
the House of Commons democracy, and as long as the balance among
the three was maintained, freedom and stability would be preserved.[13]
Locke also skillfully reconciled the separation of powers and the theory
of checks and balances implicit in the idea of mixed government. Since
the two main powers of government were in different hands—the
legislature exercising the legislative function and the king the executive one—there was a partial separation of powers. However,
unlike Harrington,[14] who advocated the pure separation of powers,
with each branch of government independent of the other and checked
by the people, Locke was more conservative and had the branches of
government check and balance each other. Although the king was the
supreme executive figure, he shared in the legislative function, and the
legislature supervised the executive. Most modern was Locke's notion
of legislative supremacy. Since making law was the most important

trust of government, the legislature was the "soul that gives Form, Life, and Unity to the Commonwealth," and the legislative function was the key power in government.[15] This was a departure from the medieval idea that Parliament found and declared law, but seldom made it. This, then, was the reservoir of basic concepts which eighteenth-century theorists tapped to support a wide variety of ideologies.

That Locke could be cited to buttress both radical and conservative political positions was superbly illustrated in an unpublished document, "A Dialogue between an American and a European Englishman," written in 1768 by Thomas Hutchinson. The American in the dialogue took the radical position that no "people under any government can be obliged to submit to what is in its nature unjust." As well as having certain inalienable natural rights which no government could violate, British subjects had the protection afforded by "certain fundamental principles of the English constitution," so that "to any act contrary to those fundamentals the people are not obliged to submit." Specifically this meant that the right to dispose of property — which taxation involved — was both a "natural right" and "a fundamental of the English constitution." Thus, Parliament's power to dispose of subjects' property — to tax — was limited by these two basic principles and the further consideration that "by the constitution it may well be questioned whether the Parliament of England can be considered as the Parliament for the colonies," since Americans were not represented in it. American rested his case with two quotes from Locke, one upholding the principle that taxation required the consent of the subject, and the other defining consent as "the consent of the majority, giving it either by themselves or their representatives chosen by them." To tax under any other circumstances would, according to Locke, invade "the fundamental law of property" and subvert "the end of government."[16]

European responded by quoting Locke to support his own more conservative view of the rights and obligations of a subject. While agreeing that government was "instituted for the sake of the people," European denied that this meant "that every individual has a right to judge when the acts of government are just and unjust and to submit or not submit accordingly." The latter doctrine he considered "repugnant to [the very idea of] government." Locke was called into service to reinforce the position that in moving from a state of nature to live under government, individuals gave up to the supreme authority powers they possessed in their natural state and contracted, in Locke's words, "to submit to the determination of the majority and to be concluded by it." On the other hand, again according to Locke, if an individual in civil society were exempted from its laws, he would be "perfectly still in the state of nature and so can be no part or member of that *civil society*." European challenged his opponent's basic premise by reasoning that "if you take the whole of Mr. Locke's work together," he condoned the right of the people as a body, not as individuals, to disregard the edicts of a government which had obviously betrayed its trust and had thereby broken its compact with the People.[17]

Hutchinson was not alone in outlining a conservative interpretation of Locke. The author of a pamphlet published serially in the *Boston Chronicle* in 1769 used rather tortured logic to attribute to Locke the idea that Parliament represented not individuals but the nation as a whole, which included all those who gave "tacit consent" to the commonwealth. "Tacit consent" was defined extremely broadly to encompass "any man that hath any possession or enjoyment of any part of the dominions of any government."[18] Though this was a very liberal doctoring of Locke, the principle that all laws must be obeyed until government was dissolved was another excellent example of the legitimate use of Locke to support a conservative view of the duties of a subject.

Court and Country Party Writers

Other British writers began with the political theories popularized by Locke and worked out their own ideologies to suit the needs of Hanoverian England which, in contrast to the seventeenth century, was characterized by stability, consensus, and self-satisfaction. The 1689 Bill of Rights and 1701 Act of Settlement had guaranteed the independence and supremacy of Parliament and the future of Protestantism. Dissenters were tolerated, freedom of speech within and outside of Parliament increased, and with the exception of a few Jacobites, most Englishmen, including the Hanoverian kings themselves, accepted the political principles of the Glorious Revolution. Conflict between a still powerful monarch and the House of Commons was avoided by the integration in practice, if not in theory, of the two branches of government. Ministers like Robert Walpole, enjoying the confidence of the king, were able to garner support for the executive in the House of Commons through astute distribution of patronage and adept manipulation of the electorate.[19]

This recently established political stability and consensus, together with the prosperity and cultural refinement produced by commercial and financial growth, encouraged Englishmen to take pride in their achievements. And they did: in essays, orations, poems, and newspapers, Englishmen complimented themselves on their achievements in commerce, warfare, and especially politics. Their self-satisfaction was reinforced by the praise of foreigners like Baron de Montesquieu, who agreed that England was the freest country of the eighteenth century, with a constitution admirable for the liberty it guaranteed to subjects.[20]

Despite the predominant tone of complacency and self-satisfaction, there was a constant, unequivocal, and often shrill and extravagant criticism leveled at current political practices by the country party, the opposition to the ministry. A disparate group which included old Tories, independent gentry, local merchants, and for a brief period the metropolitan middle class whom John Wilkes tried to represent, country party politicians were the "outs," independent members of Parliament who were not favored with ministerial patronage. What was most significant about them was the rationale they advanced for opposing the ministry. Sir Robert Walpole and others who used patronage to gain support in the House of Commons were accused by the country party of corrupting the Commons, destroying its independence, and upsetting the balance of the constitution, the all-important guarantor of liberty. The country party members who retained their independence considered themselves the only true patriots qualified to speak for the national interest.[21]

The country party's almost standardized rationale for opposing the ministry did not go unchallenged. Ministerial or court writers responded by charging that critics of government had their own designs on freedom and order in Britain. The result was a lively exchange between two quite different views of politics. Much of the debate—indeed the most lively part—occurred outside of Parliament in pamphlets, tracts, and newspapers. The literary combat was waged in a satirical, and often vitriolic vein. Opponents were castigated as

Jacobites, Republicans, libellers, demagogues, knaves, sycophants,[22] or more frequently as artful men, deceivers, betrayers, and traitors.[23] The mood was one of sinister intrigue, where designing men manipulated, beguiled, and lied themselves into power by posing as patriots and enriched themselves at the expense of their bleeding country.[24] Country party writers warned of the danger to free societies posed by standing armies or by the concentration of power in the hands of government, which always boded ill for the liberty of the subject.[25] To ward off such lurking menaces, the people had to be forever vigilant and on their guard to detect the secret motives and conspiracies of the cabals that intrigued to hoodwink the king and even his ministers and to use their powers to enslave the nation.[26]

The national drama depicted by ministerial writers was equally replete with plotting demons and diabolic machinations. The opposition, disappointed and discontented demagogues motivated by envy, malice, and ambition, courted popularity by adopting the guise of patriots and by deceiving and deluding the public through appeals to prejudice which spurred on the popular frenzy.[27] Rather than aiming at the national welfare, as the opposition professed, these intriguers used false charges to "create Discontent and Dissatisfaction" and to poison the minds of the people against their government.[28] According to court writers, the opposition party was trying to destroy the constitution by either overturning the 1688 settlement or appropriating all of the power to the Commons or to their own cabal.[29] To prevent these plots from succeeding, ministerial Whigs called on the people to turn against the pretended patriots and restore national unanimity and consensus by uniting around the principles of the 1688 settlement.[30]

The rhetoric of the debate foreshadowed that of the political disputes in New York and Massachusetts in the 1760s and was strikingly similar in tone to Loyalist and Patriot tracts of the 1770s. The mood conveyed in all of these writings was sinister and conspiratorial, and the language abusive and exaggerated. Loyalists and their intellectual forerunners used exactly the same adjectives to describe their political foes as did polemicists in England: artful, designing, disappointed, discontented, envious, ambitious. Moreover, the general thrust of the court party's case was virtually identical to that of the Loyalists and their intellectual predecessors. A basically loyal people was being duped by crafty, ambitious, and envious demagogues who appealed to popular passions and aroused unwarranted fears of tyranny. In jeopardy were freedom and order and the balance and integrity of the British Constitution.

The similarity of ideas is both significant and explicable. It is significant that Loyalists found in articles defending various British ministries arguments to counter those of the Patriots, which were in turn borrowed from British ministerial critics. For their part, the Patriots gleaned from British opposition writers the idea that liberty was fragile and constantly being threatened by power. This basic concept underpinned their liberal ideology and their ultimate conclusion that the British king and Parliament plotted to subvert American liberty. But Loyalists could find in British writing an alternative polemical tradition in response; court tracts warned that freedom and order were endangered, not by the power wielded by government but by the irresponsible and self-interested actions of critics who threatened to undermine the authority of government and plunge their communities into a debilitating and eventually oppressive anarchy. This analysis established the framework for a more conservative ideology, for the Loyalist argument about a tyranny rooted in anarchy, and for their history of the Revolution.

The resemblance in the themes running through Loyalist and ministerial tracts is not surprising since Loyalists — and Americans generally — were familiar with British court writings. Students of Patriot ideology have shown that the writings of opposition theorists were widely read in America.[31] What has been largely overlooked, however, is that the other side of the British debate was also readily available to colonists; there is evidence that court literature made its way to the colonies before the 1760s. In the controversy over King's College, New York, in the 1750s, for example, Anglican spokesmen and future Loyalists relied on British critiques of the radical opposition theorists, Trenchard and Gordon, to counter the arguments of their foes, based on Trenchard and Gordon.[32] In the 1760s and 1770s newspapers in New York and Massachusetts frequently reprinted British pamphlets and articles which defended the government of the day and advanced a more conservative view of British politics. To cite one example, Allan Ramsay's *Thoughts on the Origin and Nature of Government*[33] of 1769 was a very conservative interpretation of the role

of government and the Anglo-American relationship which Thomas
Hutchinson greatly admired and considered influential in shaping his
own political thought.[34] How did Hutchinson become acquainted
with this work, and was he the only Loyalist influenced by Ramsay?
Perhaps not; part of Ramsay's pamphlet was reprinted in the *Boston
Chronicle* in June, 1769,[35] and was therefore, more widely distributed
than has been assumed.

Moreover, it was not uncommon to find in New York and Massachusetts newspapers defenses of various British ministries and scathing attacks on antiministerial writers. A series of articles in the *Boston
Evening-Post,* for example, defended the Earl of Bute, the most notorious and unpopular minister of the 1760s.[36] A Scotsman, courtier, and
confidant of the young George III, Bute neither held a seat in Parliament nor had any political experience; he became first minister in 1761
solely because of the personal favor of the king. This fact, and his association with what was seen as an overly generous peace settlement
with France and other unpopular measures, made Bute the target for
unrelenting attacks by politicians and journalists. The rumor that he
was behind the Stamp Act made him even more repugnant to many
Americans, who hanged him in effigy on more than one occasion.[37]

Nonetheless, "A Letter in Vindication of the Earl of Bute . . ."
praised him, characterizing his ministry as showing "splendid
generosity and disinterestedness." Proof of Bute's integrity and high
principles lay in his retirement without "place or pension," ignoring
the "tempting spoils which lay at his feet." The "Letter" vehemently
denied the idea that Bute was an unconstitutional minister and
justified his status as a minister chosen by the king in a clever way.
The king, who was himself independent, being neither pro-German
nor tied to any party, had the right to choose his own minister. This
was conventional enough doctrine. Novel, however, was the reasoning that since Bute was chosen by the king, he was subject to the
check and control of Parliament, unlike a minister who came to power
at the head of a party in Parliament. Bute's fall was especially tragic to
this British author because the "learned" of his countrymen had been
searching for a "Patriot king" and "Patriot minister." In Bute and
George III—a king "too virtuous for the people"—"this country has
beheld them both and not known them."[38]

Bute's resignation, as well as many of the other troubles of the time, was attributed by this court spokesman and others to the unscrupulous and irresponsible actions of a number of government critics. "Liberty," according to Bute's defender, "is in no danger but from the growth of Licentiousness, the arrogance of Faction, and the temerity of seditious men working on the passions of their fellow subjects."[39] Government opponents most frequently singled out for criticism were Junius and John Wilkes. Junius, believed to have been Philip Francis, a War Office clerk, penned scathing and at times brutal denunciations of the ministries of the 1760s. Wilkes, renowned for his attacks on Bute and his policies, which led to Wilkes's arrest on a general warrant for seditious libel, was a popular hero for many in America. Acclaimed for his battle against general warrants and his dedication to freedom of the press, his name for some Americans was synonymous with liberty.[40] But a far less flattering image of Wilkes, Junius, and other government opponents was portrayed in various pamphlets and articles reprinted in New York and Massachusetts. It is significant that the aims, motives, and methods attributed to them were exactly the same as those ascribed to the Patriots by Loyalists and their intellectual predecessors in the 1760s.

Described by one literary foe as a "demon of discord" and "assassin of the innocent," Junius—like Wilkes—was condemned for his relentless and unfounded attacks on the government and its supporters.[41] "Junius and such writers as himself," according to another of his detractors, "occasion all the mischiefs complained of, by falsely and maliciously traducing the best characters in the kingdom."[42] Scandal, abuse, detraction, and sedition were among the methods commonly attributed to Junius and his associates.[43] Wilkes was accused of using appeals to passions and undocumented charges to discredit ministers like Bute.[44] Wilkes, it was alleged, used "fictitious patriotism" as a guide to create fears about imaginary grievances.[45] A satire on Wilkes's supporters depicted their methods as follows: "Beg leave to embarrass and perplex you with grievances which never did exist, and apprehensions which never can alarm the deserving part of the British empire." The motives of his backers were equally sordid: "unwilling to let pass an opportunity of being revenged for the insult offered to our cock-ey'd Captain, we are resolved to disturb you, plague the ministry, and render obnoxious to the people the law and the legislature; to form a precedent of arrogance and dissatisfaction, which may prove hereafter dangerous to your august family and thereby occasion the total loss of virtue, fame and freedom."[46]

Although Wilkes claimed to be upholding liberty, especially freedom of the press, his critics charged that he in fact was perverting it. "All Whigs, Lovers of liberty and steady, judicious Defenders of it," Bute's defender warned, "must forever disdain the Services of so Indecent a Writer as the North Briton."[47] Freedom of the press, in the view of one writer, did not include the right to malign public figures,[48] which Wilkes was supposedly doing. Others considered it seditious to criticize the king and his ministers.[49] In restraining Wilkes from publishing his attacks on ministers, Bute, it was argued, was curtailing "licentiousness not liberty" since liberty did not mean a license for "everyone to say what he wants" even if this meant the ruin of the government and the king.[50] But such unwarranted and unrestrained attacks on the virtue and integrity of public figures was, court writers lamented, affecting the British public. Prejudice and passion were replacing reason in public debates, licentiousness and distrust of government were becoming more common, and political standards and practices were being turned upside down as "the Respect due to Rank and Station is thought an Encroachment on the Rights of the People," while "it is considered the achievement of Liberty to impeach in the language of Billingsgate, the most exalted characters in the Nation."[51] All of this was possible because the people were being duped. They were tools of "disappointed and designing men"[52] or "imposed upon by artful and designing men, or by wretches, who, bankrupts in business, in fame and in fortune, mean nothing more than to involve this country in the same common ruin with themselves."[53]

Besides encouraging licentious behavior and disrespect for authority, Wilkes's extravagant charges against government leaders were believed to be threatening the constitution and Britain's peace and freedom. Wilkes and his followers, in the view of one detractor, aimed to "sow sedition, breed disturbances, if possible, bring about a revolution, to the total subversion of law, liberty and civil government."[54] Junius "aims the dagger at the vitals of the constitution,"[55] and was plotting "sedition and spiriting you [the public] up to rebellion."[56] Memories of past disturbances led one writer to condemn Junius for destroying the peace and unity of England: "And can

Britons applaud, can they forgive the man, who by his seditious writings would endeavour to infuse such a spirit in these times, recall former evils, and draw on our heads the curses and horrors of a civil war?"[57] The essential message of these critiques was captured nicely by one polemicist who warned, "Tremble at the thought of popular as well as Regal tyranny."[58]

Thus, the rhetoric and content of British court writings sheds some new light on the Loyalist argument. Far from representing a radical departure from previously accepted political analyses, Loyalist warnings about the evils of faction, the dangers of licentiousness, and the imminence of popular tyranny were deeply rooted not only in colonial but also in British political writing. The British court tradition which underpinned the Loyalist interpretation of the nature and origin of colonial problems was a stylized and often repeated view of eighteenth-century British politics. By the mid-1770s, it is true, it was neither novel nor dynamic. But neither was the opposing country party analysis. Indeed, the debate between Loyalists and Patriots was, to some degree at least, merely an intellectual battle between two time-worn British polemical traditions.

Real Whigs versus Bolingbroke, Burke, and Montesquieu

In addition to relying on British writers for their political analyses, both Loyalists and Patriots derived many of their ideas about basic concepts, such as the nature of liberty or the role of government, from British theorists. One main source of Patriot ideology were the radical opposition theorists—sometimes called Real Whigs or Commonwealthmen—like John Trenchard, Thomas Gordon, Thomas Hollis, Richard Baron, James Burgh, Joseph Priestley, and Richard Price. In their critiques of eighteenth-century Britain, the libertarian theories of seventeenth-century republicans like Milton, Harrington, Neville, and Sidney were blended with Lockean liberal premises.[59]

The core of Real Whig thought was Lockean, but the stress was on his bourgeois, liberal, and individualistic strains. The individual was considered the proprietor of his own person and capacities—rather than a piece of some larger social whole—who owed nothing to society for the talents he possessed.[60] Liberty was equated with freedom from restraint, self-dominion, or unencumbered control over one's abilities, and was considered necessary for the individual to develop his potential to the fullest.[61] Civil society, comprising a number of free, rational, and propertied individuals, required government to act as arbiter. Man had moved from a state of nature, where the individual's actions were unrestrained except by natural law, to form governments that would act as impartial judges to ensure protection of his inalienable rights. Government was necessary to *secure* to the individual his natural rights, which was impossible in a state of nature, but it was not an altogether desirable institution. Pervading Real Whig writings was a deeply rooted distrust of government and its power.

For Real Whigs the utopian state of nature was an ideal from which the functions and powers of government were derived. Governments, created to protect the natural rights of man, were to be restricted to performing this task. Governmental authority was to be limited, checked, and balanced to ensure that government could not infringe on man's liberty.[62] Political liberty was proportional to the people's share in the legislative branch of government and to the extent that the legislature could effectively check the executive.[63] Implicit in this view of the origins of government was the concept of popular sovereignty. Since government was formed by the people to secure their natural rights and since its power came originally from the people, it was the people, in the last analysis, who retained the supreme and ultimate power in the state.[64] These assumptions provided the theoretical framework of both Real Whig and Patriot ideology.

However, the Commonwealthmen wrote on two different, though related, levels. When discussing the origins and functions of government, their perspective was abstract, speculative, and idealistic. When they focused on the specific problems of England, the tone was critical, questioning and, to a large extent, negative. Obviously Hanoverian England fell far short of their conception of the ideal, and they concentrated on its weaknesses rather than its strengths.

The picture of England which unfolds in Real Whig literature—whether written by John Trenchard and Thomas Gordon in the 1720s or by James Burgh at midcentury[65]—is that of a society sinking into the abyss of moral degeneracy. Wallowing in luxury and debilitated by bribery, corruption, and vice, the people had abandoned their duty to guard against the encroachments of arbitrary power. Consequently, designing demagogues in the guise of "Patrons of Liberty" deceived the people and aimed "to alter the balance of government and to get it into the sole power of their creatures."[66] Salvation lay in a heroic return to a virtuous past. The people, awakened from their lethargy and pricked to use their reason, had to "exert themselves" to bring about a "general reformation" to restore national morality and public spirit.[67] A zealous and morally reformed people would then unite "in common measures to defend the Public Safety."[68]

From Commonwealthmen Patriots derived their image of Britain as a society in a state of decline and enervated by a tyranny which threatened to spread to America, a compelling reason for Patriots to seek independence. Moreover, the zeal for moral reform and the quest for the union of an enlightened and revitalized people—reminiscent of the yearnings of Commonwealth theorists—was also at the heart of American republicanism.

But the foundations for a more conservative ideology and a more positive view of England could be found in the works of other theorists. Even within the country party itself there were right-wing spokesmen whose criticism was more conservative. The most prominent of these writers was Henry St. John, Viscount Bolingbroke—philosopher, writer, and one-time Jacobite. In his newspaper the *Craftsman,* published from 1726 to 1736, Bolingbroke castigated the corruption and venality of Hanoverian society and the political practices of Walpole, which he felt violated the independence of Parliament and upset the balance of the constitution.[69] Like the Commonwealthmen, Bolingbroke envisaged a secular, millenial solution to these evils. A "Patriot king," outraged at the moral decay and political corruption of his realm, would rouse himself, restore public spirit and morality, and unite all parties under an enlightened and virtuous government, where the monarch ruled in conjunction with a purified and independent Parliament.[70]

Despite the similarities in their critiques, Bolingbroke and the Real Whigs differed fundamentally in their premises. To begin with, Bolingbroke rejected completely some of the principal assumptions of Lockean liberalism. Whereas Locke argued for the equality of man in a state of nature, Bolingbroke believed that men were born in a state of society into families and were naturally unequal. At the top of this hierarchical society was an aristocracy of wise and able men born to be "the tutors and instructors of human kind."[71] In place of the liberal individualistic view of mankind so characteristic of Real Whigs, Bolingbroke described an organic society where each person existed as part of a larger social whole and had a duty to contribute to the well-being of the whole in accord with his own abilities and station in the hierarchy.[72]

Bolingbroke also diverged from Commonwealthmen in his perspective on man, society, and government. The abstractions, idealism, and universalism that were such important parts of the Real Whig world view were virtually nonexistent in Bolingbroke's outlook. He was less concerned with mankind's natural rights than with the rights of British subjects under the constitution. In his own words, "They who talk of liberty in Britain on any other principles than those of the British Constitution, talk impertinently at best." The constitution was a "system of government suited to the genius of our nation and even to our situation" and it provided the norms by which to evaluate English society and politics.[73] Bolingbroke's aims were much less radical than those of the Real Whigs and unlike them, he had no all-pervasive suspicion of government or of executive power. Quite the contrary, his ideal Patriot king would govern in harmony with Parliament but would also restore public virtue by a wise and judicious exertion of his executive powers. Bolingbroke had no desire to curb the constitutional power of the executive. Rather he hoped for a return to first principles—those of the 1688 Revolution—whereby an independent Parliament would guarantee the liberty of the subject while working in harmony with the executive, which would perform its own role in the balanced constitution.[74]

Bolingbroke also penned a compelling critique of faction and its debilitating effects on political morality. In his eyes it was the duty of the wise and talented—the natural aristocracy—to use their abilities to promote the public good and to "preserve the moral system of the world." "To what higher station, to what greater glory can any mortal aspire," he proclaimed, "than to be, during the whole course of his life, the support of good, the control of bad government, and the guardian of public liberty?"[75] When motivated by the "spirit of liberty" national leaders fulfilled this duty; they overlooked their private ambitions and devoted their talents to promoting the "national interests." Faction, however, led man to surrender this trust and to sacrifice the public welfare to their private interests.[76] Besides, faction subverted national morality by bringing out the worst characteristics of political leaders. Instead of acting like wise and virtuous men committed to principles, factious men were designing and corrupt and courted popularity at the expense of their principles.[77] Dependent on popular acclaim to ascend to political power, leaders of factions appealed to the passions rather than to reason, thereby stifling truth under a barrage of prejudice that further ruptured the integrity of the body politic. Summarizing the morally debilitating effects of faction, Bolingbroke wrote: "Thus the corrupt lead the blind, and the blind lead one another; the still voice of reason is drowned in popular clamor and truth is overwhelmed by prejudice."[78]

His condemnation of faction was, of course, similar to the later Loyalist view. Beyond this, Bolingbroke is significant here because some of the Loyalists' more conservative beliefs resembled his views and because his writings were widely distributed in America. Several private colonial libraries contained his works; the sale of his writings was advertised in at least one colonial newspaper in the 1760s, and he was cited with approval by colonial authors.[79]

As widely read in the colonies was *L'Esprit des Lois* by Baron de Montesquieu, an ardent admirer of the British Constitution.[80] In the colonies Montesquieu's name was usually associated with the idea of the separation of powers, in which he included the concept of an independent judiciary, a body of professionals unattached to any social class or interest group. Montesquieu also stressed the importance of judicial procedure and due process to ensure the protection of the liberty of the subject.[81] In the colonies there were widely differing interpretations of Montesquieu's idea of the separation of powers. A more radical interpretation claimed that the three branches of government should carry out different functions and that people could serve in only one branch of government at a time.[82] A more conservative version of Montesquieu's theory was used by Jonathan Sewall to counter criticisms of Thomas Hutchinson's plural officeholding. Montesquieu, Sewall correctly pointed out, did not support a complete separation of powers but merely a partial one—the ideal that "a large majority" of the members of the legislative branch should not sit in the judicial or executive branch. Proof of this lay in England, where Lords were also judges and the king headed the executive but also shared in the legislative functions.[83]

Sewall was joined by Myles Cooper in approving Montesquieu's conservative definition of liberty. Cooper skillfully blended Locke's and Montesquieu's definitions of liberty, beginning with the conventional wisdom of the time that "men in a state of nature were equal" and unrestricted in their freedom except by the "laws of God." But because of the "want of a common judge" to determine and protect their rights, men united to form civil society. So that "members of this *moral person* [civil society] may cooperate to one end, they must have but one *understanding* to direct, and one *will* to chuse. This understanding and will are the *law* and the law . . . is the *soul* of society." If, however, the rule of law no longer prevailed, then man would return again to the insecure state of nature. This led logically to Locke's definition of "the liberty of men in society" as being the freedom "to be under no legislative power, but that established by consent in the common wealth" and to Montesquieu's even more conservative or negative phrasing of Locke's idea: "Liberty . . . is a right of doing what [ever] *the laws permit;* and if a citizen could do what they forbid, he would no longer be possessed of liberty, because all his fellow citizens would have the same power."[84]

Although Edmund Burke's speeches were reprinted in American newspapers and pamphlets, he apparently did not have the same degree of influence on American ideas as did Montesquieu or Blackstone. Yet at least a few of the ideas associated with Burke seeped into Loyalist thought, including his pragmatic and historical approach (in contrast to Locke's ahistorical and abstract perspective) and his organic and collectivist view of society and its institutions.

Institutions for Burke were products of history, "an unceasing and undying process, in which the generations were partners" and in which men constantly adapted to new needs and circumstances. Existing institutions were the fruits of this process and therefore embodied more sagacity than any one individual intellect at any one point in time. Political wisdom, then, lay in participating in this process — identified with nature and order — rather than in attempting to reconstruct institutions on *a priori* grounds.[85]

An integral part of this historical and organic world view was

Burke's collectivist approach to society and its institutions. In his outlook the liberal individualistic strains of Lockean thought were almost nonexistent; the family, not the individual, was the basic social unit. It was the source of the "peace, happiness, settlement and civilization of the world" and the means by which traditions, linking past and present, were transmitted from generation to generation.[86] Men existed as parts of larger social and political wholes and were molded by these institutions, at the same time adapting the institutions to meet their own needs.[87]

Burke's conception of government also diverged from that of Locke or the Real Whigs. Governments were not created by individuals on the basis of *a priori* reasoning and were not limited to protecting individual's natural rights. Moreover, there was not the same inherent tension between the individual and his liberty and the power of government, as implied by Real Whigs. Instead, governments and institutions were organic entities that had evolved in the course of history to satisfy the *needs* of mankind. As such, they changed in accord with shifts in the overall social processes and they could not be divorced from, or antagonistic toward, the numerous generations of individuals, who functioned only as parts of these larger social and political wholes.[88] Thus, in contrast to the liberal and negative view of government held by Commonwealthmen and Patriots, Burke's conception of government was more conservative and positive.

Sir William Blackstone

The most widely read and cited eighteenth-century theorist and the one who had the greatest influence on Loyalist ideology was the jurist Sir William Blackstone. His *Commentaries on the Laws of England,* written between 1765 and 1769, was the standard American text on English law and the British Constitution. The *Commentaries* were widely distributed in America and frequently cited in colonial political tracts.[89] Although on the surface Blackstone's work was descriptive in tone and legalistic in content, in fact it abounded in value judgments, and some chapters were tracts in political theory.

Blackstone personified mid-eighteenth-century England in his political assumptions, and his *Commentaries* synthesized magnificently the dominant features of the political culture. Even his tone reflected the mainstream political milieu of Hanoverian England. The critical, questioning, and almost cynical view characteristic of the Real Whigs found no place in Blackstone's work. He admired the strengths of the English polity and had little concern for its weaknesses, and he praised its achievements rather than considering in any detail its shortcomings. Blackstone was not much concerned with constructing or hypothesizing about an ideal political system and then using these derived principles to evaluate a specific polity. Instead he accepted the principles of the British Constitution as the best earthly approximation to an ideal and suggested that these were the principles by which to judge political practices and institutions. Blackstone's admiration for the constitution reflected his political premises, which were unmistakenly Hanoverian. Britain was described as "A land, perhaps the only one in the universe, in which political or civil liberty is the very end and scope of the constitution."[90] The freedom for which England was renowned was embodied in the constitution — "so wisely contrived, so strongly raised, and so highly finished"[91] — which had reached its highest pinnacle with the 1688 Revolution. It was then that the independence of Parliament was irrevocably established, the prerogative limited, and the civil and political liberties of the nation recovered and "fully and explicitly acknowledged and defined."[92]

Blackstone skillfully blended the dominant assumptions of Hanoverian England and Lockean political principles to fashion a conservative ideology which was remarkably similar to that of the Loyalists. Although he agreed with Locke that the principal aim of society was "to protect individuals in the enjoyment of those absolute rights, which were invested in them by the immutable laws of nature," he also emphasized that natural rights "could not be preserved in peace without the mutual assistance and intercourse, which is gained by the institution of friendly and social communities."[93] Man for Blackstone — and not for Locke — was inherently sociable: he was "formed for society" and was "neither capable of living alone" nor did he have "the courage to do it."[94] Since man was by nature sociable, society and government better satisfied his needs than did the state of nature.[95] Consequently, the most valuable kind of liberty was to be found in society under government and law, not in the state of nature. "This species of legal obedience and conformity," Blackstone stated, "is infinitely more desirable than that wild and savage liberty [natural

liberty] which is sacrificed to obtain it."[96] Just as he saw the state of
nature as undesirable, Blackstone had a strong aversion to the prospect
of anarchy. In contrast to seventeenth-century republicans like Neville
and Sidney, who accepted anarchy as preferable to tyranny, Blackstone
regarded it as "a worse state than tyranny itself, as any government is
better than none at all."[97]

Assuming that man was freest and happiest in society under government and law, Blackstone placed a higher priority on order, authority,
obedience, and respect for government than on individual liberty. The
freedom of the individual had to be subordinated to the "public advantage" which was the only way to preserve "our general freedom" and
"that state of society, which alone can secure our independence."[98] Implicit in this view was a positive conception of the role of government.
As well as protecting the natural rights of subjects, government had to
preserve the very state of society which was vital to human felicity and
freedom. Also, because true freedom existed only under law and
government, Blackstone categorically rejected popular sovereignty.
"For this devolution of power to the people," Blackstone wrote, "includes in it a dissolution of the whole form of government established
by that people, reduces all the members to their original state of
equality; and by annihilating the sovereign power, repeals all positive
laws whatsoever before enacted."[99] Because government was so essential to human happiness it could not anticipate its own demise nor
delegate its authority to its subjects. Thus, government rather than
the people should hold the ultimate and supreme power in the state.

The same moderate conservatism was apparent in Blackstone's ideas
about political institutions, exemplified in his explanation of the
balanced constitution. His analysis of the separation of powers was
couched in "the language of Montesquieu,"[100] and he incorporated the
independent judiciary into the theory. Yet Blackstone culled only the
more moderate aspects of Montesquieu's theory, in which a partial
separation of powers was reconciled with the theory of mixed government; he virtually ignored the more radical, pure or complete separation of powers, which Montesquieu seemed at times to be advocating.
According to the more conservative theory, the three branches of government — king, House of Lords, and House of Commons — should be
at once independent and interdependent. Political stability required
that the three work together harmoniously to promote the public

good, yet the protection of freedom required that each branch be independent so that it could effectively check the power of the other two branches.[101] This version of the balanced constitution was later cited by Henry Caner in Massachusetts. When the political opposition demanded that the governor receive his salary from the colonial, as opposed to the British, government to ensure his independence of British influence, Caner responded that if the governor was dependent on the assembly for his salary, the independence of the monarchical branch of the constitution would be compromised and the freedom of the colony threatened. He cited Blackstone to support this view.[102]

Blackstone's theory of balanced government, as Caner's argument showed, rejected the radical Patriot idea that political freedom depended on the power of the popularly elected branch of government and its ability to check the executive. Rather the balance of the constitution itself was seen as the bulwark against tyranny. Another conservative idea implicit in the theory of the balanced constitution was the idea that government and judicial institutions should remain independent of popular control so that they could limit conflict to preserve peace, order, and stability and to protect the rights and freedom of all subjects.

Basic to Blackstone's view of the constitution was his superb defense of Parliamentary supremacy, which was also fundamental in Loyalist thought. Blackstone, it should be pointed out, saw a place for custom in British political development. Like Burke, he believed that traditions and customs that had evolved over time formed part of the common law and embodied an "accumulated wisdom" that was to be prized. He rejected, however, the seventeenth-century idea of a fundamental law or ancient constitution that limited all power in the state. No custom, tradition, or natural right could limit the omnipotence of Parliament. A strong advocate of the indivisibility of sovereignty, Blackstone believed that to ensure stability every government must have "a supreme, irresistible, absolute, uncontrolled authority, in which the *jura summi imperii,* or the rights of sovereignty reside."[103] In the British Constitution, Parliament, which performed the increasingly vital function of making law, possessed this sovereign power. Parliament was the heart and soul of the body politic, where the power of the state was concentrated. It was the guardian of the constitution, entrusted with protecting liberty and with the duty to "sustain, to repair, to beautify this noble pile [British Constitution]."[104] Its trust was of the highest order—to transmit to posterity the principles of the constitution and to maintain that state of society under government and law so necessary to the freedom and happiness of man. Thus it was imperative that its power be unchallenged. "What Parliament doth," Blackstone proclaimed, "no authority upon earth can undo."[105]

Blackstone's ability to moderate potentially radical ideas was superbly illustrated in his explanation of the "rights of Englishmen," a term used frequently at the time of the American Revolution and open to varying interpretations. In the seventeenth century, when Stuart kings used prerogative powers to encroach on Parliamentary independence, writers like Locke stressed the essential right of an Englishman to resist tyrannical rulers. In the eighteenth century, however, when Parliament's rights were firmly established and the Hanoverian kings were constitutional rulers, the right of resistance became less meaningful. This important shift was reflected in the specific meaning given to the term "rights of Englishmen" by Blackstone. While admitting that resistance might be necessary in extreme cases, he focused on the constitutional guarantees against tyranny embedded in the constitution. The three "great and primary rights" of personal security, personal liberty, and private property would be maintained by the "subordinate rights of the subject." These included the constitutional powers and privileges of Parliament, the limitations on the prerogative, the right to apply to courts for redress of grievances, and the right to petition king or Parliament for redress. It was these constitutional means of gaining redress—not the right of resistance—that Blackstone felt were the essential rights of Englishmen.[106] The English system was not freed from conflict and dissent in 1688; it was just that constitutional means to deal with contention in the body politic had been firmly established.

To rely on Blackstone for legal or political theory in the 1770s, as Loyalists did, was to cite not only good, but the best, authority. No ordinary political commentator, Blackstone was an eminent jurist and theorist with a remarkable understanding of and admiration for the British Constitution. His *Commentaries* was not a time-worn tract reiterating a stylized argument. It was in the 1770s the latest and most up-to-date analysis of British institutions, and it was widely distrib-

uted and acclaimed on both sides of the Atlantic. It also reflected the
dominant values and political assumptions of Hanoverian England.
This is significant because many of the ideas stressed by Patriots—the
right of resistance, the concept of a fundamental law, and the whole
framework of political confrontation between rulers or prerogative
powers and the people or popular liberties—predated the 1688
Revolution and harked back to the seventeenth century. In contrast,
the ideas Loyalists derived from or shared with Blackstone placed them
in the mainstream of contemporary British political theory. In emphasizing the supreme authority of Parliament, the independence and
interdependence of the branches of the constitution, and constitutional
means of redress, Loyalists spoke the language of eighteenth-century
British constitutionalism.

Thus, Loyalists had no shortage of British models. To counter the
Patriot case for independence, they could utilize the writings of British
court or ministerial spokesmen, who warned that faction and anarchy
were more serious threats to order and liberty than was the power of
government. From the same source, Loyalists could also have derived
the main themes of their history of the Revolution. A more conservative ideology than that of the Patriots was to be found in the works
of well-known and respected eighteenth-century theorists. Viscount
Bolingbroke provided a holistic and elitist social ideal for at least some
Loyalists to cite approvingly. Baron de Montesquieu advanced a per-
suasive case for a limited or negative view of liberty. Edmund Burke
held the same high regard for history as did Loyalists. But it was in
Blackstone that Loyalists found an ideological kindred spirit. His antipathy to anarchy, his belief in the innate sociability of man, and his
positive view of the state were all embraced enthusiastically by Loyalist
spokesmen, who also shared Blackstone's views of the British Empire.
Common in Loyalist tracts were an idealized image of Britain and a
profound respect for the British Constitution; these were characteristic
of Blackstone, who was much more than a banal or fatuous apologist
for Hanoverian England. The concept of Parliamentary supremacy,
the indivisibility of sovereignty, and the conservative interpretation of
the balanced constitution were also at the heart of Loyalist ideology.
Blackstone's influence on Loyalist thought can be seen more clearly if
one considers another vital dimension of the ideology, the view of the
British Empire, or their Anglo-American vision.

6

THE LOYALISTS' ANGLO-AMERICAN VISION

My ancestors were among the first Englishmen who settled in America. I have no interest but in America. I have not a relation out of it that I know of. Yet, let me die! but I had rather be reduced to the last shilling, than that the imperial dignity of Great Britain should sink, or be controlled by any people or power on earth.

—SAMUEL SEABURY, *A View of the Controversy, &c. In a Letter to the Author of A Full Vindication &c.* (1774)

"YOU LOVE YOUR COUNTRY, and this affection is your duty, your honour," Myles Cooper told his New York readers in late 1773. "But remember," he continued in a classic Loyalist statement of the Anglo-American vision, "that not this, or any other province, is your country, but the *whole British Empire.* Its strength and superiority over its rival neighbours are the strength and glory of every part of its dominions, and its injuries, the injuries of all. On this ground, let us test the pretensions of some men to patriotism."[1] At the heart of Loyalist ideology was what might be called their Anglo-American vision: the basic belief in an integral and mutually beneficial union between Britain and America which had to be preserved and even strengthened. This union was considered to be rooted in history, nurtured by the colonists' pride in the British Empire and their affection for the king, and cemented by the bonds of trade.

An appreciation of the various dimensions of the Loyalists' Anglo-American vision is essential in understanding fully their ideology. Their alarm about the kinds of changes occurring in colonial America takes on an added urgency when contrasted with the many benefits they associated with the British connection. The Loyalists believed that many Americans were adopting ruinous policies and attitudes and that they were compounding their folly by jeopardizing a relationship which was so advantageous to them. Loyalists thought the British Empire and institutions offered much more than the Patriot alternatives. And the despair which at times permeated their writings can only be completely understood in the context of their deeply held conviction that they alone, as opposed to the Patriots or the people, knew the gravity and hazards of the British-American confrontation. At an emotional, intellectual, and even moral level, they were certain that America's best interest lay in membership in the British Empire. This was probably why some Loyalists were unduly optimistic about their ability to persuade the people of the merits of their position. Ironically, it was also why the realization that at least some Americans were pondering an alternative overwhelmed many Loyalists with despair.

The success of the Patriot alternative has, of course, cast a shadow over Loyalist proposals for America's future. The independence of the United States is so firmly established and universally accepted that it is virtually impossible to imagine that things could have been otherwise. Moreover, there is abundant evidence that centrifugal forces at work within the Anglo-American community were eroding the ties of interest and affection which had united the Empire.[2] At the same time, however, attachment to Britain was deeply rooted in the colonial psyche and not easily displaced. In defending the British Empire, Loyalists often had the advantage of reiterating familiar themes. Many of their arguments in the mid-1770s were merely extensions of ideas advanced in the previous decade or even earlier. Also, the divisions and problems within the empire were to a degree offset by some other centripetal forces drawing the British and American communities closer together. Trade ties between Britain and America were increasing in the eighteenth century, trans-Atlantic transportation and communication were improved significantly in the generation preceding the American Revolution, and some colonists were inclined by interest and sentiment to foster the growing British impact on colonial life.[3] The mother country was the main source for colonial political ideas,[4] and as American society matured and became more stratified, the social structure increasingly resembled Britain's.[5] Thus there was nothing impractical or utopian about the ideal of an Anglo-American community. At least some contemporary changes and long-established colonial attitudes were consistent with the Anglo-American vision, which, like other aspects of their ideology, was widely accepted by leading Loyalists from other colonies besides New York and Massachusetts.

The Nature of the British-American Relationship

Ideas about the nature of the relationship between the British and American communities were a basic point dividing Loyalists from Patriots. Admittedly, before independence most Patriots shared with the Loyalists an attachment to the British Empire based on affection for the mother country, allegiance to the British king, and an admiration for British institutions.[6] Yet even before 1776, Patriot writers tended to distinguish, often subtly, between the British and American communities, to imply that the interests of the two were not the same, and to question their own status as colonists or subordinates of the mother country. "Is there not something exceedingly fallacious in the commonplace images of mother country and children colonies?" John Adams asked pointedly. "Are we the children of Great Britain, any more than the cities of London, Exeter and Bath?"[7] The idea that equality rather than subordination was the appropriate status for America was also upheld by James Otis, who contended that "the colonists are entitled to as ample rights, liberties and privileges as the subjects of the mother country are, and in some respects, to more."[8] Virtual representation was refuted by Patriot spokesmen because, amongst other things, the interests of America could not be represented by Britons. One Patriot rejected the House of Commons' right to tax the colonies on the grounds that its members were not "our representatives, nor *members of this community*. And will Americans bear this?" he asked defiantly. "Have you not your own laws? Your own Judges? And your own Council? Why then should they command you?"[9]

The Patriot tendency to distinguish between America and its interests, on the one hand, and Britain and another set of interests, on the other hand, was reinforced by the contrasting images of the New and Old Worlds. Britain was part of the Old World, pictured as being riddled with injustices, corruption, and oppression. The New World, in contrast, was characterized by its freedom, virtue, opportunity, and peacefulness; it was "a retreat for the wretched inhabitants of the Old [World]."[10] Americans, therefore, had a duty to prevent the vices of the Old World from tainting the New. This mission to preserve America as a haven of liberty was depicted in dramatic language by one Patriot, who declared, "Preserve it [America] therefore an Asylum for the distressed of all nations, and a land of liberty for yourselves."[11]

The feelings of distinctiveness expressed by Americans were manifestations of a growing "sense of American community."[12] In the early 1760s, and even before, Americans were developing a heightened awareness of their colonial neighbors, accompanied by an emerging colonial vision of a unique and thriving North American society, or a "Rising American Empire."[13] This view of America's destiny was heralded in glowing terms by the New York Patriot William Livingston:

> For territory we need not quarrel with any power upon earth. This indispensable substratum of empire we are already possessed of! We have a country amply sufficient for hundreds of millions, and can spread out an inheritance from ocean to ocean, at a moderate expense of money, and without the guilty effusion of human blood . . . Courage then, Americans! Liberty, religion and sciences are on the wing to these shores. The finger of God points out a mighty empire to your sons.[14]

But Livingston's dreams about a "Rising American Empire" did not go unchallenged. Three future Loyalists—Charles Inglis, T. B. Chandler and Samuel Seabury—spoke for other Loyalists when they responded to Livingston. They began by acknowledging their profound attachment to America:

> No Whig that ever existed can have a warmer Attachment to the Interests of British *America,* than I have. It is the Country that gave me birth; that holds all the dear Connections of life. No one could rejoice more to see it flourish in Commerce, Arts and Sciences—in every thing that can make a people virtuous, happy and great—in the full and quiet enjoyment of all civil and religious liberty.[15]

Loyalty to America, however, was not at all inconsistent with a very deep allegiance to the empire, because the two were inseparable:

> But I cannot please myself with contemplating the Ruin and destruction of Great Britain—Avert it Heaven! May she ever continue the Mistress of the Nations—the grand Support of *Liberty,* the Scourge

of Oppression and Tyranny! May all Disgusts, Suspicions, Jealousies between the Mother Country and the Colonies, utterly cease, and be forever buried in Oblivion![16]

Unlike the Patriots, who questioned their status in the empire and distinguished between British and American interests, Loyalists assumed that there was a closely knit and thriving Anglo-American nation; their sense of community was not just American but Anglo-American. Some spoke of a specific colony or of continental America as their country and of the British Empire as their nation or state,[17] and in their minds country and nation were inseparable. America as a country was an integral part of the British nation or Empire. The Loyalists conceived of, and pledged allegiance to, America as part of a larger whole, the British Empire. This image of America as part of a larger entity was portrayed in imaginative analogies by various Loyalists. Samuel Seabury compared America to a limb which could not be detached from the body to which it belonged.[18] T. B. Chandler described the British Empire as a family in which the "sufferings" of one member affected the well-being of the group.[19] Peter Van Schaack felt that it was impossible for Americans to accuse the mother country of a usurpation of power since Britain and America were both "parts of the same state."[20] The same assumption—that the British-American crisis was a "contest between two main branches of a state"—was made by Myles Cooper.[21] Henry Caner summarized succinctly the Loyalist view when he described Massachusetts as a "subordinate Province" of "one Nation," the empire.[22]

It was impossible to distinguish between imperial and American loyalties, it was argued, because of the interdependence and mutual interests which tied together the various branches of the empire. The "reciprocal advantages" of the connection between Britain and America were stressed by Rusticus, while another Loyalist asserted that "America and Britain must conclude that their interests and security are inseparable."[23] The common interest shared by all members of the Empire was pointed out by another, who argued that since "all parts of the British Empire" were concerned in the "safety and protection of every part," all were obliged to pay for the "defence of every part."[24] And Myles Cooper felt that it was impossible "to separate (what in nature can never be disjoined) the good of particular branches of the community [America] from the good of the community itself [the British Empire]."[25]

The chasm between the Patriot sense of American community and the Loyalist Anglo-American outlook stemmed in part from their diverging interpretations of the colonial past. Patriot writers emphasized the self-reliance and independence of the first Americans as well as their quest to seek a new and better life in America. Some Patriots in New York as well as in Massachusetts felt that their ancestors had fled to America in search of the liberty denied to them in England.[26] The first Americans, in the opinion of James Otis, were "noble discoverers and settlers of a New World,"[27] and for John Adams the colonization of America marked "the opening of a grand scene and design in Providence for the illumination of the ignorant, and the emancipation of the slavish part of mankind all over the earth."[28] Their image of the New World was of a "retreat from slavery" or "an asylum for the distressed of all Nations and a land of liberty."[29] The view that the first Americans were self-reliant individuals who bore the burdens of colonization unassisted by the mother country was expressed superbly in 1773 by the Massachusetts Council:

> The dominion of the Crown over this country, before the arrival of our predecessors, was merely ideal. Their removal hither, realized that dominion, and has made the country valuable both to the Crown and nation, without any cost to either of them, from that time to this. Even in the most distressed state of our predecessors, when they expected to be destroyed by a general conspiracy and incursion of the Indian natives, they had no assistance from them.[30]

Another group of Patriots declared that "America was not sent out a Colony at the charge of *Great Britain,* and, for all the protection afforded her, might well be esteemed an orphan instead of a child."[31]

Loyalist spokesmen, however, were inclined to see the colonization of America as an extension of British civilization and imperial power into the North American continent, and they emphasized their forefathers' dependence on Britain. Rather than orphans deserted by their mother country, the first American settlers were described as children magnanimously aided by a benevolent matriarch. Great Britain, according to Isaac Wilkins, was "a kind and indulgent mother who hath nourished, protected and established us, in this land of

Canaan, this land flowing with milk and honey."[32] Charles Inglis felt that the first colonies would have perished "as an infant without its proper food, had not Great Britain offered her aid and support."[33] Although Daniel Leonard praised the "unequalled toils, hardships and dangers" faced by "our ancestors," he believed that the Crown granted them territory in North America "for purposes of colonization, which are to enlarge the empire or dominion of the parent state, and to open new sources of national wealth."[34] Similarly the *Censor* contended that Britain gave free land to the first settlers and was weakened by the loss of population; the British king made these sacrifices with the aim "of enlarging his empire."[35] The settlement of America, according to other Loyalists, was motivated by a desire to enhance the trade of the empire.[36] And a vital task undertaken by the early settlers was to bring to America the laws, institutions, and traditions of the mother country.[37] Many Loyalist spokesmen believed, then, that their ancestors had come to North America as British subjects with a mission to increase the wealth and power of the empire and to transplant British political and constitutional principles in their new environment.

Differing Loyalist and Patriot ideas about the British-American relationship were also reflected in assessments of the roles played by Britain and the colonies during the Seven Years' War. Patriot writers pointed to the colonial contributions to British successes and the benefits the war had brought to Britain. Oxenbridge Thatcher, a Boston Patriot, exemplified this interpretation:

> Nor is this objection [to taxation] removed by saying that the colonies, now enjoying the benefits accruing to them from the late war with France, ought also to share in the burdens which that war has entailed: for the war has been of no less benefit to Great Britain; while the war lasted, the colonies contributed to it their full proportion; by its territorial acquisitions, they are not particular gainers; Great Britain is a great gainer by them.[38]

Britain's role in defending the colonies was seen very differently by Loyalists. Some pointed out that British protection of colonial trade and seaports had always been a vital factor in the survival and success of the colonies.[39] Without the "impervious barrier" provided by Britain, the colonies, it was maintained, would have become prey to the French, Spanish or Dutch or have been "parcelled out, Poland like" among their various conquerors.[40] More specifically, in their accounts of the Seven Years' War, Loyalists portrayed the colonies, weak and unable to fend off enemies, as saved from destruction by Britain. "It was but a few years ago," T. B. Chandler reminded his readers, "that we believed and found by experience, that the colonies were unable to withstand the militia of Canada, supported by a few regiments of regular troops, from France." Vulnerable and unprotected, the colonies "humbly and ardently implored that Great Britain would speedily step in to their rescue, and preserve them from a destruction that threatened to overwhelm them."[41] The commanding position of Britain during the war was also stressed by Chandler: "Remember that Great Britain during the last war, did at one time carry conquest through every quarter of the Globe, and that you assisted her only in this."[42]

In light of Britain's protection of the colonies, Samuel Seabury contended, she should have the right to tax the colonies to help pay the costs of defense.[43] Others believed that the colonies' past achievements were due primarily to the aid and support provided by Britain. "By her strength, by her assistance," one wrote, "it is that we now enjoy this extensive Country, and have arrived to so great a pitch of opulence and importance."[44] A group of Loyalists in New York made the same point when they declared:

> The grand pitch of commerce we have arrived at, the progress we have made in arts and sciences, the amazing rapidity in extending, settling and improving our land estates; the magnificent appearance and flourishing condition of our towering cities, the opulence of the inhabitants, and every other blessing under GOD which we *do* and still *may* enjoy, derived their origin from, and have their existence in the laws, the lenity and the unlimited indulgence of our parent state; which has hitherto protected us, is ever able, and would be ready, if we deserve it, to defend us against all invaders of our peace and tranquility, by sending to our support the terror of the universe, the BRITISH ARMS.[45]

The clear-cut image of the mother country conveyed in these Loyalist colonial histories had been widely accepted in the colonies at the time of the Seven Years' War. Great Britain was, in the words of Seabury, Inglis and Chandler, "The Mistress of the Nations — the grand Support of Liberty, the Scourge of Oppression and Tyranny!"[46] The idea that Britain represented freedom and the Protestant religion and was at the head of a vast and glorious empire was common in both New York and Massachusetts in the early 1760s. The fall of the French Empire in North America led many colonists to express their loyalty and gratitude to the British. Bostonians lit bonfires and fired cannon as expressions of the "universal joy of this loyal and grateful people."[47] A New Yorker proclaimed that with the fall of France, North Americans were "the happiest People . . . of any People under the Sun . . . [who] glory in being sprung . . . [from Britain] and making a Part of [it] as it intitles them to many inestimable privileges."[48] New Englanders were especially grateful to the mother country for her role in destroying the French plot "to confine us to narrow bounds . . . to drive us off from our former possessions and drive us into the sea, or bring us under a slavish subjection to them."[49] For many Americans in 1763, the British Empire had reached a pinnacle of power and grandeur, "unparalleled in History," and was destined to ascend to even greater heights by increasing its sway in North America from "the Great Rivers to the Ends of the Earth."[50]

The British successes over France in the Seven Years' War were celebrated as cosmic moral victories. British-French rivalry in North America was interpreted by many colonists as a cataclysmic struggle between the forces of light and the powers of darkness.[51] The British, "upholder[s] of liberty in the world," "sons of noble freedom," defenders of Protestantism, a holy, enlightened, and tolerant religion were pitted against "cruel and oppressive" France, notorious for its despotic and arbitrary government, as well as its Roman Catholicism — anti-Christian, heathen, "Romish bigotry." The British triumph in 1763, then, was seen as a moral affirmation of the superiority of British constitutional liberty and of the Protestant religion, which the colonists, as British subjects, shared in.[52]

The Loyalists retained the idealized image of Britain that was common in the colonies in the early 1760s, although they did not hesitate to criticize specific policies or actions. Britain's military and economic might was still an important consideration to Loyalists.[53] They assumed that the mother country upheld the religious traditions common to both Britons and Americans, although this point was not stressed as much as it had been when Catholic France was still a threat on the continent.[54] But what was emphasized more than these other factors was the traditional colonial respect for British institutions.

The British Constitution

While Patriots were persuaded by the mid-1770s that the British Constitution had been subverted and corrupted in England,[55] tributes to the superiority of the constitution, similar to those of the early 1760s, were prominent in Loyalist pamphlets and articles. "I plead," Charles Inglis wrote, "for that constitution which has been formed by the wisdom of ages, is the admiration of mankind, is best adapted to the genius of Britons, and is most friendly to liberty."[56] To Henry Caner, the English Constitution was the most perfect, and most "favorable to Liberty"; under it "the subject enjoys more Liberty, is more secure in his Property, and in the enjoyment of every valuable Blessing and Privilege than the Subject of any other Nation under Heaven."[57] One group of Loyalists proclaimed they were "firmly attached to our most happy constitution," while another declared their commitment to "loyalty and our admirable constitution."[58] "We have been, and still may be," yet another group asserted, "the happiest people on earth, under the glorious and unparalleled constitution of Great-Britain."[59]

The British Constitution included key constitutional documents of the British past such as Magna Carta, the most important to Loyalists being the 1688 settlement which clearly established the concept of the supremacy of Parliament.[60] The constitution was also considered to comprise basic institutions of the British past, like trial by jury, which guaranteed to colonists, as British subjects, their basic civil and religious liberties.[61] And it included the actual form of government which existed in the colonies, modeled on that of the mother country. It was a limited monarchy in which power was balanced among three branches—governor, council, and assembly—to ensure both liberty and order.[62]

By focusing on such generally accepted strengths of the British Constitution, Loyalists could point out that Patriot political practices were inconsistent with British traditions and were thereby unconstitutional or republican. Thomas Hutchinson rejected the idea that "the common law prescribes limits to the extent of the Legislative power," since this seventeenth-century concept was inconsistent with the supremacy of Parliament, a basic tenet of the eighteenth-century constitution.[63] Another basic Patriot argument was dismissed by Seabury for the same reason: "The position that we are bound by no laws to which we have not consented, either by ourselves, or our representatives, is a novel position, unsupported by an authoritative record of the British constitution, ancient or modern. It is republican in its very nature, and tends to the utter subversion of the English monarchy."[64]

Moreover, by emphasizing the superiority of the British Constitution and the need to ensure that colonial institutions developed in accord with political traditions in the mother country, Loyalists were covering familiar territory. To Americans at that time Britain was a model for colonial values and attitudes and a standard by which American achievements could be measured.[65] Colonial laws and institutions were modeled on those of the mother country, and provincial assemblymen usually looked to the British House of Commons for precedents to guide their own behavior.[66] Besides serving as guidelines, British institutions and traditions satisfied colonial "symbolic and psychological" needs in that they epitomized not only political but also moral authority.[67] Many people in North America regarded the institutions and traditions of the mother country as an almost sacred order that defined the legitimate bounds of *all* authority and the proper relationship between subject and authority *generally*. These universal principles at the heart of the British polity and the constitution gave the British system its aura of sanctity and morality. For the colonial, conscious of existing at a distance from this moral order, being able to embrace the British system satisfied emotional and psychological needs.

A colonist's status as a British subject allowed him to identify himself with the British political system and the moral authority it symbolized. He could embrace the achievements of the British past and adopt British constitutional landmarks, like Magna Carta as his own charter of liberties. The British king, symbol of the Empire, Protestantism, and British constitutional liberty, became his king. And the victories of the British Empire over its rivals became the colonist's own triumphs. To be a British subject, sharing the British constitutional tradition, and a member of a trans-Atlantic empire was to have a place of importance in the world; it gave colonials a "sense of power."[68]

But what was vital, Loyalists pointed out, was that British liberties and traditions were part of the colonial political heritage only because they had been inherited from the mother country, and Americans enjoyed the rights of Englishmen only because they were British subjects under Parliament's jurisdiction. One of the many reasons for Samuel Seabury's denunciation of the Resolves of the Continental Congress was that they tended "to degrade and contravene the authority of the British Parliament over the British dominions; on which authority the rights of Englishmen are, in a great measure, founded; and on the due support of which authority, the liberty and property of the inhabitants, even in this country, must ultimately depend."[69] T. B. Chandler agreed that natural rights could not entitle Americans to the rights of Englishmen, that only being British subjects under Parliament could do so.[70] A group of New York Loyalists declared that their most fundamental "civil and religious liberties . . . can only be secured to us by our happy constitution."[71] Henry Caner contended that in America courts were "just, trade flourishes" and "people have property and luxury goods"; all of which were "secured to us by our happy constitution."[72]

Thus the ties binding Britain and America were extensive. History was one. Since the mother country was believed to have played an invaluable role in settling and defending the colonies, a common past as well as colonial feelings of gratitude were considered basic links in the imperial chain. Moreover, the real and perceived benefits of sharing British institutions were upheld by Loyalists as compelling reasons for Americans to cherish and cultivate the connection. Two other key ties cementing the Anglo-American relationship for Loyalists were trade and cultural ties.

Cultural or Family Ties

The idea that Britons and Americans were one people sharing the same language, religion, and institutions, members of the same trans-Atlantic family, was important in offsetting the obvious imbalance in the British-American relationship. In Loyalist writings there was no doubt that Britain was the dominant partner; besides being economically and militarily more powerful, the mother country deserved her more exalted status for reasons which were nicely summarized by Charles Inglis:

> They [the colonies] were discovered at the expense of the English Crown, first settled by English immigrants, and the governments erected here were formed on the model of the English government . . . The colonists were deemed English subjects and entitled to all the privileges of Englishmen. They were supported and defended at the expense of English blood and treasure . . . If these particulars do not entitle England to the appelation of mother-country of these colonies I know not what can.[73]

Such an unequal relationship could have been harsh or even oppressive if it were not for the affection Loyalists assumed was at the heart of the trans-Atlantic community. Great Britain was to Daniel Leonard, the "land of our forefathers' nativity, and sacred repository of their bones."[74] To Charles Inglis Britons and Americans were brothers united by the bonds of religion and kinship and sharing the same manners, habits, ideas, and institutions.[75] To Isaac Wilkins, Britons and Americans were one people with the "same laws, language, and religion, each of us, equally bound to each other by the ties of reciprocal affection."[76] Familial imagery was used frequently to suggest the intimacy of the relationship between mother country and colonies. Jonathan Sewall felt that the "true interest" of the colonies lay in being "dutiful and obedient children to the parent state."[77] Myles Cooper agreed that "the *authority* of the one should be the *beneficial* authority of a *parent;* the *obedience* of the other, the *liberal* obedience of a child."[78]

To the mother country was attributed a paternal concern for the well-being of her colonial offspring. One New York Loyalist recounted all the blessings Americans had to be thankful for and then asked "he [the colonist] is protected in his possessions by what?" The answer was as follows: " 'Tis by the paternal care, the penetrating eye, and the mighty arm of his mother country; who like a hen, when the hawk is near, hovers round her chickens, takes them under her wings, and preserves them from the enemy."[79] If Britain was the mother country, the king was the father. Colonial affection for the king was related to his being a prince of the House of Hanover — upholder of the Protestant religion and the British tradition of liberty under law — and the monarch responsible for raising the British Empire to its highest peak of glory. The essence of this image of George III was captured by an unknown poet in 1763:

> Britons rejoice while George III is king,
> In lofty strains his princely virtues sing,
> For he defends the meanest subject's cause,
> And guards religion and our glorious laws,
> . . . But know proud France and Spain, that slav'ry's chains
> Can ne'er be worn where glorious freedom reigns.[80]

The same idea was expressed more concisely by a New York Loyalist who described the British monarch as being "renowned for piety and protection for his subjects . . . His kingdom is the envy and terror of the world."[81] Undoubtedly, the British monarch could be a stern master, but his more gentle and kindly side was portrayed superbly in a poem featuring the two main figures in the British Empire—mother order and father king:

> And so, my good master, I find 'tis no joke,
> For York has step'd forward and thrown off the yoke
> Of Congress, committees and K— —g S— —S,
> Who shews your good nature, by shewing his ears;
> I trembled lest York should have join'd the mad freak,
> And formed a part of the damnable Streak--
>   The fever abated, see order arise,
> With ag'd constitutional tears in her eyes;
> Having summon'd her sons, who too wantonly stray'd,
> And calling her fair sister Grace to her aid,
> The youth she address'd in such accents of love,
> As, coming from mothers, ought always to move.
> Says she, "My dear children, ah! why should ye roam,
> "In quest of rude discord, and leave ME at home?
> "Your good father Monarchy bleeds at the heart,
> "To think that his sons should from virtue depart:
> "Consider how long we have cherish'd, protected,
> "How much we've indulg'd, and how little corrected;
> "How oft' we're provok'd, and our councils tormented;
> "What insults forgiven, what bloodshed prevented.
> "Behold your good brother, who rules in the North,
> "Examine his conduct, and copy his worth:

"Observe how Apollo presides, and you'll find,
"How lovely are mercy and power combin'd.
"His talk, tho' severe, he discharges with ease;
"And studies, like us, to preserve and to please.
"O, think how he feels between brother and brother
"When he's sent to reconcile one to the other;
"Then cease, I beseech you, no longer provoke.
"The *hand* which so tenderly wards off the Stroke
Such counsel as this, was enough, one would think,
To save them from ruin tho' just on the brink.[82]

Because of the tender guidance and protection of the parent state, Loyalists felt that affection and a sense of moral duty or filial obligation should also foster Americans' attachment to the British connection.

Trade

The most important reason for colonists to promote imperial unity, according to Loyalist spokesmen, was that they benefited in so many ways from the growing trans-Atlantic trade ties. Although this premise was highly controversial, there was no doubt that from the late seventeenth century onward the most significant factor drawing together Britain and the colonies was trade. As the colonial economies expanded and diversified, trade and economic ties with the mother country became more important. Colonial merchants in trans-Atlantic trade relied on English merchants for credit, for profitable military supply contracts, and for agents in foreign ports, and they looked to the British Parliament and navy for protection.[83] In the eighteenth century, with the beginnings of the Industrial Revolution, British manufacturers produced cheap and stylish goods, especially cloth, which were exported in increasingly large quantities to the colonies.[84] The already rising colonial demand for British manufactured goods was accentuated during the boom created by the Seven Years' War, which enhanced the purchasing power of many colonists.[85]

Not just wealthy colonials but other Americans, too, were almost obsessed with purchasing *English* manufactured goods. The image of London as a cosmopolitan center of fashion was reflected in colonial newspaper advertisements. In introducing their goods "suitable to the season," merchants were always careful to stress that the articles were fashionable and from other parts of the empire, notably London, Bristol, Hull, Liverpool, or Scotland. Colonial merchants enticed their customers with "silver buckles, London made," "an Assortment of the most fashionable Silks," a "new and elegant" London silver plate tea service, or a "Neat Assortment of Superfine cloths of the most fashionable colours now worn in London." Two went so far as to boast that their goods were from the "Royal Manufactory" or "immediately from the different manufactories." Most popular were imported cloth and articles of clothing: "rich black twilled silk, shalloons, velvets, twists, gold spangled buttons and loops," "serges, broadcloths, forest cloth, camblets, lute-strings" or "handkerchief[s], hats, umbrillos [sic]." Less prominent but still important were London and Bristol pewter, "delphware, London and Bristol grindstones," "London steel," "London stampt needles," and a whole range of items like china, ironware, paint, paper, and of course, tea. Even foodstuffs, which many northern colonies produced in abundance, were imported, and their British origin stressed: "Cheshire and Gloucester cheese, Durham mustard," "Durham flour and Mustard," or "Scottish barley and oatmeal."[86] Such advertisements suggest that Americans saw London, and to a lesser extent other British cities, as stylish, avant-garde, cosmopolitan centers, and they believed that British or Scottish goods were superior to and more desirable than those made anywhere in North America.

Newspaper announcements also indicate that some colonists were prejudiced in favor of British craftsmanship. Artisan immigrants from the British Isles, setting up shop in New York and Boston, were quick to advertise that they had learned their skills in Britain and to intimate that this resulted in more exquisite, stylish, and tasteful products. An engraver and copperplate printer from London boasted that his work was in the "most elegant taste." A New York hairdresser pointed out that he had been trained in London and "in the fashion and style of London." Two jewelers boasted that they had "served the first families of distinction in London." Perhaps the most extravagant claim was made by a watchmaker from London who stated his willingness to make watches "on an entire new plan, practised by very few in England and those esteemed the best mechanics in Europe." An announcement that William Tonge was establishing a merchant broker's office, "in the manner practised in London" implied that the American prejudice in favor of British know-how and experience extended even to mercantile transactions.[87]

Although there was no doubt that stronger economic ties meant a growing British influence on colonial life, many Americans had doubts about the desirability of these developments, mainly because of the disadvantages resulting from imports of British manufactured goods. As British imports increased, the colonies' balance of payments vis à vis Britain worsened, with a detrimental effect on the colonial economy. This situation stifled local development since colonial specie was siphoned off to the mother country to pay for imports, and British legislation restricting the use of paper money only aggravated the problem.[88] Also, because of specie shortages merchants had to rely more and more on world trade to finance British imports and this dependence made them vulnerable to trade restrictions such as those on the West Indies trade in the Sugar Act.[89] It was not just merchants who were vulnerable; indeed, indebtedness permeated to the lowest levels of colonial society, as a hierarchy of debt ascended from the most modest consumer through the local shopkeeper and the provincial importer to the merchant creditor in England.[90]

Moreover, there is evidence that the American prejudice in favor of British imports and craftsmanship adversely affected colonial artisans and merchants dealing in colonial-made products. In advertising their American manufactures, merchants argued for the superiority or the relative cheapness of their own products. James Abeel of New York, for example, stated that his hardware was better than British-made goods, as did Dennis McCready, a tobacconist, and Rickman and Browne, who dealt in native iron goods.[91] In Boston, Henry Bass advertised his grindstones as being "superior to those from Great Britain."[92]

It seems, then, that the growing British influence on American economic life was a mixed blessing. While some colonial merchants with good connections in English business circles profited by catering to the rising demand for British manufactures, others found their horizons limited by the same phenomenon. Although the growth in Anglo-American trade was an important factor in tightening the bonds between Britain and the colonies, the glaring imbalance in this

trade created serious economic problems for the American branch of
the British Empire. Thus, depending on one's perspective, trade could
be seen as an asset or as a liability to the colonies.

In the decade before independence, debate about trade was often
lively in New York and Massachusetts. One view expounded in the
1760s pointed out the costs associated with the British-American
trading nexus and argued in favor of colonial economic autonomy.
The other side of the argument, which was taken up and expanded
upon by Loyalists in the mid-1770s, focused on the benefits of colonial
membership in the British trading empire.

As early as May 1764, an anonymous New Yorker related the
"declining state" of American trade to the fact that "the balance between Great Britain and it [America] is greatly in favor of the former";
soon, he warned, Americans would find it impossible to pay their
debts because of the "immense Quantities of British Manufactures
yearly consumed by us."[93] Philo Patriae in Massachusetts agreed that
the key colonial economic problem was the imbalance in British-
American trade and the "imports of unnecessary European commodities which have late [sic] really encreased so fast as to threaten us
with general *poverty and ruin*."[94] Several other writers supported the
view that the depressed economic conditions of the 1760s were
associated with the imbalance in British-American trade, and many
criticized the increase in imports of British luxuries as an especially
alarming trend.[95] The degeneracy associated with luxurious fineries
was suggested by an unknown Bostonian who contrasted the "gaudy,
butterfly, vain, fantastick and expensive Dresses bought from Europe"
with the plain simplicity of American clothing.[96]

The most widely accepted solution to these economic difficulties in
the 1760s and 1770s was a restriction of imports and encouragement of
native manufacturing. Many appeals in favor of this form of "oeconomy" were couched in patriotic and moral terms. John Keating of
New York offered cash for rags and solicited support for his paper-
making operation with the argument that it was a patriotic duty to
promote local manufactures to retain money in the colony and improve its financial position vis à vis Great Britain.[97] Supporters of the
nonimportation schemes adopted between 1765 and 1774 also attempted to inculcate a sense of moral and patriotic duty to promote
local manufactures. Slogans like "Save your money and Save your

country" were popularized.[98] Wearing homespun came to be regarded as a sign of patriotism, while garbing oneself in the foppish finery of London was criticized as showing indifference to the fate of one's country.[99] As early as 1766 Bostonians were advised to boycott funerals where mourners wore black, which was associated with stylish imported cloth.[100] The colonial prejudice in favor of elegant and fashionable imports was depicted as a sign of moral decay. Americans were called upon to cleanse themselves by curbing their imports of foreign goods and by returning to the frugality, industry, and thrift of their Puritan ancestors.[101]

The extent of the challenge to the imperial trading network was revealed in a more detailed critique of the British-American economic relationship written in 1767 by Linen Draper. He contrasted the enormous potential for American expansion—a "Country whose Extension knows no Bounds"—with the reality of colonial indebtedness and currency shortages. The reason for this discrepancy was simple: "We follow a losing and destructive Trade to Europe . . . [that is] the ruin of our Country." According to this view, Americans were sinking into debt because of their virtually obsessive urge to purchase British manufactured articles and their disdain for American products. He observed the "the Linen made of his own [colonial] Flax is home spun; he therefore cannot endure it but . . . [must have] chintz . . . [which is] more genteel." Because American imports of manufactures exceeded exports of raw materials, the colonies labored under the burdens of debt, unemployment, and currency shortages. The villain in the drama was the American merchant who believed that only "trade makes a country great" and enriched himself "by this pernicious trade" at the expense of his country. The misconception was that imports were a sign of wealth, "when it is Exports alone that make a Country rich, and Imports that impoverish it." Americans, endowed with land, knowledge, and resources, did not have to be dependent on European or Asian imports but could become economically self-sufficient. If imports were curbed, if raw materials were processed in America, and if "Protection, Countenance and Encouragement" were given to native manufactures, then specie would remain in the colonies, development and employment would increase, indebtedness to Britain would end, and America would enjoy "Peace, Plenty, Happiness, and Independence on other Countries."[102]

Arguments like those of Linen Draper were consistent with contemporary British mercantilist ideas and, more specifically, with the
balance-of-trade theory. National prosperity and growth would be
realized by ensuring that exports exceeded imports and by bolstering
the country's economic self-sufficiency. Like British promoters of the
balance-of-trade theory — notably manufacturers worried about foreign
competition — Linen Draper favored "retrenchment in consumption"
of foreign luxuries as a way to curb imports. He also raised the specter
of retarded industrial development in order to criticize trade, especially
the export of raw materials, and to advocate instead that natural
resources be processed and developed at home. What is most striking,
however, is that the destructive imports to be curbed came from the
mother country, and the entity whose self-reliance and expansion was
to be promoted was America, not the British Empire. By the 1760s,
then, an economic rationale for independence was being suggested by
some Americans who regarded the colonies as a distinctive economic
unit, with interests different from and even antagonistic to those of
the British Empire. Patriotic Americans, within this context, would
strive to enhance the colonies' economic prospects, even if this was
detrimental to the interests of the British Empire as a whole.[103]

However, other ideas about the British-American economic relationship were expressed in the decade before independence, and these
laid the foundations for many Loyalist arguments. In both New York
and Massachusetts protests against the Sugar Act were premised on the
view that the British Empire was an interdependent trading empire
united by mutual interest, in which American agricultural products
were exchanged for British manufactures.[104] Because of the interdependence of the trans-Atlantic empire, it was argued, measures
like the Sugar Act which harmed the trade of one part affected
detrimentally the whole and were, therefore, not in the "national interest."[105] One opponent of the nonimportation schemes argued:
"Commerce is the true source of national Strength and Importance,"
and Britain was the "most opulent and powerful" commercial state.[106]
It was ridiculous, he claimed, for Americans to try to undermine
British trade through nonimportation schemes, since Britain was obviously the predominant and controlling partner in the trans-Atlantic
economic empire, while "America is scarce more than a kind of Fac-
tory to Great Britain."[107]

Other writers also admitted that Britain was the dominant partner, but instead of regarding this as a source of grievance, they stressed the beneficial aspects of Britain's superintending role. A New Yorker proclaimed that Americans

> were the happiest People . . . under the Sun: . . .Making a Part of a large Empire, we are protected in our Persons and Effects; [we have] so much Trade as the Wisdom of the Nation has thought proper to permit, as consistent with the Interest of the Whole . . . We think ourselves happier . . . in being dependent on Great Britain, than in a state of Independence, for then the Disputes amongst ourselves would throw us into . . . Confusion and bring on us all the Calamities usually attendant on civil wars.[108]

Some stressed the fact that Britain protected American trade and that "every part of an Empire that is defended by its power ought to pay a portion of such defence."[109] The essential ideas that the colonies as well as the mother country benefited from the growth in imperial power and that subordination to Britain brought benefits to America were articulated by a New Yorker: "We may safely conclude, that they [Americans] will remain steadfastly and firmly united to her [Britain]; and by contributing to her wealth and power, continue to increase their own Security, and that Dependence which they esteem their Happiness and which carries with it so many real Advantages."[110]

The various ideas expressed in the 1760s supporting the Anglo-American trading empire were tied together very effectively in 1771 by an anonymous writer with two basic premises. The first was that "the Kingdom and the Colonies are all one Dominion." The second was that "ours is a commercial Kingdom . . . The strength and wealth and happiness of it, chiefly depend on its Trade." It was necessary, therefore, for the British Parliament to regulate the trade of all the parts of the empire in the interests of the whole. Since it was "too common for each one to pursue his own private interest, without much consulting that of his neighbour or the public," it was necessary for Parliament to curtail the activities of individuals which were inconsistent with the public good. It was equally essential to restrain the colonies' trade with foreign powers since otherwise the "provinces will import the manufactures of foreign Kingdoms or States to the Strengthening and Enriching such Kingdoms; and the weakening and impoverishing their own." For these reasons, then, "the Parliament of

Great Britain . . . are certainly the most proper judges and have the best authority to make such acts concerning trade as may be most consistent with the common interest of the British Empire."[111]

Many of the ideas used in the 1760s to support British-American trade were adopted and extended by Loyalists. What is most interesting about Loyalist political economy is the small part played by the "agrarian myth."[112] Admittedly, Samuel Seabury in his pamphlet addressed specifically to farmers did offer a classic example of the myth. "Farmers," he asserted, "are of the greatest benefit to the state, of any people in it: they furnish food for the merchant, and mechanic; the raw materials for most manufactures, the staple exports of the country are the produce of their industry."[113] In the same pamphlet, however, he spoke of Americans as a "trading people,"[114] and a later tract stressed how vital merchants were to society.[115] But more common than the idealized image of the yeoman farmer or praise for the economic value of agriculture were tributes to commerce and its importance to American economic and social development. According to one Loyalist, "Commerce is that alone by which a nation supports its head . . . [it is basic to] national prosperity and grandeur . . . if merchants flourish not, a kingdom will have empty veins and flourish little . . . Empire ever has and ever will follow it."[116] Jonathan Sewall was convinced that "by Commerce and Trade alone Great Britain has arrived to such a pitch of opulence and splendour, as has scarce been equalled, never surpassed, by any Nation on the globe."[117]

Many of the arguments extolling commerce were modern in that they were more suited to a diversified, commercial economy than to one that was solely agricultural.[118] The link between commerce and progress was made by Daniel Leonard, who contrasted the poverty, backwardness, and provincialism of an agricultural economy with the sophistication, refinement, and worldliness of a more diversified economy. "Exclusive of commerce," he proclaimed, "the colonists would this day have been a poor people, possessed of little more than the necessaries for supporting life: . . . there would have been but little or no resort of strangers here; the arts and sciences would have made but small progress; the inhabitants would rather have degenerated into a state of ignorance and barbarity." In contrast to this dismal picture, Leonard portrayed the effects of our connection with, and subordination to Britain: . . . Our merchants are opulent, and our yeomanry in easier circumstances than the noblesse of some states. Population is so rapid as to double the number of inhabitants in the short period of twenty-five years. Cities are springing up in the depths of the wilderness. Schools, colleges, and even universities are interspersed through the continent; our country abounds with foreign refinements, and flows with exotic luxuries.[119]

Noteworthy is the contrast between Leonard's association of "foreign refinements" and "exotic luxuries" with progress and maturity, and the Patriots' view of these as symptoms of moral decline and degeneracy.

More specifically, the British-American trading relationship exemplified the natural interdependence that was assumed basic to commerce. To one New York Loyalist, for whom commerce was "the vitals of a nation," "every country has its share in different commodities, designed by the will of an omnipotent Being to depend on each other, linked in a chain of civil society."[120] The basic principle that there was an uncontrived symbiosis[121] between trading partners whose economies were complementary was mentioned by several Loyalists. America, it was quite rightly argued, lacked the capital and manpower possessed by Britain and required for manufacturing, but it abounded in land and resources suited to agriculture. Consequently, America needed manufactured goods and markets for its staples, while Britain required primary products and markets for manufactures. As a result, trade between the two was natural, mutually advantageous, and essential to the prosperity of both.[122]

Although the British trading empire was depicted as highly centralized and regulated by Parliament, this was considered to be neither limiting nor contrived, since Parliament was merely overseeing a natural trading relationship—in harmony with the God-given resources of the two communities and consistent with reason. The "naturalness" of mercantilism was argued by Myles Cooper in a wordy and rambling article justifying the importation of East India tea. "It is needless to observe to you," he began a most awkward and imprecise sentence which makes one wonder about his impressive scholarly credentials, "that the importance of modern states in the balance of Europe, depends on their *commercial advantages*." Since there was keen competition for the "lucrative trade of the East," and it was obvious that only a commercial monopoly like the East India Company could compete effectively in this trade, it was only reasonable for an American to "support the commercial interest in general of the State of which he is a member, by encouraging a trading company, whose welfare is so necessary to keep herein a balance with her neighbours." This meant specifically that Americans, who did not have tea of their own, should, out of a sense of duty and self-interest, import English rather than Dutch tea.[123]

Thus Cooper and other Loyalists saw the British trading empire as a corporate entity comprising various branches and regulated by the British Parliament. The idea of an economy as a "joint stock enterprise" was, Joyce Appleby has argued, a "powerful image for it provided symbolic cohesion to a society being atomized by the market."[124] In an increasingly individualistic society in which economic power was dispersed among a growing number of individuals and groups pursuing their own self-interest, it was an appealing idea that all of the diverse and competing groups in a community would join together in a broader undertaking to advance national prosperity and development. Appleby was referring to late seventeenth-century English society, but her argument could also be applied to the Loyalists and their view of the British trading empire. The Loyalists, seeing America as comprising a number of heterogeneous colonies with differing and even conflicting interests, feared that the colonies would eventually be reduced to a state of anarchy or even civil war. What was required, then, was some cohesive bond which would tie together the disparate and self-interested colonies and attach them firmly to the mother country. The ideal of the British Empire as a corporate or joint stock venture served this purpose. The various colonies and the mother country would unite in a patriotic quest to advance the prosperity and self-sufficiency of the empire relative to its rivals. Union against common economic competitors would be stressed rather than internal divisions, and the colonies and mother country would, in the words of Charles Inglis, have a mutual interest which was the "strongest bond of union."[125]

FOR MANY LOYALISTS the destinies of Britain and America were inextricably linked by extensive and deeply rooted ties. As offspring of

Great Britain, the colonists had been nurtured in their early years and protected ever since by a parent renowned for her commitment to liberty and Protestantism. The bonds of culture, language, religion, and traditions spanned the continent, as did pride in the British Empire and institutions. Added to these emotional and psychological grounds for cherishing the British connection was the very basic consideration of self-interest. To Loyalists, the benefits of membership in the trans-Atlantic trading empire constituted another compelling reason why Americans should rally behind imperial unity. But perhaps Isaac Wilkins suggested yet another and more elusive motive for Loyalists to look to Great Britain in the mid-1770s when he spoke of England as the oak around which the colonies had "twined" themselves for so long.[126] Wilkins' image of the oak, with all its connotations of strength, age, stability, and security, symbolized his and other Loyalists' most basic feelings about the mother country. For them Great Britain represented the only fixed and constant entity in a chaotic, turbulent, and uncertain world in which everything they valued most seemed threatened by profound change.

7

LOYALIST IDEOLOGY AND THE
FIRST CONTINENTAL CONGRESS

To your mighty high Congress, the Members were sent,
To lay all our Complaints, before Parliament;
Usurpation rear'd its head, from that fatal Hour,
You resolv'd, you enacted, like a sovereign Pow'r.
... Instead of imploring, their Justice, or Pity,
You treat Parliament, like a Pack, of Banditti:
Instead of Addresses, fram'd in Truth and on Reason,
They breathe nothing, but insult, rebellion and treason ...
In all the Records, of the most slavish Nation,
You'll not find an Instance, of such Usurpation.
If Spirits infernal, for dire Vengeance design'd,
Had been nam'd Delegates to afflict Human kind,
And in Grand Continental Congress, had resolv'd,
"Let the Bonds of social Bliss, be henceforth dissolved."

— *A Dialogue Between A Southern Delegate*
and His Spouse ... (1774)

T HE LOYALISTS' Anglo-American vision established the parameters for their interpretation of the Boston Tea Party and its aftermath, an interpretation which predictably was very much at odds with the Patriot one. Few Loyalists doubted that a grave crisis was brewing after the violent destruction of East India tea by Boston Patriots. The Loyalists' response to the crisis was molded by their image of the mother country and their acceptance of the dominant role of Britain in the empire. These beliefs caused them to see problems and hazards that the Patriots dismissed or overlooked. An important motive for appealing to the public was to dispel what Loyalists regarded as the myths about Britain propagated by the Patriots and to portray to their

132

fellow colonists the stark realities of their perilous situation. Also, the tenacity with which Loyalists supported Parliamentary supremacy can only be understood in the context of their sense of Anglo-American community and their unalterable conviction that the fate of the Empire rested on the supreme authority of Parliament to legislate for the whole. These basic beliefs shaped their reaction to the first Continental Congress, a major watershed in Anglo-American history generally and in the fortunes of the Loyalists particularly.

Britain versus America

The despair which surfaced at times in Loyalist appeals was generated in part by their belief that the Patriots harbored many basic misconceptions about the colonies' real strength and about the unity and the power of the British nation which they were unnecessarily provoking. In challenging British authority, the Patriots, according to T. B. Chandler, had "brought upon the *Americans* the indignation of a power, which the proudest nation in Europe reveres, and under whose resentments the strongest would tremble."[1] In any war with Britain, Daniel Leonard warned, the ill-disciplined and insubordinate provincials would face well-trained British regular troops; the British navy would control "our trade, fishery, navigation, and maritime towns," and the Canadians and "savages" would ravage the frontiers. "Whenever the sword of civil war is unsheathed," he predicted gloomily, "devastation will pass through our land like a whirlwind."[2] Samuel Seabury, like other Loyalists, worried about Britain's economic superiority: "The fleets of Great-Britain command respect throughout the globe. Her influence extends to every part of the earth. Her manufactures are equal to any, superior to most in the world. Her wealth is great. Her people enterprizing, and persevering in their attempts to extend and enlarge and protect her trade."[3] It was therefore a dangerous illusion for Patriots to think that the nonimportation and nonexportation schemes would harm Britain more than America. Britain, Seabury warned, could easily use her navy to cut off American trade to other parts of the world, and she could quickly find alternative supplies of raw materials.[4]

To these and other Loyalists, the Patriots were baiting the most powerful naval and trading nation in the world and were totally oblivious to their danger because they had foolishly underestimated British strength and vitality. Samuel Seabury lashed out at Alexander Hamilton for "always speak[ing] of Great-Britain, as of some pitiful state just sinking into obscurity . . . like an old, wrinkled, withered worn-out hag, whom every jackanapes that truants along the streets may insult with impunity."[5] Democritus ridiculed Patriot attempts to intimidate the British ministry:

> I am so tickled with the thoughts of them making Lord North tremble in his shoes . . . that I really wish myself in London with those Resolves in my Hand; in that case I would hasten into his Lordship's Preference forthwith, and throwing the paper down, cry out with an air of Triumph, "There my Lord is proof of our Union! take that and be d— —d to you!" Then would I rush out of the Room, to avoid the smell of the profuse Diarrhea, which I make no doubt would be the immediate consequence of his Fears.[6]

Ideas about Britain's weakness and decline were seen as being both misleading and dangerous. To Loyalists Britain was a kind and tender parent whose greatest fault was perhaps her leniency. Rather than asserting authority unequivocally over the colonies, the mother country had responded to appeals and had repealed legislation like the Stamp Act. But the Patriots, rather than being grateful for such concessions, saw them as signs of British weakness or were emboldened by what they misconstrued to be colonial victories.[7] Such a misinterpretation was especially dangerous because Loyalists felt that when provoked, the British parent could respond with tremendous vigor and harshness. By mid-1774 Loyalists feared that the British nation was aroused and united in its determination to crush colonial rebelliousness, or as Peter Oliver put it, "You have roused the British Lion."[8] Patriot claims that Britain was disunited and that there was widespread support in the mother country for the colonial position[9] were adamantly rejected by Daniel Leonard. "However closely we may hug ourselves in the opinion, that the parliament has no right to tax or legislate for us," he declared, "the people of England hold the contrary opinion as firmly."[10] "We hear, by every arrival from England," he wrote in January 1775, "that it is no longer a ministerial (if it ever was) but a national cause."[11]

The agonizing frustration of seeing fellow colonists trifling with a powerful, determined, and stern parent was heightened by the Loyalists' belief that America was also much less united than her potential foe. Peter Oliver warned that Massachusetts might well be abandoned by the other colonies and left to face the awesome military force of the mother country alone. He satirized the anti-New England sentiments of other colonies as follows:

> Let us therefore make them [Massachusetts] the mercenaries, — they will sacrifice every thing for money, we can pay them in paper which they are so fond of: By engaging them for soldiers, they will get knocked in the head, their wives and children will be ruined, and when we have established our empire, we shall have nothing to fear from them; they will become an easy prey to the rest of the provinces, and we can parcel them out among us as we may think proper.[12]

Several New York Loyalists stated that the colonies were far from united and that the New England extremists, "rebellious Saints at Boston" or "seditious Bostonians," were the key principals in the confrontation.[13] New York Loyalists also revealed a very negative stereotype of New Englanders, whom T. B. Chandler, for example, depicted as a band of bigots and fanatics who had in the past mercilessly persecuted minorities.[14] Antipathy to New England also surfaced in Samuel Seabury's interpretation of the events of 1774. He believed that it was the New Englanders who were guilty of rebellion. New York, on the other hand, "hath taken no decisive step" and should therefore dissociate itself from the other restive colonies and

> make the best terms that we can for ourselves. If the people of New England will kindle a fire, and then rush into it, have we no way to shew our regard and affection for them, but to jump in after them? Let us rather keep out, that we may have it in our power to pull *them* out, before they are burnt to death. A little scorching I believe will not hurt them. It may do them good: it may make them dread the fire hereafter; for, like children, they seem incapable of learning from *any* experience but *their own*.[15]

New York and Massachusetts Loyalists, then, expressed certain common attitudes about the supposed unity of the colonies in their opposition to Britain. Many believed that it was primarily New England, Massachusetts, or even just Boston engaging in rebellious activities. They did not regard the other colonies like New York as being either involved in or sympathetic with New England's activities. The assumption that the colonies in 1774, 1775, and even 1776 were very disunited stood in sharp contrast to the premises of Patriots like John Adams, who proclaimed in 1775 that in America, "one understanding governs, one heart animates the whole body . . . one great, wise, active and noble spirit, one masterly soul, [is] animating one vigorous body."[16] In short, while Patriots like Adams depicted one united American continent standing in opposition to British claims, Loyalists portrayed a continent of very different and divided colonists who diverged fundamentally in their attitudes toward the Anglo-American crisis.

Loyalists also stressed the internal divisions existing within each colony. In Massachusetts Leonard, Sewall, and others denied that the province was unanimous in its support of the Patriots. Intimidation and coercion by the Patriots, they believed, had produced a superficial unity, which would be quickly unmasked, "whenever the royal standard shall be set up," when there would be "such a flocking to it, as will astonish the most obdurate."[17] The best proof of the deep divisions in Massachusetts lay, according to Leonard, in the Patriots' persecution of Loyalists. "Do you [Patriots] wish to silence them, that the inhabitants of the province may appear unanimous?" he asked rhetorically. "The maltreatment they receive, for differing from you, is undeniable evidence that we are not unanimous."[18] The same point, that any seeming unity was the result of coercion, not consensus, was made by a New York Loyalist who denounced the Patriots for "the happy and peculiar knack, they enjoy by nature, of bullying, swearing and browbeating and of enforcing conviction without calling in the assistance of reason and justice."[19] A fellow colonist argued that true unity could only be based on "argument and conviction not terror."[20] Shattering the illusion of unanimity was, of course, essential to the Loyalist interpretation of the Revolution, which depicted a small minority misleading a basically loyal and orderly populace into violent, illegal, and disloyal measures.[21]

Nonetheless, there was enough concrete evidence of widespread disapproval of Patriot actions, especially in New York, to support the contention that Americans were divided on the eve of independence. In Massachusetts some towns denounced the Boston Tea Party, there was a debate about whether or not to pay for the tea, and the Solemn

League and Covenant provoked opposition, especially from some Boston merchants.[22] Other declarations of loyalty and of support for the legally established government included addresses to royal governors and the loyalist Association, organized by Timothy Ruggles.[23]

Signs of opposition to the Patriots and of support for the British Empire were easy to find in New York, especially in 1775, when many Loyalist associations, declarations, and addresses were signed and published. In these documents, often signed by more than a hundred citizens, rank-and-file Loyalists denounced specific Patriot actions which they considered to be aggravating the Anglo-American dispute and more generally condemned the usurpation of the authority of the colonial governments and courts by illegal and unconstitutional committees. Many signers declared their willingness to hazard their lives and property in support of their king and constitution.[24]

An "Unnatural" Rebellion

Another reason why anxiety, distress, and even frustration were apparent in Loyalist literature was that to them the Revolution was so unnatural, or as Charles Inglis put it, "The present Rebellion is certainly one of the most causeless, unprovoked and unnatural that ever disgraced any Country."[25] The adjective "unnatural," used at some point by almost every Loyalist writer, suggested two different objections to the Revolution. In the first place, it was unnatural because it was a fratricidal war between two branches of the same family, a family which for Loyalists was united by innumerable ties of history, culture, affection, and interest. In light of the natural intimacy and mutuality of the British-American relationship it was considered to be utterly unreasonable and abnormal for the colonies to seek a separation from the mother country.[26] To Isaac Wilkins, Britain had nurtured the colonies in their youth, and promoted their development. The American children should have felt gratitude and affection for the British parent; instead, the colonies were taking "part against such a parent," something which was brutal and unnatural, and showed the colonists to be nothing less than "detestable parracides."[27]

The Revolution was also seen as unnatural because it was supposedly based on such a flimsy foundation. To consider revolution legitimate, according to the Lockean compact theory of government,

Loyalists would have had to accept the Patriot view that there was a British design to deprive Americans of basic rights and freedoms. It was virtually impossible for Loyalists to accept this idea and conclude, as Patriots had by July 1776, that the Anglo-American dispute was irreconcilable. Although most, if not all, Loyalists conceded at some point that the Anglo-American relationship should be altered or that specific British acts were ill-judged, or even infringements of established American privileges, still they did not believe that British actions in the 1760s and 1770s constituted a plot to tyrannize the colonies. Peter Van Schaack, who reflected on the events of these years for some time, hit at the heart of the matter when he concluded: "But, my difficulty arises from this, that taking the whole of the acts complained of together, they do not, I think, manifest a system of slavery, but may fairly be imputed to human frailty, and the difficulty of the subject. Most of them seem to have sprung out of particular occasions, and are unconnected with each other."[28] Virtually every Loyalist in New York and Massachusetts arrived at a similar conclusion. And if revolution was not justified, then the colonists were duty bound to seek a reconciliation with Britain. It was adherence to this belief—that the British-American dispute had to be reconciled—that divided even the most hesitant Loyalist from the Patriots.[29]

Loyalists found it impossible to believe that Britain was plotting to enslave America, because such behavior would be totally inconsistent with their image of the mother country as a nation renowned for its liberty and as a kind and nurturing parent. That such a nation would turn tyrant was so irrational as to be bizarre, argued Daniel Leonard in an incisive attack on the Patriot rationale for Revolution:

> Are we, then, to rebel, lest there should be grievances? Are we to take up arms and make war against our parent, lest that parent, contrary to the experience of a century and a half, contrary to her own genius, inclination, affection and interest, should treat us or our posterity as bastards and not as sons, and instead of protecting should *enslave* us? The annals of the world have not yet been deformed with a single instance of so unnatural, so causeless, so wanton, so wicked a rebellion.[30]

Jonathan Sewall and other Loyalists charged with some accuracy that the sense of danger that the Patriots felt existed only in their imaginations[31] or, as one satirically put it, the Patriots were displaying their paranoia by constantly trying to "unveil the covert, choked design of the d— —d ministry to own us."[32]

Unconvinced of the existence of a conspiratorial design which lent a diabolical coherence to all of Britain's actions since 1765, Loyalists were amazed and horrified at the events following the Boston Tea Party. Many simply could not believe that the rather innocuous Tea Act was the spark which ignited such fires of sedition. The piece of legislation was variously interpreted by Loyalists as an attempt by the British government to enhance the competitive position of the East India Company vis à vis its Dutch rivals, as an opportunity to undermine the immoral activities of American smugglers, or as a boon to American consumers, who would pay less for their tea.[33] In other words, Loyalists viewed the Tea Act as an isolated piece of legislation unconnected with previous British measures enacted since 1765. From this vantage point, some ridiculed the Patriot suggestion that America was being tyrannized by a paltry three-penny duty;[34] others responded to Patriot cries about the tyrannical implications of landing the tea by advising upset colonists to refrain from buying the tea, which was a luxury anyway;[35] still others counseled concerned citizens to petition the British Parliament. To protest the duty by implementing nonimportation or nonexportation schemes, it was pointed out, would cost Americans a lot more than three pennies.[36] In short, for many Loyalists, the Tea Act was simply not an oppressive or a tyrannical measure.

It was from this perspective, then, that most Loyalists reacted to the events set in motion by the Boston Tea Party. If, as many assumed, the Tea duty did not represent an imminent or fatal blow to American freedom, then the violent destruction of private property it evoked was both irrational and unjustified.[37] And since many regarded the Boston Tea Party in such a light, the Coercive Acts were seen as being an understandable, though for some Loyalists a somewhat severe, British response to American provocation.[38] Thus, by the autumn of 1774, many Loyalists believed that British-American affairs had reached a crisis, apparently brought about by the Americans, and they hoped that the first Continental Congress would take steps to reconcile the dispute.

Parliamentary Sovereignty

Loyalists who looked hopefully to the first Continental Congress were sorely disappointed, mainly because of the fundamental difference of opinion between them and supporters of the Congress over the issue of Parliamentary supremacy. To virtually all articulate Loyalists, the supreme authority of Parliament to legislate for the empire was the vital constitutional ligament in the imperial connection and the most basic symbol of the oneness of the empire. In the Loyalist interpretation of American history, their forefathers had come to North America as British subjects who remained under the jurisdiction of Parliament. Americans shared the liberties, rights, and institutions of the British Constitution solely because of their status as subjects of Parliament. The most important constitutional development, the 1688 settlement, established once and for all the concept of Parliamentary supremacy.[39] And the coherence and prosperity of the Anglo-American trading empire were considered to depend upon Parliament, which regulated British and colonial interests to advance the power and self-sufficiency of the empire. For most Loyalists, then, the Anglo-American community could be preserved only if the sovereign legislative power of Parliament was coextensive with the empire.

There were, however, other reasons why Loyalists felt that Parliamentary supremacy was the linchpin in the imperial constitution. One was their unquestioning acceptance of the indivisibility of sovereignty. Peter Van Schaack cited John Locke as his authority in asserting this basic principle: "He [Locke] holds the necessity of a *supreme power,* and the necessary existence of *one legislature only* in every society, in the strongest terms."[40] This idea was supported by other Loyalists. "The supreme authority of every empire," Isaac Wilkins claimed, "must extend over the whole, and every part of that empire; otherwise there must be *imperium in imperio,* two absolute and distinct powers in one and the same government, which is impossible."[41] Assuming that the British Empire was one national unit, it was only logical that the sovereign power of that nation be coextensive with the nation. T. B. Chandler displayed impeccable logic when he argued: "Whether, if the colonies be a part of the great *British* community, they are not necessarily subject, in all cases, to the jurisdiction of that legislative power which represents this community, or, in other words, the *British* parliament?"[42]

Loyalists refuted, on two grounds, the idea that colonial governments were equal to the British Parliament in some matters because of powers granted to them in charters. First, they pointed out that the jurisdiction of colonial legislatures was restricted to purely local or internal affairs, while Parliament regulated matters affecting the empire as a whole.[43] Moreover, colonial charters were compared to charters granted in England to corporations or towns. As with grants of jurisdiction to corporations, colonial charters were intended "to grant subordinate powers of legislation, without impairing or diminishing the authority of the supreme legislature."[44] In other words, power was concentrated in Parliament and devolved in pyramid fashion to subordinate jurisdictions; if the British Empire was to continue to be one nation it was essential, from the Loyalist viewpoint, that Parliament retain its supreme power to legislate for the whole.

Not only would the unity of the empire be sacrificed if Parliamentary sovereignty were challenged, but also, it was contended, colonial unity and order would suffer. In Loyalist writings the colonies are depicted as diverse entities with different and often conflicting interests. The prevalence of trade rivalries, boundary disputes and regional jealousies was frequently stressed.[45] Because of this heterogeneity, it was deemed essential that some external body, assumed to be the British Parliament, impose a degree of coherence and unity upon America.

The idea of Parliament as the linchpin which harmonized and coordinated the energies and interests of the colonies to promote the well-being of the whole was advanced by an unknown New Yorker:

> As an American, I wish my country every blessing of freedom, But I think, we can expect more happiness, by an union with England and subordination to the supreme legislature, than by any fancied schemes of independent states. The superintendence and mediation of Great Britain seems to be necessary to balance and decide the different interests of the several plantations and colonies, and to direct, command and govern the operations and powers of *each* for the benefit and defence of *ALL*.

He concluded by contrasting the vigor and stability of America as part of the empire with the disorder and violence he associated with independence: "Protected by her navy and armies we shall rise with fresh vigour and strength, and see her free and well-balanced constitution gradually communicated to us. In a state of separation, on the contrary, ages may pass, and rivers of blood be shed, before any regular form of government could be adopted and fixed on a firm basis."[46]

But as Daniel Leonard argued, the unity and order of the empire depended on Parliamentary sovereignty. The main duty of a state was to guarantee "the security of the people from internal violence and rapacity, and from foreign invasion." In order to perform these duties, he maintained, the state had to have the power to tax its subjects. Within the empire this taxing power was vested in Parliament, the only body which could impose its will on all of the colonies and unite the strength of the various parts in defense of the whole. Left to their own devices the colonies would not contribute to the defense of the empire, so "the disjointed, discordant, torn, and dismembered state [would be] incapable of collecting or conducting its force and energy for the preservation of the whole, as emergencies might require."[47]

Another role attributed to Parliament was that of the umpire which arbitrated colonial disputes. Seabury was convinced that without Parliament's mediating influence, colonial disputes would abound and be decided only by the "sword and bayonet."[48] T. B. Chandler agreed that "without the superintending authority of Great Britain to restrain them, the colonies would . . . probably be soon at war among themselves."[49] Peter Van Schaack stated that "without such a controlling common umpire [the British Parliament], the colonies must become independent states, which would be introductive of anarchy and confusion among ourselves."[50]

The mother country generally and Parliament specifically were seen as stabilizing forces which lent a measure of order and unity to the potentially chaotic colonies. "The loyalty we owe to the best of Kings," a group of Loyalists proclaimed, "is the grand magnetic point, that will infallibly fix us on a solid basis."[51] Leonard explicitly linked order in the colonies with Parliamentary power. After depicting the anarchy he believed prevailed in Massachusetts in late 1774, Leonard expressed this uncompromising opinion: "The absolute necessity of the interposition of parliament is apparent."[52] To him the anarchy of 1774–75 merely reflected the fact that colonial governments "have no principle of stability within themselves." In turbulent times the colonial governments would become "wholly monarchical, or wholly republican, were it not for the checks, controls, regulations, and supports of the supreme authority of the empire."[53]

At the heart of the Loyalist Anglo-American vision, then, were a basic belief in the oneness of the empire and a conviction that imperial unity depended upon the supremacy of Parliament to legislate for the whole empire. Governor Hutchinson could have been speaking for virtually all Loyalists, when he wrote in July, 1774: "I have never had but one plan for the government of America. The supremacy of Parliament must never be given up. This part of the plan has lost my popularity, and brought upon me all the trouble and danger which I have laboured under for eight or nine years together."[54]

What Hutchinson said of himself was tragic, true, and applicable to Loyalists generally: their unswerving commitment to imperial unity and Parliamentary sovereignty proved to be their undoing. Parliamentary supremacy was the issue more than any other which divided them irreconcilably from the Patriots and led to civil war.

The depth of the division became apparent shortly after the first Continental Congress. Loyalists felt betrayed and embittered by the Congress, which they attacked for widening rather than narrowing the gap with the mother country and for a number of specific actions, including the supposedly treasonous addresses to the people of Quebec and Britain, the approval of the Suffolk Resolves, and the establishment of the Association.[55] Most distressing was the Congress's denial of Parliament's *right* to tax and legislate for the colonies, which to many was "effectually throwing off the mask" and declaring independence.[56] As he did so often, Leonard expressed very forcefully the sentiments of other Loyalists: "As far as was in their power, they [Continental Congress] had dismembered the colonies from the parent country. This they did by resolving, that 'the colonists are entitled to an exclusive power of legislation in their several provincial legislatures.' This stands in its full force, and is an absolute denial of the authority of parliament respecting the colonies."[57]

Weaknesses in the Loyalist Position

As news of the debates and decisions of the first Continental Congresses trickled back to the various colonies, it must have been a chilling experience for Loyalists. It was not just frustration of their hopes for a speedy resolution of the British-American crisis, it was also the perception that revolution or rebellion might lie in the future and that they as outspoken opponents of this destiny might be caught in the middle. The great strength of the Loyalists' analysis of the crisis was their accurate reading of the situation in England, perhaps because some, as royal officeholders or Anglican clergymen, had extensive connections in the mother country and were better informed about British politics than the Patriots. At any rate, when Patriots were still popularizing myths about deep divisions in England over American affairs or about widespread support for the American cause, Loyalists quite rightly saw that despite the factionalism of the previous decade, by the mid-1770s the British king, ministry, Parliament, and the vast majority of the politically aware electorate were united in their determination to deal firmly with the American "rebels."[58]

At the same time the Patriots at the first Continental Congress had staked out a position from which there was little room to retreat. Besides agreeing on a general constitutional position which was fundamentally at odds with the British one, the Congress organized intercolonial opposition to the Coercive Acts and established a system of committees to execute their policies.[59] One of the many reasons why the Revolution occurred was that neither the British nor the Patriots appreciated their opponents' determination and unwillingness to back down. From the Loyalists' unique vantage point, however, they could see the resolve or recklessness of both sides and could anticipate the collision, but they were powerless—they simply could not influence either participant in the dispute.

The inability of the Loyalists to affect the British handling of American affairs is well illustrated in the career of Thomas Hutchinson. A dedicated and experienced provincial politician and a royal officeholder with connections in England, Hutchinson proffered advice designed to stave off a confrontation to British political leaders. He was one of several prominent Americans who went to great pains to forewarn British politicians of the probable colonial reaction to the Stamp Act, and he accurately predicted many of the grounds upon which colonists opposed it, to no avail.[60] He used his influence and political cunning, at great expense to his reputation in Massachusetts, to tone down the Massachusetts petition against the Stamp Act, but the gesture was lost on British Parliamentarians.[61] In 1770 he made a point of writing to England to advise against any sudden constitutional changes in the structure of colonial governments such as were passed in the Massachusetts Government Act of 1774, but his advice was obviously unheeded.[62] In 1774 he found himself in England, trying once again to persuade British leaders, now to repeal the Boston Port Act, which closed the port of Boston. This time, however, he was an exile from his native colony.[63]

After the first Continental Congress, it was all too apparent that Loyalists like Hutchinson not only lacked influence in Britain but also had minimal ability to affect decisions in the colonies. An obvious question is why did Loyalists have so little influence on colonial decisions? This in turn raises broader questions about the Loyalists' Anglo-American vision and their interpretation of the Continental Congress and the events leading up to it. Were the Loyalists so out of touch with public opinion that their ideas were irrelevant to the concerns of colonists in this period? Were the colonists so eager to usher in independence that there was no scope for a defense of the empire? Were there serious shortcomings in the Loyalist argument and in the methods they used to communicate it to the people?

Most colonists were not ready to accept independence before 1776, and there probably was some room for a rekindling of loyalties to the empire. The best proof of this lies in the first Continental Congress. While making manifest their sympathy with Boston and indicating their resolve to resist the Coercive Acts, delegates to the Congress were also careful to appear to be acting only on the defensive.[64] They portrayed themselves as defenders of American rights rather than as aggressors provoking a British-American confrontation. This strategy, of course, led to independence because the hard-line posture adopted by Britain undercut the position of moderates and further alienated the colonists from the mother country.[65] But this process occurred gradually from mid-1774 to mid-1776. Before independence, there probably was still quite a reservoir of colonial feeling for the British Empire which Loyalists could tap. And they did.

Their vision of an Anglo-American Empire was in tune with many important contemporary changes and consistent with well-established colonial attitudes. Along with the increase in trade, the expansion of the Anglican church in New York and New England meant that more and more colonists had ties to England as members of a trans-Atlantic

religious community.[66] British influence on colonial culture was increasing in the eighteenth century;[67] good connections in England
were important to an aspiring colonial politician as well as to an ambitious merchant;[68] and other local institutions and practices, such as
colonial criminal law, were increasingly modeled on British precedents.[69] Moreover, in extolling British institutions Loyalists were
reiterating what was conventional wisdom in the colonies and else-
where at the time. Pride in the vast and powerful British Empire and
affection for the king were equally traditional colonial beliefs. And the
Loyalists' political economy included a modern and well-argued brief
on behalf of a more enlightened mercantilism. Why, then, were there
problems selling this view of the empire to colonial readers?

Loyalists were writing about a vision or an ideal, about how the
empire could or should operate in theory, but the practice, the reality
unfolding before colonists' eyes, diverged markedly from the ideal. It
might have been possible for the empire to be run in the interests of
America as well as of the mother country, but this was manifestly not
happening in the 1760s and 1770s. For all kinds of reasons, American
interests were not adequately represented in Britain; British politicians
and bureaucrats responsible for colonial policy were not well enough
informed about American affairs and attitudes; because of the earlier
British policy of "salutary neglect" there were serious discrepancies
between British and American ideas about how the empire should
operate, which were brought to the fore by British attempts to tighten
up the empire before and after the Seven Years' War.[70] At least some
Englishmen on both sides of the Atlantic were grappling with solutions to these chronic problems.[71]

But there were also short-term problems: at a time when the aim of
British policy was to centralize the empire, there were grave weaknesses at the center. The 1760s was a decade of instability, as George
III asserted his prerogative to choose his own ministers, and American
affairs became enmeshed in factionalism. The opposition in Parliament
fanned the flames of discontent and protest in America by launching
well-publicized and often outlandish attacks on the ministry's handling of American affairs, not because of any substantive disagreement
with the government's policy, but as a way to discredit and defeat the
ruling faction.[72] This served only to mask the reality: British politicians, with a few exceptions, were basically unanimous about British-

American relations, and the generally accepted views, though outdated, were never seriously discussed or questioned in the 1760s and
were therefore never changed or updated—until it was too late.[73]

The short- and long-term problems in the empire help to explain the
irony that the greatest liability to the Loyalists in the mid-1770s was
the mother country. British ideas about colonial matters were so out
of touch that the policies adopted only angered and provoked
Americans. But because the British leaders' beliefs were so closed, they
were not open to advice from informed Loyalists, who were dedicated
to preserving the empire and Parliamentary supremacy. And Loyalist
appeals were tarnished by British mismanagement of colonial affairs.
In effect, Loyalists had to convince Americans that the empire could
work to their advantage and fulfill all their expectations of it, even
though it was obviously being mismanaged at that moment. It was
the same as having to persuade people of the value of monarchical institutions when the king on the throne is a fool or worse. The subtle
distinction between present policies and personalities and the long-
term value of institutions and traditions can be made, but not easily.

There are two other possible explanations for the Loyalists' apparent
lack of influence on colonial decisions. One was their organizational
weaknesses. This has been related to a variety of factors, such as their
disdain for illegal and extraconstitutional bodies like committees of
correspondence.[74] A very simple and obvious reason for their organizational deficiencies, however, lies in the definition of a Loyalist. As
Americans who opposed independence and supported the British Empire, Loyalists were active only when the possiblity of independence
reared its head at the time of the first Continental Congress. But 1774
was too late to begin to organize. By this time, the Patriots had a network of committees spanning the continent so that they could communicate with each other, devise and execute strategies, and coerce or
silence opponents. Thus in organizational terms alone the Patriots
were in command by 1774.

Lack of organization proved to be a real weakness. Although virtually all Loyalist writers opposed the actions of the first Continental
Congress, they had no intercolonial organization to translate their
ideas into actions: most Loyalist writers did not even know or communicate with their counterparts in other colonies. Consequently,
Loyalists could not respond effectively to Patriot actions: they could

not band together to outline and execute alternative policies and counter Patriot coercion. Most of them probably took up their pens in 1774 because there was little else to be done, and many had trouble doing even that without inviting Patriot harrassment.

But equally devastating was the effect of having virtually no organization on potential followers. After the first Continental Congress the Patriots had in place committees to weed out dissidents or waverers and indirectly to show them and others the price of loyalty. By 1774 in Massachusetts and 1775 in New York, to show signs of supporting the Loyalist cause or even to refuse to sign the Association left one exposed to Patriot tribunals.[75] Salvation from this fate lay in only two directions. One choice was to seek the protection of the British army; but this was a weak reed to rely on outside of the few cities where the army was based. The alternative was exile either to British lines in the colonies or to some part of what is now Canada. How many potential Loyalists were transformed into obedient Patriots—those who signed the Association—by such sobering prospects? This was the question raised in an excellent poetic parody of Hamlet's soliloquy:

> To sign, or not to sign!—That is the question:
> Whether 't were better for an honest man
> To sign—and so be safe; or to resolve,
> Betide what will, against "associations",
> And, by retreating, shun them. To fly—I reck
> Not where—and, by that flight, t'escape
> Feathers and tar, and thousand other ills
> That Loyalty is heir to: 'tis a consummation
> Devoutly to be wished. To fly—to want—
> To want?—perchance to starve! Ay, there's the rub!
> For, in that chance of want, what ills may come
> To patriot rage, when I have left my all,
> Must give me pause! There's the respect
> That makes us trim, and bow to men we hate.
> For, who would bear th' indignities o' th' times,
> Congress decrees, and wild Convention plans,
> The laws controll'd, and inj'ries unredressed,
> The insolence of knaves, and thousand wrongs
> Which patient liege men from vile rebels take,
> When he, sans doubt, might certain safety find,
> Only by flying? Who would bend to fools,

And truckle thus to mad, mob-chosen upstarts,
But that the dread of something after flight
(In that blest country, where, yet, no moneyless
Poor wight can live) puzzles the will,
And makes ten thousands rather sign—and eat,
Than fly—to starve on Loyalty!
Thus, dread of want makes cowards of us all;
And, thus, the native hue of Loyalty
Is sicklied o'er with a pale cast of trimming;
And enterprises of great pith and virtue,
But unsupported, turn their streams away,
And never come to action.[76]

It is possible, then, that Loyalist ideology did have a significant impact on American attitudes—there may have been many in their closets secretly praying for the king—but when supporters were unable or unwilling to rally behind the Loyalist cause or even voice their dissenting views, the Patriot control of colonial decision making remained unchallenged.

The lack of Loyalist influence was probably also a reflection of some aspects of their ideology and of the means by which they communicated it to the people. What Loyalist spokesmen hoped to do was to unmask the unscrupulous machinations of the Patriots so that the Revolutionary ferment would subside and a peaceful resolution of the British-American crisis could be achieved. This required, however, mobilizing the masses behind their cause. Yet, relative to the Patriots, Loyalist writers were often handicapped in trying to communicate effectively with plain Americans. One problem was what might be called their traditionalism. Their thought reflected superbly the dominant assumptions of the contemporary Anglo-American world. What was lacking, however, was innovation. Loyalists were not breaking new ground or going beyond generally accepted political theories. This tendency to cling to the conventional was also apparent in the methods used to convey their message to the people. Most Loyalists restricted themselves to pamphlets, newspapers, and broadsides, the accepted media for political debates in contemporary Britain and America. The Anglicans in New York supplemented the written word with oral presentations, and the views of rank-and-file Loyalists were expressed in addresses and declarations. Missing, however, were the popular symbols, rituals, and mass

rallies which were so important in making common people feel involved in the Revolutionary movement. The Patriot practices of reading aloud key documents, of having people sign the Association, and
of holding public assemblies in which common people participated fostered an emotional as well as intellectual commitment to the Revolution. The same was true of rituals, such as the hanging in effigy of enemies of American freedom, which allowed for popular participation
and evoked in some cases memories of evangelical religious rituals.[77]

Some Loyalists disdained or ridiculed the use of symbols, rituals,
and popular assemblies. One writer was disturbed and even mystified
to find that people were moved by mere "sounds" rather than ideas.
"The words king, parliament, ministers, governors, mandamus councillors, revenue, tea & c." he declared, "carry the idea of slavery with
them, while with as little color or reason the words congress, charter,
patriots, delegates, charter councillors, independence, coffee & c. carry
with them all powers of necromancy to conjure down the spirit of
tyranny." Another was chagrined to see people carried away by the
"cry of Liberty." Disdained as well were ritualistic public gatherings
which featured symbols of the Revolution like the liberty pole and
praise for colonial defiance of British authority, such as the rejection by
ninety-two members of the Massachusetts General Court of Lord
Hillsborough's order to rescind the Circular Letter. These practices
were ridiculed by an unknown writer, who stated: "Are there not
many among them whose case we may lament . . . who at some
seasons appeared frantic, superstitious and in some degree idolators by
their veneration for a tree and the number 92 . . . [and] their sacrifice
on the annual solemnity or feast of dedication of the juice of lemons,
wine & c. which, with the temper and behaviour of the votaries, appear to have some resemblance of the ancient Bacchanalia?"[78]

Loyalist spokesmen were also at a disadvantage in mobilizing
widespread support for and a sense of popular involvement in their
cause because of some of their ideas. Basic to their ideology was a
distrust of the masses, an elitist view of political leadership, and an interpretation of the Revolution which emphasized that the people were
being manipulated by a Patriot cabal. This meant, for one thing, that
there was a contradiction between trying to rouse the common people
to stem the tide of Revolution and the assumption that the common
people should defer to the leadership of those best qualified to guide

the community. And although rank-and-file Loyalists did express views about the Revolution, they tended to defer to the wisdom of traditional political leaders.[79]

Moreover, the Loyalists' distrust of the masses and their elitist view of political leadership sometimes showed through in a condescending tone to the common people, whom they treated as subordinates. Jonathan Sewall displayed a sincere concern for the fate of the people in his native colony, but he also spoke to them in a paternalistic manner. "When I see your fears alarmed, your tempers irritated, and passions inflamed, without any just cause; by men, the sole motives of whose conduct are envy, malice, or ambition, I think myself justifiable in attempting to expose the errors and defeat the inimical designs of such men." In another article he exclaimed, "Fain would I shield you from the surrounding flames; fain would I save you from the threatened destruction."[80] Thus, Sewall's concern was like that of a father trying to protect or bring to their senses his wayward children.

But Sewall's apparent arrogance was in part inherent in the message he was trying to convey. The Loyalists' conspiracy theory of the origins of the Revolution meant that they had to persuade the masses that they were naive or malleable enough to be hoodwinked by unprincipled Patriot upstarts who did not merit the respect of discerning citizens. The "infatuated blindness" or "impudent and rash behaviour" of the American people were cited as key ingredients in the Revolutionary ferment.[81] The difficulty that some readers might have in embracing such ideas and in changing their own attitudes and actions is obvious.

Such contradictions undoubtedly lessened the popular appeal of the Loyalist position. A final problem lay in their interpretation of the role and aims of the first Continental Congress. Loyalists denounced the Congress for betraying its trust, which they assumed was to narrow not widen the gap between Britain and America. However, the generally accepted view was that the Congress's main job was to organize colonial opposition to the Coercive Acts and to stake out the American constitutional position.[82] The Loyalist view—that a minority of radicals cajoled other delegates into supporting such drastic action as the challenge to Parliamentary supremacy—was simply not accurate. By the time of the Congress, it has been argued persuasively, many Americans had serious reservations about Parliament's power in America.[83] The Congress delegates merely reinforced these doubts. Believing that the Congress did not reflect the views of the majority was, of course, essential to the Loyalist interpretation of the Revolution as the work of an aggressive and totally unscrupulous minority.

Yet it is not surprising that many Loyalists clung so tenaciously to their conspiracy theory. The whole edifice of Loyalist ideology would crumble if it were replaced by the idea that Patriot actions were popularly supported. This would mean, among other things, that most Americans agreed with the Congress's denial of Parliamentary sovereignty in America. But by denying Parliament's supreme authority in the colonies, the Congress threatened all that Loyalists writers cherished most. At stake were the civil liberties of the British Constitution, the prosperity and glory associated with the imperial tie, the order, peace and unity of America, and the Loyalists' very identity as Anglo-Americans. In short, if the actions and ideas of the Congress were ever to gain general acceptance, only doom awaited America—and the Loyalists. This feeling was aptly conveyed by an unknown poetess, who condemned the actions of the Congress, and very appropriately compared herself to Cassandra—the prophetess of misfortune who was destined never to be believed:

> Oh! My Country! remember, that a Woman unknown,
> Cry'd aloud,—like *Cassandra* in Oracular Tone,
> Repent! Or you are forever, forever undone.[84]

Some Loyalists were disappointed, apprehensive, and angry because the Congress failed to even discuss a plan of accommodation outlined by the Pennsylvania Loyalist Joseph Galloway. Although not all Loyalist writers endorsed Galloway's specific plan, they did support his general aims. Basic to Loyalist ideology were their recommendations for resolving the British-American dispute and their proposed alternatives to independence and republicanism. It is necessary to examine the Loyalists' distinctive vision of America's future to complete this study of their ideology.

8

THE LOYALIST ALTERNATIVE

*After many more centuries shall have rolled away, long after we,
who are now bustling upon the stage of life, shall have been received
to the bosom of mother earth, and our names are forgotten, the colonies may be so far increased as to have the balance of wealth,
numbers, and power, in their favour, the good of the empire make it
necessary to fix the seat of government here; and some future
George, equally the friend of mankind, with him that now sways the
British sceptre, may cross the Atlantic, and rule Great Britain, by an
American parliament.* —[DANIEL LEONARD], *Massachusettensis,*
JANUARY 9, 1775

L OYALIST SPOKESMEN were firmly convinced that the British Empire
and constitution offered more to Americans in terms of freedom,
security, and prosperity than did Patriot proposals for the future. Yet
Loyalism should not be equated with preservation of the status quo.
Loyalist writers were captivated by the *ideal* of the British Empire and
by the *theory* of how British institutions should operate. When it came
to scrutinizing the actual functioning of the empire and its institutions
in America—specifically colonial governments—many pointed to
shortcomings and advocated significant changes. Despite some differences among them about the exact nature of the changes, it is possible
to trace the general outlines of a Loyalist vision of America's future.
As was true of so many aspects of their ideology, the modifications
they proposed were not new and were supported not only by New
York and Massachusetts Loyalists. Similar changes had been suggested
earlier in the century, and by the time of the Revolution, Loyalists
from other colonies, as well as a number of English officials and
writers, supported reforming the empire. Upholders of imperial unity

153

on both sides of the Atlantic agreed that the bonds uniting the colonies and the mother country had to be solidified and colonial governments strengthened. While Patriots favored initially reducing and eventually breaking completely the tie with the mother country, Loyalist leaders wanted to increase the integration between the two branches of the empire. Likewise, while Patriots strove to make government more responsive to the people, Loyalists wanted to do exactly the opposite — to strengthen the nonelected branches and make government less vulnerable to popular pressure. Thus, the Loyalist alternative to the Revolution was a reformed British Empire and revitalized colonial institutions.

The Restoration of Order

Many Loyalists believed that the British-American crisis was in part produced by chronic shortcomings in colonial and imperial institutions. Because the British Empire failed to satisfy the changing needs of growing colonies and because colonial governments were too easily influenced by the populace, the way was open, it was argued, for self-interested Patriots to foment unrest. Any permanent reconciliation between colonies and mother country would require changes to strengthen the empire and American institutions. But how could the Loyalists bring about these greatly needed reforms? The British and the Patriots were hardening, not softening, their positions, and the crisis was worsening. Reconciliation and reform could only occur if polarization and confrontation were replaced by negotiation and compromise. Thus a basic first step in any reform scheme, for many Loyalists, was to moderate the colonists' behavior and steer protest into legal channels.

Restoring "peace and order among ourselves," Jonathan Sewall believed, was a prerequisite for gaining redress of colonial grievances, and Isaac Wilkins linked the restoration of order with the return of freedom.[1] Such appeals reflected the belief of many Loyalists that as long as the British-American dispute was handled by radical and illegal Patriot-led committees and congresses, reconciliation and reform would be impossible to achieve. The committees and congresses were assumed to be dedicated to widening the gap with Britain. Moreover, they believed Britain would not make concessions to the Patriots who, in the words of Henry Caner, acted "peevishly" like "froward children" and displayed "high handed opposition and repugnance to government." Another Loyalist satirized the insolence which he felt characterized Patriot addresses to the mother country: "Resolved . . . That the best way of Approving [sic] our Loyalty is to spit in the King's face, as that may be the means of opening his Eyes."[2] Negotiations for change could only begin after Americans had, as Samuel Seabury put it, "Renounce[d] all dependence on Congresses and Committees" and turned their eyes to their wise and experienced "*Constitutional* representatives," who would know the most "reasonable, constitutional and effectual" means of proceeding. Other Loyalists agreed that if Americans stated their case on constitutional grounds, sought a constitutional settlement of the dispute, or made "humble and dutiful representations," the British government would respond positively to appeals for change.[3]

Many rank-and-file Loyalists supported the notion that wresting control of the colonial protest movement from the Patriot leadership was necessary to settle the British-American dispute. In addresses, resolves, declarations, and associations, hundreds pledged their support for legally constituted authority, committed themselves to undermining the effectiveness of the illegal Patriot-led bodies, and took concrete actions to support these aims. When Patriots in rural New York called for a meeting to elect a committee, more than three hundred Loyalists—many apparently tenant farmers—responded by convening a counter meeting at which they declared their "abhorrence" of all committees and congresses, their support for the king and constitution, and their determination to "acknowledge no representatives but the General Assembly."[4] Other Loyalists attended town meetings en masse to vote against the election of committees or to pass resolutions denouncing those that already existed.[5] Some shopkeepers publicly announced their intention to sell their wares at whatever price they pleased, regardless of attempts by local Patriots to regulate prices.[6] Loyalists in Ulster County, New York, even had the temerity to challenge the dominance of the Patriot liberty pole by flying the royal standard.[7] One organization that might have been most effective in challenging Patriot committees and congresses if it had operated on an intercolonial basis was the Association. Effective only at the local level, Loyalist Associations were compacts in which signers pledged to support each other in defying Patriot committees, congresses, and even mobs. Most began with a solemn declaration of mutual support: "We do hereby associate and mutually covenant and engage to and with each other." In addition to protecting each other against mobs, the signers promised to uphold each other's liberty "in eating, drinking, buying, selling, [and] communing" in defiance of restrictions on such activities in the Patriot Association. Some swore that they would assist magistrates in executing the law, and one group even promised in 1775 to furnish Britain with whatever aid was necessary to restore order.[8] What is most remarkable about these expressions of popular support was that rank-and-file Loyalists strove to heal the British-American breach by reestablishing former institutions and by turning the direction of colonial affairs over to traditional, experienced, constitutional leaders. Beyond this, most average Loyalists were willing to defer to the wisdom of established leaders who would be entrusted with the delicate task of gaining redress of colonial grievances and negotiating changes in the empire.

Loyalist Criticisms of the Imperial Status Quo and Early Reform Proposals

Settlement of the dispute between Britain and America, most Loyalist leaders were convinced, had to involve significant changes in the imperial relationship. They were neither blind to some of the substantive American complaints about the imperial status quo nor in complete agreement with the British view of the empire. This fact is easy to overlook since Loyalists did support essential parts of the British position, notably Parliamentary supremacy. Moreover, when Patriots were painting a totally negative picture of the mother country and her designs, Loyalist writers were almost forced to convey an equally distorted, idealized image of Britain. However, interspersed with their praise for the English king, constitution, and empire were criticisms of Parliament's policy and conduct. Understanding what Loyalists thought was wrong with the empire helps to explain the nature of the changes they proposed.

Some Loyalists criticized specific measures adopted by the British government in the decade before independence. Isaac Wilkins denounced the Stamp Act as being "impolitic and Oppressive." Another Loyalist spoke of the "mistaken system of taxation," and William

Smith, Jr., decried the "palpable Blundering" of the ministry which sought to tighten the imperial system through "exceptionable Taxations, and an imbarrassed, partial Commerce." According to Seabury, sending the East India tea to America was an unlucky step which "increased our discontent" because added to their opposition to the three-penny duty was the Americans' "dread of a monopoly."[9]

Several Loyalists, however, made more substantive complaints about British colonial policy and widely accepted attitudes toward the colonies. What is especially interesting is the accuracy of their comments, showing that they were well-informed and astute critics of the imperial status quo. William Smith, Jr., writing in the mid-1760s, blamed the misguided British taxation policies on the minister's "want of Knowledge concerning the Nature and State of our Trade." British ministers saw only the colonies' prosperity and their apparent ability to give financial aid to the mother country, overlooking the benefits derived from trade with the colonies. Another devastating charge was that the British single-mindedly pursued their own interests, often at the expense of the well-being of the colonies. This was illustrated, Smith believed, in British support for the concept of virtual representation. The scheme, he stated, was "manifestly defective, because it does not provide for the Safety of the Colonies; It discovers an overweaning Attachment to their own Interest."[10] In other words, British ignorance of colonial conditions and lack of concern for American interests were key deficiencies which had to be overcome if the empire was to survive.

Daniel Leonard and Peter Oliver criticized the factionalism of British politics and the vacillation of British ministries. "Thinking Minds," Oliver wrote, "compared the Proceedings of the parent State to the whirligig Toy wch. plays backward & forward for meer Amusement." What was so alarming to Loyalists like Oliver was that because of factional infighting, British ministries and measures were in an almost constant state of flux. Lacking was any consistency or determination to enforce what policies did exist. Leonard was similarly disillusioned with the British government for not backing the administrations of Governors Bernard and Hutchinson. "When they found that government here could not support itself . . . [they] wrote home for aid sufficient to do it . . . And let me tell you, had the intimations in those letters, which you are taught to execrate, been timely attended to, we had now been as happy a people as good government could make us."[11]

Several other Loyalists blamed Britain for not defining more precisely the imperial relationship, which was seen as especially necessary because the colonies had grown so much. This point was made superbly by an unknown Loyalist who criticized Parliament more for "what is left *undone*, than for what it did, for having left things, at the end of near seven years in the very same unsettled state in which it found them, rather than for having done what is scarce possible, put them in a worse [state]." While the British government was afraid "of weakening the fundamentals if they endeavour to explain them," the bewildered Americans showed in "votes of [the] Assembly" that they "had no precise ideas of the relation in which they stand to the mother country." The result was that "whilst parliament was so cautious of reasoning about fundamental constitutions, the Americans reasoned so long and so widely, that at length they found out, there were no common fundamental[s] between us at all."[12] Another anonymous writer agreed that colonial "grievances" were rooted in "an indefinite constitution of government," and Jonathan Sewall proclaimed that "the time is come explicitly to define and settle the rights of *Americans*, and the bounds of Parliamentary authority."[13] A restructuring of the imperial relationship was necessary, many believed, because of the maturity of the colonies, which in Seabury's view were "incapable of being governed in the same lax and precarious manner as formerly." Instead, their "mature state of manhood" required a different and more exact political framework. "Without obtaining this," he concluded emphatically, "it is idle to talk of obtaining a redress of the grievances complained of. They naturally, they necessarily result from the relation which we at present stand in to Great-Britain."[14]

It is striking that few Loyalists believed imperial problems could be solved by merely returning to a policy of "salutary neglect."[15] Indeed, most argued exactly the opposite. Not defining the British-American relationship and allowing the colonies to drift was seen as damaging to imperial unity and harmony. Establishing clearly defined lines of authority and tightening up the empire were the basic components of reform. Yet, achieving what Isaac Wilkins called a stricter imperial framework had to be balanced by other changes to meet colonial complaints.[16] On a practical level, this meant devising a scheme whereby the colonies could provide financial aid to the British Empire without being taxed directly by a Parliament in which they were unrepresented.

A more subtle problem was ensuring that colonial ideas and feelings were more fully understood and taken into account in the mother country. When Loyalists criticized British measures as being impolitic, unwise, or misguided, they were implying that officials were not well enough informed about colonial matters or sensitive enough to their anxieties. Correcting this problem involved finding ways to improve the communication between the two branches of the empire, to guarantee that American interests were better represented and protected in imperial decision making, and to ensure that colonists felt the empire benefited them as well as Britain. In the 1770s, Loyalist writers were groping for formulas which would overcome these perceived problems, but their quest was by no means a new one. Since the early eighteenth-century observers had pinpointed similar difficulties in the British-American relationship and advocated various schemes to solve them. These earlier proposals for reform foreshadowed many of the arguments advanced by Loyalist spokesmen in the 1770s.

In the eighteenth century various proposals were made for tightening up the imperial relationship, which had been advocated in the seventeenth century primarily for defense purposes.[17] Martin Bladen, a British Member of Parliament and a long-time member of the Board of Trade, proposed in 1739 to strengthen the empire by creating an American parliament. The Plantation Parliament, to include a crown-appointed captain general and council and an elected lower house with representatives from each colony, was designed to bolster royal authority in America and to promote colonial obedience to British legislation. But Bladen also hoped that the captain general would convey to British officials more accurate information about the colonies and thereby ensure that imperial policymakers were better informed about American affairs and more attuned to the colonists' sensibilities.[18] There were other British schemes which resembled Bladen's;[19] however, another dimension was added by William Shirley, governor of Massachusetts during the Seven Years' War. Shirley advocated a simple change to solve the problem of Americans being taxed by a Parliament in which they were unrepresented: the colonies could send members to Parliament.[20]

American proposals for altering the imperial framework included one by the future Patriot Benjamin Franklin who devised various schemes in the 1750s and 1760s to reorganize the British Empire in North America. It is interesting that his ideas resembled more closely what would become Loyalist ideology than Patriot thought. Franklin hoped to see a British-American relationship which would reflect the growing importance of the colonies within the Empire and bring them closer to being partners with Britain. Like Shirley and many other writers in the 1760s, he advocated sending colonial representatives to the British Parliament. This change would cement the union between the two countries, teach Americans and Britons to think in terms of a common imperial interest, and help to avert British-American strife by improving communication and understanding. Moreover, the ideal of a trans-Atlantic union had significant emotional appeal for Franklin as well as for other Americans at the time of the Seven Years' War. Enthusiastic about the prospect of colonial growth and expansion after the defeat of the French in North America, Franklin was even more inspired about combining American potential with British experience and achievements within a revitalized British Empire.[21]

The contrast between Franklin's and Bladen's vision of a reformed British Empire is significant. Franklin envisaged a relationship in which the colonies were almost equals with Britain, and he strove to give America a voice in directing the Empire. Bladen too was a reformer; he wanted to tighten up the empire and he realized the need for enhancing British awareness of colonial conditions. Yet he assumed that the colonies were subordinate to the mother country and that Britain should retain the exclusive power to govern. Bladen was merely reflecting attitudes and ideas that were widely accepted in contemporary England. In an in-depth study of the use of the term "British Empire" on both sides of the Atlantic, Richard Koebner concluded that to the vast majority of mid-eighteenth-century Britons, the term denoted the majesty of Britain based on trade, shipping, and the navy, but not on colonization. Lacking was the sense, felt so powerfully by Franklin and many other Americans in the early 1760s, that the colonies were integral and vital parts of the empire. When most British officials spoke of the empire they meant only the kingdom of Great Britain, made up of England and Scotland. The colonies were seen as outlying dependencies to this kingdom, and their subordination was taken for granted. This did not necessarily mean that all of the benefits of the connection were to accrue to England. The navigation system, for example, promoted colonial trade, expansion, and prosperity. But most crucial were the assumptions that British interests should unquestionably take precedence over those of the colonies and that the empire should be run exclusively by the mother country.[22]

Not *all* English officials and writers shared this attitude. Dissenting views were expressed in the 1760s by a minority of British officials familiar with the colonies and in anonymously written British articles reprinted in American newspapers. What is most significant is that these writers in the 1760s were moving away from the mainstream ideas about the colonies and closer to Franklin's vision of the British Empire. In so doing, they were laying the foundations for Loyalist proposals for imperial reform.

In the 1760s the governor of Massachusetts, Francis Bernard, outlined a comprehensive scheme for reforming the British Empire which contained elements of earlier British and American ideas. Like his British predecessors, he sought to tighten up the empire, strengthen royal authority, and continue the subordination of the colonies. But he also saw the need to reconcile Parliamentary supremacy with colonial self-government, especially when it came to taxation. Though Parliament, he was convinced, had to retain control of defense and the right to levy taxes for that purpose, Bernard was willing to allow the colonies to determine the means for collecting such revenues and to control taxes for internal purposes.[23] Bernard also advocated — as did Shirley, Franklin, and William Knox, a British bureaucrat who had a hand in devising Britain's colonial policy[24] — sending American representatives to the British Parliament. Such a prospect, he wrote, "greatly enlarges my View of the Grandeur of the British Empire."[25]

Bernard's ideas were carried a step further by a former governor of Massachusetts, Thomas Pownall, in his *Administration of the Colonies*, first published in 1764. He explicitly rejected the mainstream British attitude toward the colonies: "Our kingdom may be no more considered as the mere kingdom of this isle, with many appendages of provinces, colonies, settlements, and other extraneous parts." The ideal he embraced instead was of "a grand marine dominion, consisting of our possessions in the Atlantic and in America united into a one interest, in a one center where the seat of government is." Concern about British taxation prompted Pownall to endorse imperial union. He believed that Parliament had the right to tax Americans, yet he worried about the wisdom of such levies, even if local legislatures were given exclusive control over taxes on property. Americans would still be taxed by a Parliament in which they were not represented, and this conflicted with Pownall's belief that British subjects on both sides of the Atlantic should have the same rights and privileges. A complete union would solve this problem, and by 1768 this was what Pownall enthusiastically endorsed. Where he went far beyond Bernard was in his conviction that the proposed British-American union could not remain static but had to evolve in accord with shifts in power within the empire. In the 1760s the seat of empire would be in England and Americans would send representatives to Parliament because Britain was obviously the dominant power. If, however, the colonies prospered and expanded to outdistance Britain, then he envisaged an empire directed from the American side of the Atlantic.[26]

Ideas conflicting with mainstream British attitudes were also found in British articles reprinted in colonial newspapers in the 1760s. Some supported ending restrictions on colonial trade; but most noteworthy were the reasons behind these proposals. Rather than assuming that the empire should be run in the mother country's interest, these authors extolled the virtues of an empire based on mutual interest, in which colonial prosperity and expansion would be welcomed as important contributions to imperial might and power.[27] Other authors supported granting Americans jurisdiction over internal taxes or allowing them to be represented in Parliament.[28] One especially eloquent writer heralded the ideal of a British Empire headed by the British parent but rooted in justice and liberty. Although America had the potential to become a mighty empire, both the colonies and Britain would be happier in a union "on equal terms to the end of time." Such a union promised to advance the British Empire "to the highest pinnacle of earthly glory," so that it would be "the sovereign of the world" and the "protector of the liberties of mankind."[29]

The ideas of Bernard, Pownall, and the unknown British writers are very significant for two reasons. In the 1760s, in some cases in response to colonial protests over British legislation, at least a few British observers came to recognize the necessity of accommodating

American growth and even American ambitions within a reformed imperial framework. They saw the need not only to tighten up the empire, but also to incorporate Americans into it by, for example, giving them some role in directing imperial affairs. These writers placed less emphasis on colonial subordination and more on the vision of an empire bound together by mutual interests and common ideals. These ideas were a direct challenge to the dominant British attitudes, but even more remarkable is that very similar thoughts were being expressed at exactly the same time on the American side of the Atlantic.

In the 1760s in America several proposals were made for improving the British Empire. Candidus spoke for many when he declared that a "general union of all parts" of the British Empire was most desirable since "our mutual interests are so inseparable."[30] Several anonymous Bostonians argued that the British-American dispute could be solved by "being united to the British legislature"; such a union, they believed, would strengthen the uniformity of interests between the two countries. The most widely accepted concrete proposal for union, as in Britain, was sending American representatives to Parliament.[31] An alternative approach, however, was offered by Americanus, who was probably the Pennsylvania Loyalist Joseph Galloway. In 1766 he urged Americans either to petition for the right to send members to the British Parliament or to begin making plans for an American parliament.[32] The spirit in which many of these suggestions were made was captured nicely by an unknown writer who proclaimed that together Britain and America could "rise to the highest pitch of grandeur and opulence."[33]

At least two other colonists writing at the time linked improvement of the Empire with creation of an American or a new imperial parliament. An unknown author in 1769 wanted to create an imperial body, to be located in England, to which each colonial assembly would send delegates with power to make "national" decisions and to levy taxes for "national" purposes. "National" concerns were those which affected the Empire as a whole, such as defense, trade, and naval matters. Local affairs as well as internal taxes would be left to provincial governments. Obviously inspired by the promise of the scheme, this writer predicted that it would allay American anxieties about taxation and remove a major source of discord in the empire. Greater unity, stability, "Peace and Concord" would pervade the empire to "disappoint the vain Hopes of the common restless Enemy; who would be proud to take Advantage of a *House* divided against itself."[34]

In the mid-1760s the future Loyalist William Smith, Jr., adopted the idea of creating an American parliament as a way to improve the empire. Believing as he did that the British-American controversy merely showed the inability of the empire to meet the needs and aspirations of expanding and maturing colonies, Smith wanted to devise a new imperial constitution "linking Great Britain and her Colonies together, by the most indesoluble [sic] Ties." The cornerstone of his plan was the continental parliament,to be composed of a crown-appointed lord lieutenant and council and a house of commons, whose deputies would be chosen by the colonial assemblies. One advantage of Smith's framework was that Parliamentary supremacy would be reconciled with colonial self-government, especially in taxation matters. The crown would requisition the American parliament for taxes for imperial purposes, and the American parliament would fix the contribution to be made by each colony; the colonial governments would then decide the best means of raising these taxes and would also have control of local matters and taxation for internal purposes.[35]

Smith believed that the continental parliament would stabilize and unify the colonies, promote British-American understanding, and give the colonies a role in directing the empire. One problem with the empire, according to Smith, was that "our Assemblies are unequal to the Task, of entering into the Views of so wise, and so great a Nation as Great Britain is." As he explained, assemblymen often represented "little obscure Counties," lacked independent means, and were too easily influenced by their constituents. Because they were parochial in their outlook and self-interested in their aims, politics in America frequently degenerated into factional infighting in which the common interest was lost to "private Piques or Partial aims." In the continental parliament, however, delegates would be chosen by the assemblies rather than elected directly and would therefore be less vulnerable to popular pressures. The "Wisdom of the whole Continent," Smith predicted, would be collected in this body, whose members would be more wordly, capable, principled, and able to set aside petty squabbling and dedicate themselves to promoting the general welfare of the empire. He saw the parliament as a stabilizing influence which would foster order and unity in America, and because of its more dignified nature, it would be taken more seriously in Britain. Thus, communication and understanding between the two countries would be improved, and the colonies would have more weight in imperial decision making. But the "Capital" advantage of the scheme for Smith was that it would restore mutual trust and esteem and provide for the kind of input from the colonies which would allow Britain to "regulate and improve this vast, dependant, growing Territory, as to unite every Branch of the Empire, by the Cords of Love and Interest, and give Peace, Health and Vigor to the whole."[36]

Loyalist Ideas about Imperial Union and Reform

Proposals made before the 1770s to reform and unite the British Empire set the stage for Loyalist ideas on the subject. Like earlier British writers, Loyalist spokesmen advocated tightening up the empire and defining more precisely its power structure, a basic principle of which was the supreme authority of Parliament to legislate for the whole. Yet Loyalist writers also realized that a restructured empire would have to take into account colonial priorities and anxieties about the imperial framework. They were aware of the high value Americans placed on local self-government—considered synonymous with the autonomy of colonial legislatures—and they were sensitive to American grievances about British taxation. Though few went so far as to admit that the taxation was unconstitutional, many recognized it as a serious problem. Typical was T. B. Chandler's comment that although Americans were not being deprived of the privileges of Englishmen in being taxed by Parliament, still "it is time that we were exempted, in a regular way, from parliamentary taxation, on some generous and equitable plan." Daniel Leonard also conceded that the taxing powers of Parliament might be a legitimate source of uneasiness to Americans, and he hoped that a constitutional arrangement could be worked out "whereby the constitutional authority of the supreme legislature, might be preserved entire, and America be guaranteed in every right and exemption consistent with her subordination and dependance." Some Loyalists equated this kind of constitutional change with writing an American constitution which, as one put it, had to be "agreed to and fixed by both sides." Chandler too stressed the mutual agreement which had to underpin an American constitution: "The great object in view should be a general *American Constitution,* on a free and generous Plan, worthy of Great Britain to give, and of the colonies to receive." What all these writers wanted to see was a restructured empire which guaranteed to the colonies control over internal taxation and local concerns, with Parliament retaining its sovereign power to legislate on imperial matters. The benefits associated with reform of this kind were very similar to those envisaged by earlier writers: American fears about potentially oppressive taxes would be allayed, and future disputes about the exact bounds of Parliament's authority would be prevented.[37]

Support for American control of local matters and taxation did not mean that Loyalists envisaged a devolution of imperial powers. On the contrary, they favored the further integration of the two branches of the empire through some form of constitutional union. This aim was applauded by Charles Inglis: "From our former connection with Great Britain, we have already derived numberless advantages and benefits; from a *closer* union with her, on proper principles, we may derive still greater benefits in future." Samuel Seabury supported the idea of a constitutional union in which "the mother-country and all her colonies will be knit together, in ONE GRAND FIRM AND COMPACT BODY." Isaac Wilkins hoped that Americans would "secure to ourselves a free Constitution" in which "a line of government" was "stretched out and ascertained," the end result being the "closest and most intimate union" between America and Britain. The basic goals of constitutional union, as outlined by an anonymous Loyalist, were to find some means to represent American ideas in Parliament so Americans could enjoy "the blessings of the British constitution, so far as their local circumstances would permit." These ends could be achieved, he believed, if the "same relation" existed "between the House of Commons and the colonies as between the House of Commons and inhabitants of Great Britain." He concluded, very appropriately, "I hope it is not impossible."[38]

A more detailed proposal was Joseph Galloway's plan of union, presented to the first Continental Congress. Its main feature was an American parliament, consisting of a president general to be appointed by the crown and a grand council, whose members were to be chosen by the assemblies every three years. Like other Loyalist schemes,

Galloway's aimed to secure control over local affairs and taxation. Giving the American parliament power to tax and legislate in local matters would, Galloway believed, calm American fears. But to protect Americans even further and to give them a voice in running the empire, Galloway's projected parliament was to be an "inferior and distinct Branch of the British Legislature united and incorporated with it." This meant specifically that legislation affecting the colonies could be initiated by either the American or the British parliament, but would require the consent of both bodies. Parliament would retain its power to legislate on imperial matters, colonial self-government would be preserved, and Americans would have more scope to affect imperial decision making.[39]

What needs to be stressed about Loyalist plans for imperial union is that they did not foreshadow the British Commonwealth, with dominion status for former colonies. What they proposed was more like a federal union spanning the Atlantic. Jurisdiction over provincial matters and taxation would be assigned to the colonies, which were to be similar to the present-day state and provincial governments in the United States and Canada. The British government would be like a national government in a federal system, since Parliament would retain sovereign power to legislate in matters affecting the whole empire. But the federal union proposed by Loyalists would be more like the Canadian one than the American. Because local governments would be in effect the creations of the national or imperial government, their jurisdiction would be restricted to purely local affairs. The imperial government, on the other hand, was to be supreme in all other matters or, to put it another way, all residual powers would accrue to it.

Support for imperial reform and for a federal trans-Atlantic union could also be found in England in the 1770s. The most interesting of the British proposals was a plan, reprinted in New York and Massachusetts in 1774, to unite the colonies under an American parliament. The recommendations and even the language and phraseology used were almost identical to those of William Smith's plan of the mid-1760s. The only foundation for a permanent British-American relationship, it was asserted, was "mutual satisfaction and friendship." Specifically this meant that Britain had to abandon virtual representation—a point stressed by Smith—and find "some scheme of accommodation, some solid, lasting compact, built upon upright, generous

principles, and founded in interest and affection." As in Smith's proposal, an American parliament was basic to the British scheme;
delegates to the lower house, called by both "deputies," were to be
chosen by the colonial assemblies; and the head of the government,
again called by both "lord lieutenant," was to be appointed by the
crown, as was the upper house. Moreover, the union was federal in
nature. Parliament would still have the power to legislate on imperial
matters, but local concerns and taxes would be under the American
parliament, which would also grant aid to the British government for
imperial expenses. The advantages seen by Smith were also stressed by
the British writer; colonial unity and order would be promoted;
Americans would not be taxed by bodies in which they were
unrepresented, and the colonies would have some influence in governing the empire.[40]

By the 1770s, then, a consensus was emerging among a small but
not insignificant number of writers on both sides of the Atlantic about
the general framework of an alternative British-American relationship.
The basic features included some concessions to the colonies about
jurisdiction over taxation and local matters, some restructuring to improve communication between the two branches of the empire, and
some formula to strengthen the union. The essential principles of this
reform scheme were outlined well before the Loyalist-Patriot debate of
1774–1776. In this debate Loyalists merely adopted or elaborated upon
ideas that had been expounded in Britain and America for some time.
Thus by 1774 it seemed that the foundations were laid for an alternative to independence which would have at least some support in
both Britain and America.

There were, however, many obstacles to the realization of this
Loyalist dream. Virtually all of the proposals were premised on
Parliamentary supremacy, a concept rejected by the first Continental
Congress. Negotiations could not occur while Britain took a hard-line
position regarding the colonies, and Loyalists did not succeed in
wresting control of the colonial protest movement from the Patriot
leadership. But there was also a problem with many of the Loyalist
proposals themselves: unlike earlier schemes, those of the 1770s were
very vague and generalized. Before the mid-1760s, the proposal to
send American representatives to Parliament was simple and straightforward, and it solved the most pressing problems of taxation without

representation and of providing for a common legislature. However, this idea was discredited in 1766 when the Stamp Act Congress explicitly rejected it as being impractical because of the distance involved.[41] In the 1770s the idea was still mentioned, but infrequently; the Maryland Loyalist Jonathan Boucher referred to it in 1774, but even he suggested an alternative reform plan.[42] It was probably no coincidence that the popularity of American Parliamentary representation declined in the mid-1760s immediately after the Stamp Act Congress rejected it. This was a serious blow to the Loyalist position: what was lacking in the 1770s was a specific and easily understood proposal around which a consensus could develop. Had the Loyalist-Patriot debate lasted longer, perhaps widespread support would have emerged for Galloway's more complex plan. But in the mid-1770s, although there was some agreement in Britain and America about the aims of imperial reform, what was missing was a consensus about the exact means to achieve these goals.

To fully appreciate their significance, Loyalist proposals for imperial reform have to be seen in the context of the contemporary theory and practice of the British Empire. Theoretically, the empire was highly centralized. Since Parliament had the right to legislate for and tax all parts of the empire, the foundation existed for a unified and well-integrated Anglo-American political system. In practice, however, the empire was quite decentralized and laxly run for many reasons. Before 1768 there was no single central body in England with authority to govern the colonies, and those governing bodies that did exist were open to pressure from British interest groups. Royal authority in the colonies was also very weak. There was, for example, no effective means to enforce imperial statutes, especially unpopular ones. Moreover, during the administration of Sir Robert Walpole, the colonies had been given a great deal of practical freedom to run their own affairs. Parliamentary supremacy had, by the mid-eighteenth century, been exercised so rarely that Americans had come to assume that there were practical limits on what Parliament or the British government could do. Jack Greene has argued that the colonists believed Britain should facilitate, not restrict or inhibit, their ability to prosper and to advance their own interests.[43]

Because of the discrepancy between theory and practice, the door was open for disagreements about the nature of the British-American relationship. The Patriots embraced the practical relationship that had developed in the early eighteenth century and rejected the theoretical principles of the imperial system. They rejected Parliamentary supremacy—a basic principle of the eighteenth-century British constitution and empire—and they strove to increase the autonomy of the colonies, eventually, of course, by seeking independence. But also important is that they had come to see the British tie as a negative force which curbed or restricted colonial development. Many Patriots may have believed in the early 1760s, as Benjamin Franklin had, that America's resources could be developed within the framework of the empire. By 1776, however, that ideal had been replaced by the prospect of a voluntary union among the colonists, who hoped to realize America's potential by creating an American empire.[44]

The British, in contrast, strove to put into practice the theory of a centralized empire. Parliament was to exercise its power by, for example, taxing the colonies, tightening up the administration of the empire, and enforcing imperial regulations like customs duties. What the British failed to provide for was a new imperial framework that would accommodate the growth and maturity of the colonies. Immediately before the Seven Years' War, British officials, as Greene showed, were aware that the colonies were expanding and becoming economically important to the mother country. But instead of seeing this as a boon to the empire, British officials saw it as a threat. Motivated in part by fears that America might seek independence, the British sought to tighten their hold over the colonies and enforce colonial subordination in a restrictive and even coercive way, and this, ironically, pushed many Americans to seek independence.[45]

Relative to the British and Patriots, the Loyalists were truly Anglo-Americans. Like the British, they wanted to tighten up the empire, based on Parliamentary supremacy, and to increase the integration of the British and American branches. Unlike the British, they saw the empire, as Franklin had in the early 1760s, as almost an Anglo-American partnership, with benefits for both. Charles Inglis believed that if Britain and America were united, "Both countries, supporting and supported by each other, might rise to eminence and glory, and be the admiration of mankind till time shall be no more."[46] America's growth, prosperity, and economic potential need not be a threat to imperial unity. If Americans' hopes and ambitions could be realized within the framework of a reformed empire, colonial prosperity would benefit Britain as well as the colonies. Loyalist writers, unlike the Patriots, had faith in the flexibility of the British Empire and in the ability of the colonies to thrive within it. The Loyalists' vision of a reformed and united empire was an expression of their American patriotism.

Like the Patriots, Loyalists displayed an almost unbridled confidence in the potential of the colonies. As maturing communities, whose horizons had been enlarged immeasurably by the defeat of the French Empire in North America, the colonies were regarded as having substantial human and material resources to be developed. Unlike the Patriots, however, Loyalist spokesmen were less confident about the colonies' ability to *harness* this potential. Besides lacking the economic and military might of the mother country, the colonies were not seen as a homogeneous or united continental force. Instead, the Loyalists depicted the colonies as potentially unstable, very different, heterogeneous communities with a history of trade rivalries, and boundary disputes, unable to unite even in the face of a common foe. The British Empire could provide the unity, sense of direction, and order which the colonies lacked. Presiding over the whole, Parliament could perform the same role in the empire as government could within a particular society. Parliament could intervene to restrict conflict among members of the British-American community, to impose order on the whole, and to prevent one part of the empire from dominating at the expense of others. Thus, the bonds uniting the colonies would not be, as they were for the Patriots, forged from a colonial consensus. Instead, Loyalists envisaged a union from above: Parliament would impose the unity and order necessary to ensure that America's energies could be harnessed and its potential realized.

This path promised a more orderly and structured development of American resources and a more secure future along a familiar and well-traveled road. As members of the empire, T. B. Chandler believed, "the colonies have hitherto flourished beyond example. They have become populous, both by natural increase, and the yearly influx of foreigners, the sure indications of a happy country . . . And were they to pursue the same path which has brought them thus far, there is no doubt but that they would go on to flourish and prosper in the same proportion, till, in the process of time, they would excite either the admiration or envy of the whole human race."[47]

The familiar order and security of the empire no doubt appealed to the conservative temperament of many Loyalists. Yet, as Chandler suggested, it offered more; it promised America an inspiring and exalted future as part of an empire with a role of cosmic significance. By combining the energy and resources of America and Britain, the empire could reach a pinnacle of power and grandeur and outdistance any rivals. "One cannot take the State, Nature, Climates and prodigious Extent of the American Continent into Contemplation," William Smith, Jr., declared, "without high Prospects in favor of the Power, to which it belongs." America's prospects might be inspiring, yet as part of a trans-Atlantic empire its destiny was unparalleled in the history of mankind.[48] Charles Inglis and Daniel Leonard were so convinced of America's potential that they predicted that the future British Empire might well be centered there. According to Leonard, at some future time "the colonies may be so far increased as to have the balance of wealth, numbers, and power, in their favour . . . and some future George . . . may cross the Atlantic, and rule Great Britain, by an American parliament."[49] Thus a reformed and strengthened British Empire was the vehicle by which Loyalists expressed their own exalted aspirations for America and their confidence in its destiny.

The Reform of Colonial Institutions

Many Loyalist writers believed that Imperial reform would not by itself solve the problems in the British-American relationship. Colonial institutions also must be altered and strengthened. Although American institutions were modeled on those of the mother country, the nonelected branches were much weaker than their British counterparts. Colonial governors, though theoretically very powerful, did not have the same patronage at their disposal as did the king to soothe the fractiousness and lull the critical faculties of potential critics. The councils also lacked the permanence and stability of the House of Lords.[50] Rather than being hereditary peers, councillors were either appointed by the crown or elected. In Massachusetts the council was nominated by the assembly subject to the veto of the governor. The relative weakness of the upper branches of government contributed to the weakness of royal authority in America. Governors, for example, often had to ignore their instructions from the British government in order to gain support for their administrations from very powerful lower houses.[51] Moreover, because appointed institutions in America lacked independence, they could not offset the instability produced by factional infighting in the assemblies, nor could they unify and impose order on society. For these reasons, many Loyalists contended that the power of the assemblies had to be lessened or at least offset by strengthening the other branches of the constitution. Loyalist proposals to reform colonial institutions were, like so many of their ideas, not original. They had been anticipated prior to the mid-1770s by writers on both sides of the Atlantic.

Martin Bladen and Francis Bernard were two British officials who advocated strengthening colonial governments. One key aim of Bladen's union of the colonies proposed in 1739 was to lessen the power of colonial assemblies, particularly those in the charter colonies. His Plantation Parliament was to be given broad power to legislate for America as a means of limiting the jurisdiction of the assemblies to strictly local and relatively unimportant matters.[52] Bernard, who was concerned in the 1760s about the democratic tendencies in the charter governments, suggested establishing a uniform royal structure for all of the colonies. His aim was to make colonial governments resemble more closely their British model by increasing the power and independence of the upper house. By establishing a civil list whereby the salaries of the executive would be guaranteed and not subject to assembly control, he hoped to enhance the autonomy of the executive. Moreover, he wanted to bolster the independence of the upper house by creating "A *Nobility* appointed by the *King* for life, and made independent." His goal was to "give strength and stability to the *American* governments."[53]

Bernard's aims were shared by colonial writers in the 1760s and early 1770s. The "Dougliad," the series critical of Alexander McDougall, complained in 1770 that while local government was modeled on Britain's, "the Crown here wants the balance against the popular weight, which distinguishes the parent kingdom." He explained that the nobility, in the balanced constitution of government, was to maintain the equilibrium "between the prerogative of the

Crown and privileges of the people." However, since the New York Council lacked the "stability and privileges" of the House of Lords, the government of New York suffered from chronic instability. The alternatives, as he saw them, consisted of moving toward a democracy or republic — a prospect which horrified him — or "to rise in Time, to a perfect copy of that bright original, which is the Envy and Admiration of the world" — the British Constitution. In concrete terms, this meant creating a hereditary upper house in New York so that the council would more closely resemble the House of Lords and be a more influential, stabilizing factor in the polity.[54]

Similar ideas were expressed in Massachusetts. A defender of Francis Bernard attacked the assembly in 1767 for usurping a long-established crown prerogative by pardoning those responsible for using violence to protest against the Stamp Act. Another Massachusetts writer argued that the independence of the judiciary would be preserved if judges were dependent for their salaries on the king, who was three thousand miles away, rather than on the assembly. If the assembly paid judicial salaries, then it would have "the power to starve them [judges] into compliance" with its wishes, and judges would become the "assemblies' judges not the king's."[55]

The goal of enhancing the power of nonelected institutions was supported in other colonies. In Connecticut there was a movement among Anglicans to have the charter revoked and a royal government established.[56] Support for this idea could also be found in Rhode Island, as evidenced by a 1764 article from the *Newport Mercury* reprinted in a Boston newspaper. In a vituperative critique of Rhode Island politics, the author singled out factionalism as the colony's main problem. In "democratical" governments — as Rhode Island's was assumed to be — power was attained only by "virulence and faction," which meant being governed by the "most wicked, ambitious, avaricious and mischievious" politicians. Moreover, because parties were motivated by the quest for political advantage, not principles, there was no uniformity or consistency in public life so that "law instead of being a permanent and uniform rule to society, is ever vague and transitory and adjusted to the annual complexion and passions of a party." Added to this was the rancor and bitterness, narrow and illiberal sentiments that parties fostered. This critic, whose arguments were almost identical to those later made by Loyalists, proposed a remedy that was also similar to what Loyalists would recommend. Since the factionalism and instability resulted from the charter which gave too much power to the people and too little to the crown, the colony's salvation lay in the crown resuming the charter and imposing a less democratic royal government.[57]

Loyalist plans to bolster the authority of appointed institutions in America resembled those of earlier British and American writers. William Smith's proposed American parliament was, like Bladen's, designed in part to lessen the influence of local assemblies. The councillors were to be almost like life peers; "to preserve their Independency" they were to be "Men of Fortune" who were to be appointed by the crown for life, and "some honorable Distinctions" were to be given to their families "as a Lure to prevent the Office from falling into Contempt."[58] Although Joseph Galloway's 1774 Plan of Union did not provide for an upper house, his later plans did. In his 1779 scheme, for instance, councillors in the American parliament were to be appointed by the crown for life and were to have "some degree of Rank or Dignity above the Commons." Galloway stated his philosophy explicitly: "An entire Democracy without the checks of Aristocracy and Monarchy would be dangerous to the State."[59]

Loyalist proposals to strengthen nonelected institutions were especially common in Massachusetts because of what was considered to be the inordinate power of the lower house in the colony. As the *Censor* and others pointed out, the House of Representatives had in 1766 used its power to nominate councillors to purge executive officeholders from the upper house; by blacklisting supporters of the administration in the House itself, dissidents in that body were either silenced or defeated at the polls. By the early 1770s the House was challenging the governor's prerogative to call and prorogue the General Court and his duty to obey his royal instructions. What all of this meant, the *Censor* warned, was that the Patriots, like Cromwell, had "overturned the very constitution of our civil government." The *Censor* hit at the heart of the matter when it argued that although American institutions were designed to be miniatures of British ones, only the assembly possessed the full powers of the House of Commons. The governor, council, and even judiciary lacked the independence and power of their British counterparts.[60] The solution, then, was to bolster the authority of the governor, the judiciary, and especially the council and to make them impervious to popular pressure.

Recommendations to achieve these goals came from several Massachusetts Loyalists. The *Censor* stressed the need to appoint councillors for life rather than electing them indirectly. Jonathan Sewall agreed about the importance of increasing the council's independence, and he shared Peter Oliver's view that the British government's policy in the 1770s to pay crown salaries to judges and governors was an important first step in establishing their independence. As Oliver explained, by making judges independent of the lower house for their salaries, the British government was "striking at the Root of that Slavery which the Judges had always been held under [by the Assembly]." Since colonial institutions were tainted by republicanism, rendering the judiciary and executive independent of the lower house merely made the local government more consistent with the British Constitution, which was "founded on the soundest Principles of Government."[61]

Daniel Leonard went so far as to support the changes in the structure of the Massachusetts government contained in the Coercive Acts. Like other Loyalists, Leonard traced the instability of colonial governments to the fact that they were but "faint sketches" of their British model. In America the judiciary was unable to enforce the law and "distribute impartial justice" as in England, and the lower houses "lent no aid to the executive power"; but the crux of the problem was with the council. The "original defect" of the Massachusetts government, which became obvious "when the political storm arose," was that the council was not an independent branch of government. "The board which was intended to moderate between the governor and the house, or perhaps rather to support the former," Leonard wrote, "was incapable of doing either by its original constitution." This problem had, however, been solved by the British government in 1774 when it created mandamus councillors who were beyond the control of both the governor and the assembly and were therefore able to fulfill their independent role in the Massachusetts constitution.[62]

Proposals to change colonial institutions must be seen in relation to Patriot ideology. As the *Censor* perceptively observed in 1772, there was an unbreachable chasm between what were to become Loyalist and Patriot ideas about the structure of colonial governments.[63] Patriots accepted the argument of the British country party that the integrity of the British Constitution had been destroyed by an excessively powerful executive which had effectively undermined the independence of the House of Commons. The focus in Patriot thought was on guarding against an independent executive with overweening power and on making government more responsive to and dependent on the popular will. The much heralded theory of a balanced constitution wich included elected and appointed parts was explicitly rejected in 1776 by Thomas Paine.[64] Embraced instead was the ideal of republicanism. All branches of government were to be responsible, directly or indirectly, to the people, and the people themselves were to be reformed and knit together by the bonds of consensus and public spirit.

Loyalist writers, in contrast, retained their admiration for the British Constitution, which they associated with highly prized legal rights like trial by jury and landmarks in British constitutional history such as the 1689 Bill of Rights. But what most attracted Loyalists was the conservatism of the Constitution. As a set of institutions which had evolved over time to meet the changing needs and values of Englishmen, the British Constitution had weathered the tests of time and guaranteed to its subjects order as well as liberty. However, a basic part of its conservatism was its actual form of government — the balanced constitution. A free government, according to the *Censor,* was not one in which all branches were responsible to the people. On the contrary, imperial unity required that the governor retain his independence and obey his instructions from England.[65] Moreover, stability and freedom within each colony could be preserved only if all three branches of government retained their independence from one another, and in the case of the governor and council, their independence from popular control.[66] Because the balance of colonial constitutions had been upset by excessively powerful lower houses, reform to Loyalist writers meant strengthening the weak upper branches of government. Once revitalized, colonial governments would have the authority to perform their trusts of unifying and stabilizing society. But the unity to be achieved within each colony was — like the union of the colonies under the British Parliament — to be imposed from above by government. Thus, the Loyalists' alternative to republicanism was a reformed British Constitution.

Loyalist proposals to strengthen the British Empire and American institutions tied together the various dimensions of their ideology and symbolized the depth of their division from the Patriots. The Loyalist aim to strengthen the bonds between Britain and America reflected their view that history, culture, and a common pride in the British empire and constitution united the two communities. They also argued for the economic benefits to the colonies of remaining within the British trading empire. This idea was totally at odds with the aims of the Patriots, who strove to increase the autonomy of the colonies, but it was quite consistent with many contemporary realities. In the eighteenth century, economic, religious, and other ties between Britain and America were increasing. Communication was improving, and many Americans were captivated by various aspects of British culture, from political theories to fashionable consumer goods. In advocating a closer union between the two countries, Loyalist writers were seeking to extend to the political sphere a process already under way in other areas. This ideal of imperial union was supported by at least some British writers and officials.

Loyalist spokesmen, however, also wanted to reform the British Empire and to give the colonists some role in directing its affairs. Unlike the majority of British officials responsible for colonial policy, they took into acccount the growth and maturity of the colonies and Americans' continental interests and aspirations. These goals, which were also shared by some British writers and officials, were consistent with the Loyalist view of the origins of the Revolution. Patriots were seen as being able to foment unrest and to discredit established colonial leaders because of the shortcomings in the imperial framework. By passing legislation like the Stamp Act, misguided or uninformed British ministers unwittingly made it easy for unscrupulous factions to arouse popular fears of British oppression. If Americans were given more say in imperial decision making, then Britain would be more informed about colonial conditions and attitudes, American interests would be better protected, and opposition factions in the colonies would have less scope to use British blunders to their own political advantage.

But the Loyalist attachment to the British Empire and to the concept of Parliamentary supremacy also symbolized their desire to foster unity and order in America. An underlying theme for them was that in the colonies order was precarious and unity fragile. They were apprehensive lest rivalries among the colonies fragment the continent into a number of competing communities, each pursuing its own self-interest. Weakened by internal divisions, they would be vulnerable to an American or foreign tyrant. Salvation from such an ignominious fate lay with the British Empire. A sovereign British Parliament could intervene to settle colonial disputes, could preside over the continent to stabilize and unify the colonies, and could harness the potential of the continent under a common leadership. The idea that the British trading empire should operate like a corporate or joint stock venture was for Loyalists a compelling unifying image. The colonies would be united in their commitment to advancing the prosperity and might of the British Empire vis à vis its rivals. So important to Loyalists was the association between the British Empire and stability and unity.

The same general aim—to impose order and unity from above—underpinned Loyalist proposals to strengthen colonial institutions. Loyalist ideas about colonial institutions were rooted in their interpretation of the Revolution and in their attitudes toward man and his nature. At the heart of this ideology was the conviction that Americans had more to fear from self-interested Patriot factions in their midst than from the power of the British government. These factions, according to Loyalist writers, aroused popular passions as part of a plot to undermine deference for established leaders and institutions. Once reduced to anarchy by such tactics, the colonies would be ripe for a new regime, called by some Loyalists a popular or democratic tyranny. That the new order being ushered in by Patriot committees, congresses, and mobs was far more tyrannical than the British government was buttressed by some rather compelling evidence. The excessive power of the committees, their violation of basic rights of Englishmen, and their repression of dissent seemed concrete proof that tyranny was emanating not from Britain but from the Patriot faction in America.

Yet Loyalists regarded the Revolution as just one of many manifestations of human weakness in the history of mankind. Because people were frail creatures too prone to seek their own self-interest, it was almost to be expected that some, like the Patriot leaders, would aspire to advance their own fortunes at the expense of their country and that the malleable and unpredictable masses would be deluded by the passionate appeals of these self-interested leaders. But the threat to social peace and political stability posed by factions was especially acute in America. The tremendous economic potential of the continent, coupled with the unprecedented growth and expansion of the eighteenth century, fostered the ambitions of ordinary Americans and prompted them to behave in unabashedly self-interested ways. What alarmed Loyalists was that self-interest was manifesting itself in public life in the form of factions, and these threatened to fragment colonial society into competing groups engaged in an amoral struggle for wealth and power. Viewing man and contemporary American society from this vantage point, Loyalist writers looked to government to impose upon society the unity and order which was vital to its well-being.

Strengthening nonelected institutions in America was seen by Loyalists as essential to stability and order and to the freedom of the citizens. Within the colonies the Revolution had been facilitated by the weakness of colonial institutions. Designing factions had been able to mislead the populace and undermine the authority of government because there was no effective brake on the power of the colonial lower houses. Only by making colonial institutions resemble more closely their British counterparts could such schemes be frustrated in future. Government would then be in some measure independent of popular control and able to fulfill its positive role in society. It could counteract the negative effects of faction by minimizing conflict and contention; it would impose order on the community and unify the people by imparting some sense of common purpose and meaning. But a strong and independent government could also preserve freedom by ensuring that basic British rights like trial by jury were guaranteed to all citizens. Even those citizens who supported unpopular political ideas would be guaranteed the rights to life, liberty, and property. And it could prevent organized and powerful groups within the community from denying to dissenters such rights as freedom of speech and of the press. This was the liberty which Loyalists sought but did not find in Revolutionary America.

NOTES

INDEX

ABBREVIATIONS

AHR	*American Historical Review*
BC	*Boston Chronicle*
BEP	*Boston Evening-Post*
BNL&NEC	*Boston News-Letter and New England Chronicle*
BPB	*Boston Post-Boy*
BWNL	*Boston Weekly News-Letter*
CSMP	*Colonial Society of Massachusetts Publications*
EG	*Essex Gazette*
Am. Arch.	*American Archives*, 9 vols., ed. Peter Force (Washington, D. C.: 1837–1853)
JAH	*Journal of American History*
JCS	*Journal of Canadian Studies*
MG	*Massachusetts Gazette*
MGBNL	*Massachusetts Gazette and Boston News-Letter*
MGBPB&AD	*Massachusetts Gazette, Boston Post-Boy and Advertiser*
MGBWNL	*Massachusetts Gazette and Boston Weekly News-Letter*
MHS	*Massachusetts Historical Society*
NEQ	*New England Quarterly*
NYC	*New-York Chronicle*
NYG	*New-York Gazette*
NYGWM	*New-York Gazette and Weekly Mercury*
NYH	*New York History*
NYHSQ	*New York Historical Society Quarterly*
NYJGA	*New-York Journal and General Advertiser*
NYM	*New-York Mercury*
RIV	*Rivington's New-York Gazetteer, or the Connecticut, New Jersey, Hudson's River and Quebec Weekly Advertiser*
WMQ	*William and Mary Quarterly*

NOTES

1. Loyalist Writers, the Media, and the Message

1. Accounts of the American Revolution in Massachusetts include: Bernard Bailyn, *The Ordeal of Thomas Hutchinson* (Cambridge, Mass., 1974); Robert E. and Katherine B. Brown, *Middle-Class Democracy and the Revolution in Massachusetts, 1691–1780* (Ithaca, N.Y., 1955); Richard D. Brown, *Revolutionary Politics in Massachusetts: The Boston Committee of Correspondence and the Towns, 1772–1774* (Cambridge, Mass., 1970); Stephen E. Patterson, *Political Parties in Revolutionary Massachusetts* (Madison, Wis., 1973); Pauline Maier, *From Resistance to Revolution: Colonial Radicals and the Development of American Opposition to Britain, 1775–1776* (New York, 1974), pp. 218–219; John J. Waters, *The Otis Family in Provincial and Revolutionary Massachusetts* (Chapel Hill, N.C., 1968); Frances G. Wallet, "The Massachusetts Council 1766–1774: The Transformation of a Conservative Institution," *WMQ*, 3rd ser., 15 (1958): 508–520; Donald C. Lord and Robert M. Calhoon, "The Removal of the Massachusetts General Court from Boston, 1769–1770," *JAH* 55 (1969): 738–755; Hiller B. Zobel, *The Boston Massacre* (New York, 1970); Richard L. Bushman, "Massachusetts Farmers and The Revolution," in *Society, Freedom and Conscience: The Coming of the Revolution in Virginia, Massachusetts, and New York,* ed. Richard M. Jellison (New York, 1976), pp. 77–124; L. W. Labaree, *Colonial Massachusetts: A History,* (Millwood, N.Y., 1979).

2. Accounts of the Revolution in New York include: Bernard Mason, *The Road to Independence: The Revolutionary Movement in New York, 1773–1777* (Lexington, Ky., 1966); Carl Becker, *The History of Political Parties in the Province of New York, 1760–1776* (Madison, Wis., 1909); Roger Champagne, "New York Politics and Independence," *NYHSQ* 46 (1962): 281–304; Champagne, "New York Radicals and the Coming of Independence," *JAH* 51 (1964): 21–40; Champagne, *Alexander McDougall and the American Revolution in New York* (Schenectady, N.Y., 1975); Milton Klein, "Prelude to Revolution in New York: Jury Trials and Judicial Tenure," *WMQ*, 3rd ser., 17 (1960): 439–462; Klein, "New York's Reluctant Road to Independence," in *The Politics of Diversity: Essays in the History of Colonial New York,* ed. Milton Klein (Port Washington, N.Y., 1974); R. Ashton, "The Loyalist Experience: New York, 1763–1789," Ph.D. diss., Northwestern University, 1973; Alexander C. Flick, *Loyalism in New York During the American Revolution*

(New York, 1901); Richard B. Morris, "The American Revolution Comes to John Jay," in *Aspects of Early New York Society and Politics*, ed. Jacob Judd and Irwin H. Polishook (Tarrytown, N.Y., 1974), pp. 96–117; Esmond Wright, "The New York Loyalists: A Cross Section of Colonial Society," in *Loyalist Americans: A Focus on Greater New York*, ed. Robert A. East and Jacob Judd (Tarrytown, N.Y., 1975), pp. 74–94; Michael Kammen, "The American Revolution as a *Crise de Conscience*: The Case of New York," in Jellison, *Society, Freedom and Conscience*, pp. 125–189.

3. Three studies of Puritanism are Darrett B. Rutman, *American Puritanism*: *Faith and Practice* (Philadelphia, 1970); Perry Miller, *Orthodoxy in Massachusetts, 1630–1650* (Cambridge, Mass., 1933); and Perry Miller, *Errand into the Wilderness* (Cambridge, Mass., 1958). Alan Heimert, "Puritanism, the Wilderness and the American Frontier," *NEQ* 26 (1953): 361–382, discusses changing views of the American wilderness and the development of a sense of mission to Christianize the wilderness. Sam Shortt, "Conflict and Identity in Massachusetts: The Louisbourg Expedition of 1745," *Social History* 5 (1972): 165–185, discusses the development of an "incipient provincial awareness characterized by secular pride and confidence in the vitality of Massachusetts," p. 176. See also Patterson, *Political Parties*, pp. 3–33; and Richard D. Brown, *Massachusetts: A Bicentennial History* (New York, 1978).

4. John Jay to Gouverneur Morris, April, 1778, quoted in Morris, "Revolution Comes to John Jay," p. 111.

5. Recent studies of New York are Milton Klein, "New York in the American Colonies: A New Look," in *Politics of Diversity*, pp. 183–204; Klein, "Shaping the American Tradition: The Microcosm of Colonial New York," *NYH* 59 (1978): 173–197; Patricia U. Bonomi, "The Middle Colonies: Embryo of the New Political Order," in *Perspectives on Early American History: Essays in Honor of Richard B. Morris*, ed. Alden T. Vaughan and George A. Bilias, (New York, 1973), pp. 63–94; Bonomi, *A Factious People: Politics and Society in Colonial New York* (New York, 1971); Michael Kammen, *Colonial New York: A History* (New York, 1975); Philip J. Schwarz, *The Jarring Interests: New York's Boundary Makers, 1664–1776* (Albany, N.Y., 1979). Review or historiographical essays include Jack P. Greene, "The Making of New York," *Times Literary Supplement* (Sept. 2, 1977); John M. Murrin, "Pluralism and Predatory Power: Early New York as a Social Future," *Reviews in American History* 6 (1978): 473–479; Nicholas Varga, "The Historiography of Colonial New York: Whiggish and Otherwise," *NYHSQ* 8 (1969): 182–186; Douglas Greenburg, "The Middle Colonies in Recent American Historiography," *WMQ*, 3rd ser., 36 (1979): 396–427.

6. Samuel Seabury, *Free Thoughts on the Proceedings of the Continental Congress* (New York, 1774), pp. 60–62.

7. Bruce E. Steiner, *Samuel Seabury, 1729–1796: A Study in the High Church Tradition* (Oberlin, Ohio, 1971); E. E. Beardsley, *Life and Correspondence of the Right Reverend Samuel Seabury, D.D., 1729–96* (Boston, 1881); Robert M. Calhoon, *The Loyalists in Revolutionary America, 1760–1781* (New York, 1973) pp. 244–252. Seabury wrote four pamphlets: *Free Thoughts; The Congress Canvassed: or, An Examination into the Conduct of the Delegates, &c., to the Merchants of New York* (New York, 1774); *A View of the Controversy, &c. In a Letter to the Author of a Full Vindica-*

tion &c. (New York, 1774); and *An Alarm to the Legislature of the Province of New York* (New York, 1775). A fifth pamphlet by the Westchester Farmer, *The Republican Dissected*, was advertised, but either it was never published or no copies have survived; see Moses Coit Tyler, *The Literary History of the American Revolution,* 2 vols. (New York, 1957), I: 348. Subsequent references to the pamphlets are from Seabury, *Letters of a Westchester Farmer,* ed. Clarence H. Vance (White Plains, N.Y., 1930).

8. John Wolfe Lydekker, *The Life and Letters of Charles Inglis* (London, 1936); Judith Fingard, *The Anglican Design in Loyalist Nova Scotia, 1783-1816* (London, 1972); Tyler, *Literary History,* I: 480-481. Charles Inglis wrote *The True Interest of America Impartially Stated* . . . (Philadelphia, 1776). Philip Davidson suggests that Inglis also wrote a series of articles signed A New York Freeholder, which appeared in *NYGWM* from August to October 1774; see Davidson, *Propaganda and the American Revolution 1763-1783* (Chapel Hill, N.C., 1941), pp. 253-254.

9. Carl Bridenbaugh, *Mitre and Sceptre, 1689-1775* (New York, 1962), pp. 204-206; Davidson, *Propaganda,* pp. 252-253; Steiner, *Samuel Seabury,* p. 107, p. 125. Chandler wrote four pamphlets: *A Friendly Address to All Reasonable Americans* (New York, 1774); *The American Querist or Some Questions Proposed Relative to the Present Dispute Between Great Britain and Her American Colonies* (New York, 1774); *The Strictures on the Friendly Address Examined and a Refutation of its Principles Attempted* (New York, 1775); *What Think Ye of the Congress Now? Or, An Enquiry How Far the Americans are Bound to Abide by and Execute the Decisions of the Late Congress?* (New York, 1775).

10. Becker, *Political Parties in the Province of New York,* p. 103; Steiner, *Samuel Seabury,* p. 400n.; David C. Humphrey, *From King's College to Columbia 1746-1800* (New York, 1976). The pamphlet was called *The Patriots of North America: A Sketch* (New York, 1775). The broadsides were: Poplicola, *To the Worthy Inhabitants of the City of New-York: Every good citizen* . . . (New York, 1773); *To the Worthy Inhabitants of the City of New-York: No subject* . . . (New York, 1773); *To the Worthy Inhabitants of the City of New-York: The cause* . . . (New York, 1773). They were also published in *RIV,* Nov. 18, Dec. 2, Dec. 23, 1773.

11. Steiner, *Samuel Seabury,* p. 130; Isaac Wilkins, *Short Advice to the Counties of New York* (New York, 1774), speech to the Assembly of New York, *RIV,* Apr. 6, 1775.

12. Listings of Sewall's letters to the press, except for the Phileirene letters, and analyses of his ideas are in Ann Gorman Condon, "Marching to a Different Drummer: The Political Philosophy of the American Loyalists," in *Red, White and True Blue, The Loyalists in the Revolution,* ed. Edmond Wright (New York, 1976), pp. 1-18, 175-177, Carol Berkin, *Jonathan Sewall: Odyssey of an American Loyalist* (New York, 1974), pp. 31-34, 37-43, 87-89, 97-100; and Berkin, "Jonathan Sewall: One Tory's Conception of the Press," paper read at the St. Augustine Conference on American Loyalism, St. Augustine, Fla., Feb. 8, 1975. Sewall's pamphlet was *A Cure for the Spleen, or Amusement for a Winter's Evening: Being the Substance of a Conversation on the Times, over A Friendly Tankard and Pipe* (Boston, 1775). Other studies of Sewall are Hiller B. Zobel, "Jonathan Sewall: A Lawyer in Conflict," *Publications*

of the Cambridge Historical Society, 40 (1964–1966); and Clifford K. Shipton, *Sibley's Harvard Graduates* (Boston, 1933–1973), 12: 306–325.

13. See Bailyn, *Ordeal*; Peter Orlando Hutchinson, *Diary and Letters of Thomas Hutchinson* (London, 1883); James K. Hosmer, *The Life of Thomas Hutchinson: Royal Governor of the Province of Massachusetts Bay* (Boston, 1896) (Appendix B includes Hutchinson's speeches to the Council and House of Representatives in 1773); Peter Oliver, "An Address to the Soldiers of Massachusetts Bay who are now in Arms against the Laws of their Country," *MGBWNL*, Jan. 11, 1776; Douglass Adair and John A Schutz, eds., *Peter Oliver's Origin & Progress of the American Rebellion: A Tory View* (San Marino, Calif., 1961) and Shipton, *Sibley's,* 8: 737–743.

14. Harrison Gray, *The Two Congresses Cut Up* (New York, 1774); Lorenzo Sabine, *Biographical Sketches of the Loyalists of the American Revolution* (Boston, 1847), p. 334; James H. Stark, *The Loyalists of Massachusetts and the Other Side of the American Revolution* (Boston, 1910), pp. 225–229; Charles W. Akers, *Called Unto Liberty: A Life of Jonathan Mayhew, 1728–1766* (Cambridge, Mass., 1964), pp. 56, 184, 205, 223–224; "The Reasons of the Honourable Brigadier-General [Timothy] Ruggles for voting against the establishment of Manufactures in general in this province," *BEP*, Feb. 29, 1768, *BC*, Mar. 7, 1768; Loyalist Association, in *MGBPB&AD*, Dec. 19–26, 1774.

15. [Daniel Leonard and John Adams], *Novanglus and Massachusettensis: or Political Essays Published in the Year 1774 and 1775 on the Principal Points of Controversy Between Great Britain and Her Colonies* (New York, 1968), Jan. 2, 1775, p. 163 (hereafter cited as Leonard, *Mass.*); Bernard Mason, ed., *The American Colonial Crisis: The Daniel Leonard–John Adams Letters to the Press, 1774–1775* (New York, 1972).

16. *Massachusettensis* was published in *MGBPB&AD* between Dec. 5, 1774 and Jan. 30, 1775, and in *RIV*, Dec. 22, 1774 to Jan. 26, 1775; as a pamphlet, *The Origin of the American Contest with Britain,* it was published in New York in 1775; London, 1776; and Boston, 1775 and 1776.

17. *The Works of John Adams. With a Life of the Author,* ed. C. E. Adams (Boston, 1856), II, 405, quoted in Tyler, *Literary History,* I, 357.

18. Leonard, *Mass.,* Dec. 14, 1774, p. 146.

19. Tyler, *Literary History,* I: 295–296.

20. Ralph Davol, *Two Men of Taunton* (Taunton, Mass., 1912); Shipton, *Sibley's,* 14: 640–647.

21. Tyler, *Literary History,* I: 356–368; Davol, *Two Men*; Shipton, *Sibley's,* 14: 640–647.

22. Leonard, *Mass.,* Jan. 2, 1775, p. 163.

23. Ibid., Jan. 2, 1775, p. 167.

24. See Tyler, *Literary History,* I: 295; Jack N. Rakove, "The Decision for American Independence: A Reconstruction," *Perspectives in American History* 10 (1976): 217–278; Rakove, *The Beginnings of National Politics: An Interpretive History of the Continental Congress* (New York, 1978), pp.21–62.

25. Bernard Bailyn, *The Ideological Origins of the American Revolution* (Cambridge, Mass., 1967), p. 1; Davidson, *Propaganda*, pp. 216–223.

26. Tyler, *Literary History,* I: 20; Davidson, *Propaganda*, p. 210; Bailyn,

Ideological Origins, p. 23.

27. Recent studies of the colonial press include: Stephen Botein, " 'Meer Mechanics' and an Open Press: The Business and Political Strategies of Colonial American Printers,"*Perspectives in American History* 9 (1975): 127-225; Botein, "Printers and the American Revolution," in *The Press and the American Revolution,* ed. Bernard Bailyn and John B. Hench (Worcester, Mass., 1980), pp. 11-57; Richard Buel, Jr., "Freedom of the Press in Revolutionary America: The Evolution of Libertarianism, 1760-1820," ibid., pp. 59-97; Janice Potter and Robert M. Calhoon, "The Character and Coherence of the Loyalist Press," ibid., pp. 229-271; Thomas Tanselle, "Some Statistics on American Printing, 1764-1783," ibid., pp. 315-363; Timothy M. Barnes, "The Loyalist Press in the American Revolution, 1765-1781," Ph. D. diss., University of New Mexico, 1970; "Loyalist Newspapers of the American Revolution: A Bibliography," *Proceedings of the American Antiquarian Society* 83 (1974); William F. Steirer, "Losers in the War of Words: The Loyalist Press in the American Revolution," paper read at the St. Augustine Conference on American Loyalism; Thomas C. Leonard, "News for a Revolution: The Exposé in America, 1768-73," *JAH* 67 (1980): 26-40.

28. Davidson, *Propaganda,* p. 225.

29. Alfred Lawrence Lorenz, *Hugh Gaine: A Colonial Printer-Editor's Odyssey to Loyalism* (Carbondale, Ill., 1972), p. 26. See also Davidson, *Propaganda,* pp. 225-245; A. M. Schlesinger, "Colonial Newspapers and the Stamp Act," *NEQ* 8 (1935): 63-83. A *Pennsylvania Ledger* subscription cost 10 shillings per year, *RIV,* Feb. 2. 1775.

30. See, for instance, Philanthrop [Jonathan Sewall], in *BEP,* Dec. 1, 15, 22, 29, 1766; Jan. 5, 12, 26, Feb. 9, Mar. 2, July 27, Aug. 3, 10, 1767; Dec. 24, 1770; Jan. 14, 28, Feb. 4, 18, 1771; A True Patriot, in *BEP,* Dec. 21, 1767; Feb. 29, 1768; M.Y., in *BEP,* May 12, 1766; "Letters in Answer to the Farmer's," *BEP,* Feb. 13, 20, 27, Mar. 6, 20, 27, Apr. 3, 10, May 15, 22, 29, 1769.

31. John E. Alden, "John Mein: Scourge of Patriots," *CSMP* 24 (1937-1942): 571-599; Leonard, "News for a Revolution," pp. 33-34.

32. See Bailyn, *Ordeal,* pp. 199-201.

33. See Lorenz, *Hugh Gaine;* Anne Y. Zimmer, "Hugh Gaine: Loyalist Printer," paper read at the St. Augustine Conference on American Loyalism.

34. Chronus [Henry Caner], *MGBPB&AD,* Dec. 2, 1771; Jan. 6, 1772; *MGBWNL,* Nov. 28, Dec. 12, 1771; Jan. 23, Feb. 12, 1772. Two Loyalist newspapers published in the 1770s were named *The Massachusetts Gazette.* One, the *Massachusetts Gazette and the Boston Post-boy and Advertiser* (MGBPB&AD) was called the *Boston Post-Boy (BPB)* in the 1760s. The other, the *Massachusetts Gazette and Boston Weekly News-Letter (MGBWNL)* was called the *Boston News-Letter and New England Chronicle (BNL&NEC)* until mid-1763, when it became the *Massachusetts Gazette and Boston News-Letter (MGBNL).*

35. Lawrence Henry Gipson, *American Loyalist: Jared Ingersoll* (New Haven, 1971), pp. xiii, xiv; see also Leroy Hewlett, "James Rivington: Tory Printer," in *Books in America's Past,* ed. David Kaiser (Charlottesville, Va., 1966).

36. Judge Thomas Jones, *History of New York during the Revolutionary War and*

of the Leading Events in the Other Colonies at That Period. 2 vols., ed. Edward Floyd DeLancey (New York, 1968); Adair and Schutz, *Oliver's Origin.*

37. R. M. Calhoon, "William Smith Jr.'s Alternative to the American Revolution," *WMQ*, 3rd ser., 22 (1965): 105–118; see also William H. Sabine, ed., *Historical Memoirs from 16 March 1763 to 9 July 1776 of William Smith* (New York, 1956); L. F. S. Upton, *The Loyal Whig: William Smith of New York and Quebec* (Toronto, 1969); Michael Kammen's introduction to William Smith, *The History of the Province of New York* 2 vols. (Cambridge, Mass., 1972), I: xvii–xxxvii.

38. William S. Bartlett, *The Frontier Missionary: A Memoir of the Life of the Reverend Jacob Bailey, A.M., Missionary at Pownalborough, Maine, Cornwallis and Annapolis, Nova Scotia with Illustrations, Notes, and an Appendix* (New York, 1852); Nina M. Tiffany, ed., *Letters of James Murray, Loyalist* (Boston, 1901); Andrew McFarland Davis, *The Confiscation of John Chandler's Estate* (Boston, 1903); Henry C. Van Schaack, *The Life of Peter Van Schaack LLD Embracing Selections from his Correspondence and Other Writings during the American Revolution and His Exile in England* (New York, 1842); Carl Becker, "John Jay and Peter Van Schaack," in *Everyman His Own Historian* (New York, 1935), pp. 284–98; George F. Dow, *The Diary and Letters of Benjamin Pickman, 1740–1819, With a Biographical Sketch and Genealogy of the Pickman Family* (Newport, R.I., 1928); George A. Ward, ed., *Journal and Letters of Samuel Curwen: Judge of Admiralty, etc., An American Refugee in England from 1775–1784 to Which Are Added Biographical Notes of Many American Loyalists and Other Eminent Persons* (New York, 1842); Andrew Oliver, ed., *Samuel Curwen's Journal and Letters* (Cambridge, Mass., 1972); Sydney W. Jackman, ed., "Letters of William Browne, an American Loyalist," *Essex Institute Historical Collections* 96 (1960): 1–46; Edward Oliver Fitch, ed., *The Diary of William Pynchon, Salem: A Picture of Salem Life, Social and Political, A Century Ago* (Boston, 1890).

39. Samuel Seabury claimed that he traveled extensively in rural New York attempting to rouse people to denounce the First Continental Congress: Davidson, *Propaganda,* p. 265. The same was true of Charles Inglis; ibid., pp. 253–254. Isaac Wilkins also worked with another Loyalist, Frederick Philipse III, an assembly representative and manor lord of the 90,000-acre Philipsburgh estate, to organize Westchester county freeholders and tenants. A Loyalist declaration signed by 312 individuals was headed by the names of Wilkins and Seabury; see *RIV,* Apr. 20, 1775; and Jacob Judd, "Frederick Philipse III of Westchester County: A Reluctant Loyalist," in East and Judd, *Loyalist Americans,* pp. 25–43. A letter in *RIV,* Apr. 20, 1775, claimed that Wilkins and Philipse were the prime movers behind the declaration, and a second letter by Lewis Morris, in *RIV,* May 11, 1775, claimed that some of the original signers were tenants rather than freeholders. In Rye, Westchester County, another Anglican cleric, Timothy Wetmore, was active in organizing members of his community and clarifying their response to the Revolution. In *RIV,* Nov. 3, 1774, he pointed out that a previous declaration of loyalty signed by 82 Rye citizens did not mean that they approved of all British measures.

40. W. H. Nelson, *The American Tory* (London, 1961), pp. 85–115; Esther C. Wright, *The Loyalists of New Brunswick* (Fredericton, N. B., 1955), appendix. Statistics show that the vast majority of New York Loyalists were not well to do,

since of an estimated 35,000 exiles, only 1,107 filed claims: Edmond Wright, "The New York Loyalists: A Cross Section of Colonial Society," in East and Judd, *Loyalist Americans*, p. 78.

41. Webster's Dictionary, quoted in Clifford Geertz, "Ideology as a Cultural System," in *Ideology and Discontent*, ed. David E. Apter (London, 1964), p. 47. For another discussion of ideology, see Joseph Ernst, " 'Ideology' and an Economic Interpretation of the Revolution," in *The American Revolution: Explorations in the History of American Radicalism*, ed. Alfred F. Young (DeKalb, Ill., 1976), pp. 157-185.

42. F. X. Sutton, S. E. Harris, C. Kaysen, and J. Tobin, *The American Business Creed* (Cambridge, Mass., 1956), pp. 4-5, quoted in Geertz, "Ideology," p. 58.

43. Geertz, "Ideology," p. 58.

44. Gordon Wood, *The Creation of the American Republic, 1776-1787* (Chapel Hill, N.C., 1969), pp. 47-48; Robert E. Shalhope, "Toward a Republican Synthesis: The Emergence of an Understanding of Republicanism in American Historiography," *WMQ*, 3rd ser., 29 (1972): 49-80.

45. E. S. Morgan, "The Puritan Ethic and the American Revolution," *WMQ*, 3rd ser., 24 (1967): 3-18.

46. Bushman, "Massachusetts Farmers and the Revolution," p. 123.

47. Milton Klein, "New York's Reluctant Road to Independence," in Klein, *Politics of Diversity*, pp. 209-211.

48. Preserved Smith, "Chronicles of a New England Family," *NEQ* 9 (1936): 424; J. M. Bumsted, "Orthodoxy in Massachusetts: The Ecclesiastical History of Freetown, 1683-1776," *NEQ* 43 (1970): 274-284. Bumsted considered the history of a very unorthodox and largely Loyalist community which included pedobaptists, antipedobaptists, and a Congregational parish which refused to pay support to its preacher and requested an Anglican minister. It was Bumsted who observed that for such minorities the British government was the "final line of defense against unwanted encroachments by the Massachusetts authorities," p. 275.

49. Gage to Guy Johnson, Feb. 5, 1775, quoted in Barbara Graymont, *The Iroquois and the American Revolution* (Syracuse, N.Y., 1972), p. 61.

50. Sung Bok Kim, *Landlord and Tenant in Colonial New York: Manorial Society, 1664-1775* (Chapel Hill, N.C., 1978), pp. 346-367.

51. Jack P. Greene, "An Uneasy Connection: An Analysis of the Preconditions of the American Revolution," in *Essays on the American Revolution*, ed. Stephen G. Kurtz and James H. Hutson (New York, 1973), pp. 32-80.

52. Phileirene, in *MGBWNL*, Jan. 12, 1775.

2. "Democratic Tyranny"

1. Richard Cartwright, Jr., "A Journey to Canada," in *Loyalist Narratives from Upper Canada*, ed. J. H. Talman (Toronto, 1946), pp. 44-53, 45.

2. John E. Ferling, *The Loyalist Mind: Joseph Galloway and the American Revolution* (University Park, Pa., 1977), p. 33; Calhoon, *Loyalists in Revolutionary America*, pp. 161-164; Petition of Loyal Rangers, Isle aux Noix, July 24, 1783, Haldimand

Papers, Public Archives of Canada; Anne Y. Zimmer, *Jonathan Boucher: Loyalist in Exile* (Detroit, 1978).

3. A Citizen of New York, in *NYGWM,* Mar. 6, 1775; A Freeholder of Essex and real Lover of Liberty, in *RIV,* Jan. 5, 1775; America's Real Friend, in *RIV,* Feb. 16, 1775; "County of Ulster (resolution)," *RIV,* Jan. 26, 1775; Poplicola, *The cause . . .*; Seabury, *Free Thoughts,* p. 66; Agrippa, in *RIV,* Mar. 30, 1775; Major Benjamin Floyd and a great number of others, in *RIV,* Apr. 6, 1775; A New York Freeholder, in *NYGWM,* Oct. 3, 1774.

4. A Suffolk Yeoman, in *MGBWNL,* Dec. 29, 1774; X. W., in *MGBWNL,* Jan. 5, 1775; Phileirene, in *MGBWNL,* Jan. 12, 1775.

5. Bailyn, *Ideological Origins;* Maier, *From Resistance to Revolution;* Wood, *Creation of the American Republic;* Morgan, "The Puritan Ethic"; Gordon Wood, "Conspiracy and the Paranoid Style: Causality and Deceit in the Eighteenth Century," *WMQ,* 3rd ser., 39 (1982): 401-441.

6. Poplicola, in *RIV,* Nov. 18, 1773; Philo-Libertas, in *RIV,* Oct. 20, 1774.

7. Oliver, "An Address." Also X, in *MGBWNL,* June 16, 1774; "Declaration of the Grand Jury and Magistrates of Tryon County," *RIV,* Apr. 6, 1775.

8. A New York Freeholder, in *NYGWM,* Oct. 3, 1774; Timothy Ruggles's Association, in *MGBPB&AD,* Dec. 19-26, 1774; Seabury, *A View,* p. 133.

9. Bailyn, *Ideological Origins,* pp. 94-143.

10. Thomas Hutchinson, *History of the Colony and Province of Massachusetts-Bay,* 3 vols., ed. Lawrence Shaw Mayo (Cambridge, 1936); see also, Catherine Barton Mayo, ed., "Additions to Thomas Hutchinson's *History of Massachusetts-Bay,*" *Proceedings of the American Antiquarian Society* 59 (1949), pp. 11-74.

11. Leonard, *Mass.,* Mar. 6, 1775, p. 208.

12. Oliver, "An Address."

13. Rev. Henry Caner to Governor Wentworth, Nov. 8, 1773, in *The Price of Loyalty: Tory Writings from the Revolutionary Era,* ed. Catherine S. Crary (New York, 1973), p. 19; see also Phileirene (Apr. 1775), in *Am. Arch.,* 4th ser., 2: 325-329.

14. M., in *RIV,* Dec. 1, 1774.

15. Jones, *History of New York,* I: 5, 35, 37, 39.

16. Chandler, *What Think Ye,* p. 26; see also Seabury, *A View,* pp. 108-109; A Whig, in *RIV,* Jan. 26, 1775; Ferling, *Loyalist Mind,* p. 38.

17. Leonard, *Mass.,* Dec. 19, 1774, p. 146; Mar. 6, 1775, pp. 208-209.

18. Adair and Schutz, *Oliver's Origin,* pp. 35, 50, 35.

19. Hutchinson, *History,* 3, p. 64.

20. Phileirene, in *MGBWNL,* Mar. 2, 1775; Jan. 12, 26, 1775. See also Philo Patria, in *MGBWNL,* Dec. 22, 1774; Plain Heart, in *MGBWNL,* Feb. 16, 1775; A Suffolk Yeoman, in *MGBWNL,* Dec. 29, 1774.

21. Jones, *History of New York,* I: 16, 224.

22. Charles Inglis to the Rev. Richard Hind, D.D., Oct. 31, 1776, in Lydekker, *Life and Letters of Charles Inglis,* pp. 157-158; also Seabury to the secretary of the SPG, May 30, 1775, *ibid.,* p. 149.

23. Chandler, *American Querist,* p. 24; "Remarks on the late manoeuvres in America, by a real friend to his King and country and an American," *RIV,* Mar. 2,

1775; Seabury, *A View*, pp. 123–124; Bellisarius, in *RIV*, Mar. 9, 1775; "Declaration of Grand Jury," *RIV*, Apr. 6, 1775; A New York Freeholder, in *NYGWM*, Oct. 10, 1774; America's Real Friend, in *RIV*, Feb. 16, 1775; Zimmer, *Jonathan Boucher*, p. 119.

24. Anti-Licentiousness, in *RIV*, Apr. 20, 1775.

25. *RIV*, Jan. 5, 1775; see also Philo Patria, in *MGBWNL*, Dec. 22, 1774.

26. Chandler, *American Querist*, p. 24; Philo-Libertas, in *RIV*, Oct. 20, 1774. See also "Remarks on the late manoeuvres," *RIV*, Mar. 2, 1775.

27. Mercator, in *RIV*, Aug. 11, 1774.

28. Philo-Libertas, in *RIV*, Oct. 20, 1774.

29. Leonard, *Mass.*, Mar. 6, 1775, p. 209.

30. Poplicola, *The cause* . . . .

31. "An Epigram," *RIV*, Jan. 26, 1775.

32. "To the Principal Gentlemen and Merchants of New York," *RIV*, Sept. 29, 1774; "Declaration of Grand Jury," *RIV*, Apr. 6, 1775; Philo Patria, in *MGBWNL*, Dec. 22, 1774; Phileirene, in *MGBWNL*, Jan. 12, 1775; Jones, *History of New York*, I: 3, 35; Chandler, *American Querist*, p. 24; "A Loyalist Description of Leading Members of the Revolutionary Party in Boston," *MHS*, 2nd ser., 2 (1897–1899): 139–142.

33. Jones, *History of New York*, I: 3, 4, 30; Jones did not consider William Smith, Jr., to be a sincere Loyalist.

34. Adair and Schutz, *Oliver's Origin*, pp. 44, 37, 41, 40.

35. Oliver, "An Address"; see also Ferling, *Loyalist Mind*, p. 32.

36. Leonard, *Mass.*, Dec. 19, 1774, p. 150.

37. Adair and Schutz, *Oliver's Origin*, p. 39.

38. Philo Patria, in *MGBWNL*, Dec. 22, 1774; Inglis to Hind, in Lydekker, *Life and Letters of Charles Inglis*, p. 157; see also Phileirene, in *MGBWNL*, Jan. 12, 1775; Plain Heart, in *MGBWNL*, Feb. 16, 1775; "Ulster," *RIV*, Mar. 2, 1775; "One of the Associations in Dutchess County," *RIV*, Mar. 30, 1775; "A Protest of Some of the Inhabitants of the Town of Plymouth against the Town Resolves," *BEP*, Dec. 27, 1773.

39. Adair and Schutz, *Oliver's Origin*, p. 65; Seabury, *Free Thoughts*, especially p. 54.

40. Conciliator, in *MGBPB&AD*, Feb. 6–13, 1775.

41. Wood, "Conspiracy and the Paranoid Style."

42. A Suffolk Yeoman, in *MGBWNL*, Dec. 29, 1774; Adair and Schutz, *Oliver's Origin*, p. 120; Philo Patria, in *MGBWNL*, Dec. 22, 1774.

43. Thomas Hutchinson to Sir Francis Bernard, Mar. 9, 1774, in Hutchinson, *Diary and Letters*, p. 131; A Suffolk Yeoman, in *MGBWNL*, Dec. 29, 1774; see also Grotius, "To the Honourable Peyton Randolph, esq., late President of the American Continental Congress," *MGBPB&AD*, Jan. 9–16, 1775.

44. *RIV*, Oct. 6, 1774; Mercator, in *RIV*, Aug. 11, 1774; see also A Suffolk Yeoman, in *MGBWNL*, Dec. 29, 1774; Major Benjamin Floyd and a great number of others, in *RIV*, Apr. 6, 1775.

45. J. G. A. Pocock, "The Classical Theory of Deference," *AHR* 81 (June

1976): 516–523.

46. Phileleutheros, in *RIV*, Apr. 21, 1774; see also Philalethes, in *MGBWNL*, June 24, 1773; *RIV*, Jan. 5, 1775.

47. Plain English, in *RIV*, Mar. 9, 1775; Seabury, *Free Thoughts*, p. 43; Oliver, "An Address"; "Form of an Association in Cortlandt's Manor," *RIV*, Feb., 16, 1774; Wilkins, *Short Advice*, p. 8; "To all the Inhabitants of the Earth," *MGBPB&AD*, May 31–June 6, 1774.

48. Leonard, *Mass.*, Feb. 13, 1775, pp. 192–193; Plain English, in *RIV*, Mar. 9, 1775.

49. Poplicola, in *RIV*, Nov. 18, 1773; also, Poplicola, *No subject . . .* ; Anti-Licentiousness, in *RIV*, Apr. 20, 1775; Seabury, *Congress Canvassed*, p. 91.

50. A Poor Man, in *RIV*, Dec. 22, 1774.

51. Maier, *From Resistance to Revolution*.

52. A Freeman, in *RIV*, July 21, 1774; *MGBWNL*, Aug. 4, 1774; "To the Principal Gentlemen and Merchants of New York," *RIV*, Sept. 29, 1774; "Queen's County, Long Island," *RIV*, Jan. 19, 1775; Agrippa, in *RIV*, Mar. 30, 1775; America's Real Friend, in *RIV*, Feb. 16, 1775; Philo-Libertas, in *RIV*, Oct. 20, 1774; R. L., in *RIV*, Dec. 22, 1774; X, in *MGBWNL*, June 16, 1774, Sept. 15, 1774; Leonard, *Mass.*, Jan. 2, 1775, pp. 160–167; "A Letter from a Gentleman at Cambridge to One in this Town," *MGBWNL*, Dec. 1, 1774; Zimmer, *Jonathan Boucher*, p. 163.

53. Poplicola, in *RIV*, Nov. 18, 1773; Leonard, *Mass.*, Jan. 2, 1775, p. 166. See also Seabury, *A View*, p. 145; Seabury, *An Alarm*, p. 158; America's Real Friend, in *RIV*, Feb. 16, 1775.

54. Seabury, *Congress Canvassed*, p. 89.

55. A Freeholder of Essex and real Lover of Liberty, in *RIV*, Jan. 5, 1775; see also Seabury, *Congress Canvassed*, pp. 84–85; "Here, gentlemen, is a court established upon the same principles with the *papish Inquisition*."

56. Seabury, *Free Thoughts*, p. 62; see also Zimmer, *Jonathan Boucher*, p. 161.

57. Adair and Schutz, *Oliver's Origin*, p. 111; *MGBWNL*, Feb. 16, 1775; see also Chandler, *American Querist*, p. 25.

58. Phileirene, in *MGBWNL*, Feb. 9, 1775; see also T.V.V. in *RIV*, Dec. 15, 1774; Seabury, *A View*, pp. 106–107.

59. Agricola, *To The Public: The Above* (New York, 1774); see also "Marshfield Town Meeting," *MGBPB&AD*, Jan. 31–Feb. 7, 1774; "Protest against the Solemn League and Covenant," *MHS* 10–13 (1871–1873): 46–47; A Converted Whig (Mar. 1775), in *Am. Arch.*, 4th ser., 2: pp. 104–106.

60. Steiner, *Samuel Seabury*, pp. 159–166; Calhoon, *Loyalists in Revolutionary America*, pp. 251–252.

61. Leonard, *Mass.*, Jan. 2, 1775, p. 166.

62. Inglis, *True Interest*, pp. 36–44.

63. Major Benjamin Floyd and a great number of others, in *RIV*, Apr. 6, 1775.

64. *BC*, Aug. 21, 24, 31, Sept. 4, Oct. 16, 1769; Bailyn, *Ordeal*, pp. 134–135; Alden, "John Mein," p. 587; Leonard, "News for a Revolution," pp. 33–34; Gip-

son, *American Loyalist,* p. xv, Lorenz, *Hugh Gaine,* pp. 99–100.

65. *MGBWNL,* Mar. 2, 1775.

66. "The Resolves of a Certain Patriotic Committee in a Neighboring Colony," *RIV,* Mar. 30, 1775; see also, T.V.V., in *RIV,* Dec. 15, 1774; "Major Benjamin Floyd to committee at Smithtown, Brookhaven, Suffolk County, New York," in *Am. Arch.,* 4th ser., 2, pp. 36–37; Mercator, in *RIV,* Aug. 11, 1774; A Suffolk Yeoman, in *MGBWNL,* Dec. 29, 1774; Ferling, *Loyalist Mind,* p. 33.

67. Agrippa, in *RIV,* Mar. 30, 1775.

68. *RIV,* Dec. 8, 1774.

69. Phileirene, in *MGBWNL,* Jan. 26, 1775; see also Seabury, *Congress Canvassed,* p. 97; America's Real Friend, in *RIV,* Feb. 16, 1775; Zimmer, *Jonathan Boucher,* p. 171.

70. Chandler, *Friendly Address,* pp. 49, 53.

71. Wilkins, "Speech," RIV, Apr. 6, 1775; see also Leonard, *Mass.,* Jan. 30, 1775, pp. 184–185; Seabury, *A View,* pp. 116–117; Chandler, *American Querist,* p. 26.

72. Oliver, "An Address."

73. Thomas Paine in *Common Sense* described "those who espouse the doctrine of reconciliation" as follows: "Interested men, who are not to be trusted, weak men who *cannot* see, prejudiced men who will not see, and a certain set of moderate men who think better of the European world than it deserves," *Selected Writings of Thomas Paine,* ed. Richard Emery Roberts (New York, 1945), p. 22. See also Lester H. Cohen, "Explaining the Revolution: Ideology and Ethics in Mercy Otis Warren's Historical Theory," *WMQ,* 3rd ser., 37 (1980): 200–218.

74. John Ferling, "The American Revolution and American Security: Whig and Loyalist Views," *The Historian* 40 (1978): 492–507.

75. See, for example, Bonomi, *Factious People;* Waters, *Otis Family;* Patterson, *Political Parties;* and R. L. Bushman, *From Puritan to Yankee: Character and the Social Order in Connecticut, 1690–1765* (Cambridge, Mass., 1967).

76. Bonomi, *Factious People,* pp. 229–267; Bailyn, *Ordeal,* pp. 111–117; Patterson, *Political Parties,* p. 61; Edmund S. Morgan and Helen M. Morgan, *The Stamp Act Crisis: Prologue to Revolution* (Chapel Hill, N.C., 1953), pp. 121–122. See Elizabeth P. McCaughey, *From Loyalist to Founding Father: The Political Odyssey of William Samuel Johnson,* (New York, 1980), pp. 62–63, for a similar discussion about Connecticut.

77. James Kirby Martin, *Men in Rebellion: Higher Governmental Leaders and the Coming of the American Revolution* (New Brunswick, N.J., 1973); Robert Zemsky, *Merchants, Farmers and River Gods: An Essay on Eighteenth Century American Politics* (Boston, 1971); Bruce G. Merritt, "Loyalism and Social Conflict in Revolutionary Deerfield, Massachusetts," *JAH* 57 (1970–1971): 277–289. Robert William Venables, "Tryon County 1775–1783: A Frontier in the Revolution," Ph.D. diss., Vanderbilt University, 1967, contended that social conflict was also a factor in determining allegiances in Tryon County, New York. Because the Johnson family and their associates dominated the county, other capable and ambitious men found themselves relegated to district and local, rather than county, offices. Patriots, then,

were protesting against British measures but also against the Johnsons' dominance and the closed structure of leadership in the county. Similarly in Barnstable, Massachusetts, it appears that Loyalist-Patriot divisions were influenced by local rivalries and jealousies. Francis T. Bowles, "The Loyalty of Barnstable in the Revolution," *CSMP* 25 (1922–1924): 265–345, suggests that while the economically and politically dominant Otis family actively supported the Revolution, the main opposition was led by Edward Bacon, an old rival and antagonist of the Otises. See also Waters, *Otis Family,* and Waters and John A. Schutz, "Patterns of Massachusetts Colonial Politics: The Writs of Assistance and the Rivalry Between the Otis and Hutchinson Families," *WMQ,* 3rd ser., 24 (1967): 543–567, for a discussion of the role played by rivalry between the Otises and Hutchinsons.

78. Marc Egnal and Joseph A. Ernst, "An Economic Interpretation of the American Revolution," *WMQ,* 3rd ser., 29 (1972): 3–32, especially pp. 21–24; see also Ernst, *Money and Politics in America, 1755 to 1775: A Study in the Currency Act of 1764 and the Political Economy of Revolution* (Chapel Hill, N.C., 1973); C. M. Andrews, "Boston Merchants and the Non-Importation Movement," *CSMP* 19 (1916–17): 159–259; Virginia D. Harrington, *The New York Merchants on the Eve of the Revolution* (New York, 1935), chap. 8.

79. The Association urged Americans to "discountenance and discourage every species of extravagance and dissipation, especially all horse-racing, and all kinds of gaming, cock-fighting, exhibitions of plays, shews, and other expensive diversions and entertainments": Worthington C. Ford, ed., *Journals of The Continental Congress, 1774–1789* (Washington, D.C., 1904), I, 78, quoted in David Ammerman, *In The Common Cause: American Response to the Coercive Acts of 1774* (Charlottesville, Va., 1974), p. 84.

80. See, for example, W. L. Scott, "A U. E. Loyalist Family," *Ontario Historical Society Papers and Records* 32 (1937): 140–161; Petition of Mary Deforest, Dec. 1778, Haldimand Papers, Public Archives of Canada.

81. Kammen, "Revolution as a *Crise de Conscience,*" pp. 144–155.

3. The Loyalists' Conservatism

1. See Ferling, *Loyalist Mind,* pp. 67–80; Zimmer, *Jonathan Boucher,* pp. 160–192; Calhoon, *Loyalists in Revolutionary America,* pp. 76–84, 159–169, 191–196.

2. Paine, *Common Sense,* p. 8; Philip Livingston, *The Other Side of the Question* (New York, 1774), pp. 12–13; James Otis, *The Rights of the British Colonies Asserted and Proved* (Boston, 1764), p. 35, quoted in James R. Ferguson, "Reason in Madness: The Political Thought of James Otis," *WMQ,* 3rd ser., 36 (1979), p. 200; Alexander Hamilton, *A Full Vindication of the Measures of the Congress from the Calumnies of their Enemies; in Answer to a Letter under the signature of A. W. Farmer* (New York, 1774), p. 5; [Adams], Novanglus, Jan. 23, 1775, in Leonard, Mass., pp. 11–12; see also Charles W. Akers, "Religion and the American Revolution: Samuel Cooper and the Brattle Street Church," *WMQ,* 3rd ser., 35 (1978), p. 494.

3. Peter Van Schaack to Henry Van Schaack, Jan. 2, 1769, in *Life of Peter Van Schaack,* p. 9; Phileirene, in *MGBWNL,* Jan. 26, 1775; see also Philalethes, in

MGBWNL, Aug. 5, 12, 1773; Wilkins, "Speech," *RIV,* Apr. 6, 1775; Zimmer, *Jonathan Boucher,* pp. 292–293. Bailyn, *Ordeal,* p.27, points out Hutchinson's interest in history and observes that Hutchinson's "mind was remarkably historicist." Also, it is interesting to note that three prominent Loyalist writers—Thomas Hutchinson, William Smith, Jr., and Judge Thomas Jones—were historians of their native colonies.

4. See "An Address to the Inhabitants of Cortlandt's Manor," *RIV,* Feb. 16, 1775; A Suffolk Yeoman, in *MGBWNL,* Dec. 29, 1774; Plain English, in *RIV,* Mar. 9, 1775; Colburn Barrell, in *BC,* Dec. 4, 7, 11, 1769; Seabury, *Free Thoughts,* p. 44; Seabury, *Congress Canvassed,* pp. 90–91; Leonard, *Mass.,* Feb. 6, 1775, p. 188; Ferling, *Loyalist Mind,* p. 74; Zimmer, *Jonathan Boucher,* p. 173.

5. "Anecdotes on Patriotism," *NYJGA,* Oct. 13, 1774; Paine, *Common Sense,* p. 29; see also William Wood, *New England's Prospect* (Boston, 1764); Garry Wills, *Inventing America: Jefferson's Declaration of Independence* (New York, 1978), p. 288.

6. *MGBWNL,* Feb. 11, 1773; A Friend to Great Britain, in *MGBWNL,* Jan. 14, 1773; "Of True Happiness and how to Attain It," *MGBPB&AD,* Jan. 25, 1773; see also Berkin, *Jonathan Sewall,* p. 38; Calhoon, *Loyalists in Revolutionary America,* pp. 175–187.

7. The Anatomist, in *NYJGA,* supplement, Feb. 23, 1769; *Censor,* Dec. 14, 1771; Philanthrop, in *BEP,* Jan. 14, 1771; Seabury, *An Alarm,* p. 160; see also Conciliator, in *MGBPB&AD,* Feb. 6–13, 1775; A New York Freeholder, in *NYGWM,* Sept. 12, 1774.

8. Calhoon, *Loyalists in Revolutionary America,* contrasted the temperaments of Samuel Quincy, a Loyalist, and his brother, Josiah, a Patriot. Samuel admitted that "a love of ease and retirement" was his own predominant passion; Josiah was described as possessing "zeal and fervor of imagination, strength of genius and love of glory" and a desire to achieve "fame through the turmoils of *public action*": Samuel Quincy to Josiah Quincy, June 1, 1774, May 13, 1775, quoted in Calhoon, p. 160. Also, according to Bailyn, *Ordeal,* p. 17, "caution, control and prudence" were the "guiding principles" of Thomas Hutchinson's life; see also N. E. H. Hull, Peter C. Hoffer, and Steven L. Allen, "Choosing Sides: A Quantitative Study of the Personality Determinants of Loyalist and Revolutionary Affiliation in New York," *JAH* 65 (1978): 344–366.

9. Leonard, *Mass.,* Feb. 20, 1775, pp. 196–197; Lieutenant Governor Oliver to Secretary Dartmouth, Sept. 10, 1774, in *CSMP* 22 (1930–1933), p. 488; "The Humble Address of the Council of the Province of Massachusetts Bay to the King's Most Excellent Majesty," July 20, 1774, ibid., p. 495; see also Jacob Bailey to SPG Secretary, 1776, in Bartlett, *Frontier Missionary,* pp. 112–113; Colburn Barrell, in *BC,* Dec. 4, 7, 11, 1769; *Censor,* Nov. 30, 1771; T.V.V., in *RIV,* Dec. 15, 1774; A Farmer, in *RIV,* Dec. 9, 1773; A Spectator, in *MGBWNL,* Feb. 24, 1774; Agrippa, in *RIV,* Mar. 30, 1775; Conciliator, in *MGBPB&AD,* Feb. 6–13, 1775; Philalethes, in *MGBWNL,* June 24, 1773; Poplicola, in *RIV,* Nov. 18, 1773; *MGBWNL,* Mar. 2, 1775. For a discussion of the role of conscience in the Revolution in New York, see Kammen, "Revolution as a *Crise de Conscience,*" pp. 125–189.

10. Van Schaack, "Letter to the Convention," Jan. 25, 1777, in *Life of Peter*

Van Schaack, p. 73; see also Becker, "John Jay and Peter Van Schaack"; W. A. Benton, *Whig-Loyalism: An Aspect of Political Ideology in the American Revolutionary Era* (Cranbury, N.J., 1969), pp. 165–168; *RIV*, Aug. 11, 1774; "The Resolves of a Certain Patriotic Committee in a Neighboring Colony," *RIV*, Mar. 30, 1775.

11. Van Schaack, "Journal," Aug. 15, 1778, in *Life of Peter Van Schaack*, p. 130.

12. Censor, in *RIV*, May 6, 1773, Apr. 22, 1773.

13. "A Whip for the American Whig," *NYGWM*, Apr. 11, 1768; Leonard, *Mass.*, Dec. 19, 1774, pp. 146–151; Phileirene, in *MGBWNL*, Mar. 30, 1775.

14. Seabury, *Congress Canvassed*, p. 82. See also Calhoon's excellent discussion of Seabury's views on reason and passion, *Loyalists in Revolutionary America*, pp. 247–251.

15. Chandler, *Friendly Address*, p. 23; see also I. H., in *MGBWNL*, Nov. 26, 1772; Leonard, *Mass.*, Jan. 2, 1775, p. 167.

16. Censor, in *RIV*, Apr. 22, 1773.

17. Censor, in *RIV*, Apr. 29, 1773; Leonard, *Mass.*, Feb. 20, 1775, p. 197; A Friend to Great Britain, in *MGBWNL*, Jan. 14, 1773.

18. Phileirene, in *MGBWNL*, Jan. 12, 1775; Conciliator, in *MGBPB&AD*, Feb. 6–13, 1775.

19. *RIV*, Feb. 16, 1775, Jan. 19, 1775; Andrew Oliver, May 11, 1768, in *The Letters of Governor Hutchinson and Lieutenant Governor Oliver; Printed at Boston and Remarks Thereon*, 2nd ed. (London, 1774), p. 28.

20. Chronus, in *MGBPB&AD*, Jan. 6, 1772; A Converted Whig, in *Am. Arch.*, 4th ser., 2: 103; Philanthrop, in *BEP*, Jan. 28, 1771; Grotius, in *MGBPB&AD*, Jan. 9–16, 1775; Hutchinson to Sir Francis Bernard, Mar. 9, 1774, in Hutchinson, *Diary and Letters*, p. 131.

21. Chronus, in *MGBWNL*, Feb. 13, 1772; Hutchinson, "Speech," Jan. 6, 1773, in Hosmer, *Life of Thomas Hutchinson*, p. 368; Dr. Peter Oliver to Elisha Hutchinson, June 1, 1775, in Hutchinson, *Diary and Letters*, p. 459; see also Censor, in *RIV*, May 20, 1773, who wrote that "tranquility and contentment of mind" were "the purest and most substantial human enjoyment"; "An Address to the Inhabitants of Cortlandt's Manor," *RIV*, Feb. 16, 1775.

22. Grotius, in *MGBPB&AD*, Jan. 9–16, 1775; Observator, in *MGBWNL*, Feb. 25, 1773; ZZ, Mar. 9, 1775, *Am. Arch.*, 4th ser., 2: 1747–1748; "Protest by Forty-Three Voters and Freeholders, June 20, 1774, at Worcester Town Meeting," in Davis, *Confiscation of John Chandler's Estate*, pp. 252–253.

23. Leonard, *Mass.*, Jan. 2, 1775, p. 166; Conciliator, in *MGBPB&AD*, Feb. 6–13, 1775.

24. ABC, in *BEP*, Sept. 20, 1773; see also Phileirene, in *MGBWNL*, Apr. 6, 1775; Van Schaack, "Journal," 1777, in *Life of Peter Van Schaack*, p. 88.

25. Leonard, *Mass.*, Dec. 12, 1774, p. 146; A New York Freeholder, in *NYGWM*, Oct. 10, 1774; Oliver De Capitum, in *RIV*, Jan. 13, 1774. Chandler, *Friendly Address*, p. 31, compared the Bostonian "hairbrained fanaticks" with the Anabaptists at Munster.

26. "A Whip," *NYGWM*, June 13, Oct. 24, 1768; "People of America,"

RIV, Feb. 9, 1775; America's Real Friend, in *RIV,* Feb. 16, 1775.

27. Leonard, *Mass.,* Dec. 26, 1774, p. 153.

28. Phileirene, in *MGBWNL,* Apr. 13, 1775; Philanthrop, in *BEP,* Jan. 14, 1771; *MGBPB&AD,* May 3-10, 1773; see also *Censor,* Nov. 23, 1771; "The Damsel of Montagoras," reprinted from *Massachusetts Gazette,* in *RIV,* Oct. 6, 1774.

29. Chronus, in *MGBWNL,* Feb. 13, 1772; A Spectator, in *MGBWNL,* Feb. 24, 1774; Crito, in *MGBWNL,* Mar. 18, 1773; *BC,* Sept. 7, 1769; *RIV,* Dec. 22, 1774; A New York Freeholder, in *NYGWM,* Oct. 10, 1774; "A Whip," *NYGWM,* Apr. 4, Apr. 11, June 13, 1768; Ferling, *Loyalist Mind,* p. 70; Zimmer, *Jonathan Boucher,* p. 146.

30. See Chapter 2.

31. Philanthrop, in *BEP,* Jan. 14, 1771; Poplicola, *No subject* . . . ; Poplicola, in *RIV,* Nov. 18, 1773; see also "An Address to the Inhabitants of Cortlandt's Manor," *RIV,* Feb. 16, 1775; "A Whip," *NYGWM,* Jan. 16, 1769; "On Idleness," *MGBPB&AD,* Dec. 28, 1772; *MGBWNL,* Feb. 11, 1773.

32. C. B. MacPherson, *The Political Theory of Possessive Individualism: Hobbes to Locke* (Oxford, 1962); Poplicola, in *RIV,* Nov.18, 1773; Adair and Schutz, *Oliver's Origin,* pp. 6-7; "On Idleness," MGBPB&AD, Dec. 28, 1772; Phileirene, in MGBWNL, Jan. 12, 1775; Censor, in *RIV,* June 6, 1773; Colburn Barrell, in *BC,* Dec. 4, 7, 11, 1769; "On Avarice and Patriotism," *MGBPB&AD,* Jan. 17-24, 1774; A Card, in *RIV,* Mar. 9, 1775; Philanthrop, in *BEP,* Jan. 14, 1771; Bellisarius, in *RIV,* Mar. 9, 1775; Rusticus, in *NYGWM,* Jan. 16, 1775; *RIV,* Oct. 20, 1774; A Suffolk Yeoman, in *MGBWNL,* Dec. 29, 1774.

33. "To the Principal Gentlemen and Merchants of New York," *RIV,* Sept. 29, 1774; Censor, in *RIV,* Apr. 29, 1773; "A Whip," *NYGWM,* Apr. 4, Apr. 25, 1768; A New York Freeholder, in *NYGWM,* Oct. 10, 1774; *Censor,* Feb. 22, Mar. 7, 1772; Wilkins, "Speech," *RIV,* Apr. 6, 1775; *BC,* Sept. 7, 1769; Pacificus, in *BC,* Feb. 19, 1770; Conciliator, in *MGBWNL,* Feb. 13, 1775; T.V.V., in *RIV,* Dec. 15, 1774.

34. Chronus, in *MGBWNL,* Dec. 12, 1771; Leonard, *Mass.,* Dec. 19, 1774, p. 149; see also Censor, in *RIV,* Aug. 5, 1773; Plain Heart, in *MGBWNL,* Feb. 16, 1775; Crito, in *MGBWNL,* Mar. 18, 1773; A Tradesman of Philadelphia, reprinted from *Pennsylvania Journal,* in *RIV,* Aug. 25, 1774; Ferling, *Loyalist Mind,* p. 72.

35. Leonard, *Mass.,* Dec. 19, 1774, p. 149.

36. Patterson, *Political Parties,* pp. 3-32; Richard Hofstadter, *The Idea of a Party System: The Rise of Legitimate Opposition in the United States, 1790-1840* (Berkeley, 1970), chap. 1.

37. Bonomi, "Middle Colonies," pp. 87-90.

38. Wood, *Creation of the American Republic,* pp. 15-36; Shalhope, "Toward A Republican Synthesis."

39. Hofstadter, *Idea of a Party System,* chap. 1; Archibald Foord, *His Majesties' Opposition, 1714-1830* (Oxford, 1964).

40. A. B., reprinted from *Pennsylvania Journal,* in *RIV,* Aug. 25, 1774; see also Chronus, in *MGBWNL,* Feb. 13, 1772.

41. *RIV,* Apr. 6, 1775; A Spectator, in *MGBWNL,* Feb. 24, 1774.

42. Mercator, in *RIV*, Aug. 11, 1774; "A Cure," *RIV*, Dec. 22, 1774; "A Whip," *NYGWM*, Apr. 4, 1768; Philalethes, in *MGBWNL*, July 1, 1773.

43. A. B. reprinted from *Pennsylvania Journal*, in *RIV*, Aug. 25, 1774; Censor, in *RIV*, Apr. 29, 1773; Americanus, in *BC*, Feb. 12, 1770; see also Wilkins, "Speech," *RIV*, Apr. 6, 1775; A New York Freeholder, in *NYGWM*, Oct. 10, 1774; *Censor*, Feb. 22, 1772; A Spectator, in *MGBWNL*, Feb. 24, 1774; Ferling, *Loyalist Mind*, p. 72.

44. Censor, in *RIV*, Aug. 5, 1773.

45. Marc Egnal, "The Economic Development of the Thirteen Continental Colonies, 1720–1775," *WMQ*, 3rd ser., 32 (1975): 191–222. For a critique of Egnal's article and his reply, see John R. Hanson, II, "The Economic Development of the Thirteen Continental Colonies, 1720–1775: A Critique," *WMQ*, 3rd ser., 37 (1980): 165–175; James A. Henretta, *The Evolution of American Society, 1700–1815: An Interdisciplinary Analysis* (Lexington, Mass., 1973).

46. Greene, "Uneasy Connection," p. 56; Joyce Appleby, "The Social Origins of American Revolutionary Ideology," *JAH* 64 (Mar. 1978): 935–958.

47. Joyce Oldham Appleby, *Economic Thought and Ideology in Seventeenth-Century England* (Princeton, 1978), pp. 255, 198; Appleby, "Social Origins"; Greene, "Uneasy Connection," pp. 50–61.

48. Appleby, "Social Origins"; Appleby, *Economic Thought and Ideology*, pp. 27–28, 150–151.

49. Bushman, *From Puritan to Yankee*; Gary B. Nash, *The Urban Crucible: Social Change, Political Consciousness and the Origins of the American Revolution* (Cambridge, Mass., 1979); Alan Heimert, *Religion and the American Mind from the Great Awakening to the American Revolution* (Cambridge, Mass., 1966); William G. McLoughlin, *Revivals, Awakenings and Reform: An Essay on Religion and Social Change in America, 1607–1977* (Chicago, 1978); Philip Greven, Jr., *Four Generations: Population, Land and Family in Colonial Andover* (Ithaca, N.Y., 1970). For another view of the family, see James A. Henretta, "Families and Farms; *Mentalité* in Pre-Industrial America," *WMQ*, 3rd ser., 35 (1978): 3–32.

50. Paul Lucas, "A Note on the Comparative Study of the Structure of Politics in Mid Eighteenth Century Britain and Its American Colonies," *WMQ*, 3rd ser., 28 (1971): 301–309; Bernard Bailyn, *The Origins of American Politics*, (New York, 1968), pp. 66–80.

51. See, for example, Bonomi, *Factious People*; Waters, *Otis Family*; Patterson, *Political Parties*; and Bushman, *From Puritan to Yankee*.

52. Nash, *Urban Crucible*; Pauline Maier, "Popular Uprisings and Civil Authority in Eighteenth Century America," *WMQ*, 3rd ser., 27 (1970): 3–35; Jesse Lemisch, "Jack Tar in the Streets: Merchant Seamen in the Politics of Revolutionary America," *WMQ*, 3rd ser., 25 (1968): 371–407; Dirk Hoerder, *Crowd Action in Revolutionary Massachusetts, 1765–80* (New York, 1977); John Phillip Reid, *In a Rebellious Spirit: The Argument of Facts, the Liberty Riot, and the Coming of the American Revolution* (University Park, Pa., 1979); John Lax and William Pencak, "The Knowles Riot and the Crisis of the 1740s in Massachusetts," *Perspectives in American History* 10 (1976): 163–214.

53. Bailyn, *Ideological Origins*, pp. 55–93.

54. Shalhope, "Toward a Republican Synthensis"; Appleby, "Social Origins," pp. 953–958.

55. Leonard, *Mass.*, Feb. 6, 1775, p. 188; Seabury, *A View*, p. 109; Thomas Hutchinson, "A Dialogue between an American and a European Englishman" (ed. and intro. Bernard Bailyn), *Perspectives in American History* 9 (1975), p. 393; Bartlett, *Frontier Missionary*, pp. 148–149.

56. Paine, *Common Sense*, p. 9.

57. "Answer of the Council to the Speech of Governor Hutchinson of Jan. 6," Jan. 25, 1773, in Hosmer, *Life of Thomas Hutchinson*, p. 372; see also Hamilton, *Full Vindication*, p. 4.

58. A Card, in *RIV*, Mar. 9, 1775.

59. Wilkins, "Speech," *RIV*, Apr. 6, 1775; see also Philanthrop, in *BEP*, Jan. 14, 1771; Bellisarius, in *RIV*, Mar. 9, 1775; Rusticus, in *NYGWM*, Jan. 16, 1775; *RIV*, Oct. 20, 1774.

60. Phileleutheros, in *RIV*, Apr. 21, 1774; see also Philalethes, in *MGBWNL*, July 8, 1773; Chronus, in *MGBPB&AD*, Dec. 2, 1771; Censor, in *RIV*, July 15, 1773; *RIV*, Oct. 6, 1774; Mercator, in *RIV*, Aug. 11, 1774.

61. Lelius, in *MGBWNL*, June 6, 1771.

62. Staughton Lynd, *The Intellectual Origins of American Radicalism* (New York, 1968), chap. 1; Dr. James Tilton to Samuel McMasters, in *Am. Arch.*, 4th ser., 3: 1551; "Answer of the House of Representatives to the Speech of the Governor of February sixteenth," Mar. 2, 1773, in Hosmer, *Life of Thomas Hutchinson*, p. 418; "To the Inhabitants of the Massachusetts Bay . . . From the County of Hampshire," in *Am. Arch.*, 4th ser., 2: 99–100; Benevolus, in *NYJGA*, Jan. 12, 1775.

63. Inglis, *True Interest*, p. 52; Leonard, *Mass.*, Mar. 27, 1775, p. 221; Inglis, *True Interest*, p. 10; see also Causidicus, in *RIV*, Oct. 6, 1774; "A Whip," *NYGWM*, May 2, 1768; May 23, 1768; Zimmer, *Jonathan Boucher*, p. 277; "To The People of Pennsylvania," *NYGWM*, Apr. 29, 1776.

64. Hutchinson, "Dialogue," pp. 400–401.

65. Censor, in *RIV*, May 6, 1773; see also Henretta, "Families and Farms," for a discussion of the role of the family in molding values in eighteenth-century America.

66. A Card, in *RIV*, Mar. 9, 1775; see also "A Whip," *NYGWM*, Nov. 14, 1768; Aug. 15, 1768; Censor, Jan. 4, 1772; A Congregational Clergyman, in *MGBWNL*, Mar. 16, 1775; *RIV*, July 21, 1774.

67. Inglis, *True Interest*, pp. 1–13; see also "On Avarice and Patriotism," *MGBPB&AD*, Jan. 17–24, 1774; "An Address to the Inhabitants of Cortlandt's Manor," *RIV*, Feb. 16, 1775; *MGBWNL*, Feb. 16, 1775; Poplicola, in *RIV*, Dec. 23, 1773; Philanthrop, in *BEP*, Jan. 14, 1771; Oliver, "An Address"; The Querist, in *MGBWNL*, Nov. 24, 1774; Chronus, in *MGBWNL*, Feb. 13, 1772; "From a Friend to Peace," in *MGBWNL*, Jan. 14, 1773.

68. Van Schaack, "Journal," Jan. 1776, in *Life of Peter Van Schaack*, p. 56; see also Leonard, *Mass.*, Mar. 20, 1775, p. 213.

69. See "From a Friend to Peace," *MGBWNL,* Jan. 14, 1773; Philanthrop, in *BEP,* Dec. 1, 1766; Chronus, in *MGBPB&AD,* Jan. 6, 1772; The Querist, in *MGBWNL,* Nov. 24, 1774; Seabury, *Free Thoughts,* p. 67; Wilkins, *Short Advice,* p. 15; "Flushing, Queen's County, Long Island," *RIV,* Jan. 19, 1775; Plain English, in *RIV,* Mar. 9, 1775.

70. Hutchinson, "Dialogue," pp. 397-398; see also William E. Nelson, "Emerging Notions of Modern Criminal Law in the Revolutionary Era: An Historical Perspective," *New York University Law Review* 42 (1967): 450-482. Nelson contended that the more modern and secular view of law as an instrument for maintaining social and political order first emerged in colonial America in the arguments of Loyalists in the 1760s and 1770s.

71. Seabury, *Congress Canvassed,* pp. 90-91; see also Leonard, *Mass.,* Feb. 6, 1775, p. 188; "On Avarice and Patriotism," *MGBPB&AD,* Jan. 17-24, 1774; Phileirene, in *MGBWNL,* Jan. 12, 1775; *BEP,* Jan. 23, 1775; *RIV,* Mar. 9, 1775; *Censor,* Dec. 7, 1771.

72. Josiah Quincy, Jr., "Observations on the Boston Port Bill," in Josiah Quincy, *Memoir of the Life of Josiah Quincy, Junior, of Massachusetts: 1744-1775* (Boston, 1874), p. 304, quoted in Wood, *Creation of the American Republic,* p. 23.

73. See Appleby, "Social Origins," pp. 953-958.

74. Rowland Berthoff and John M. Murrin, "Feudalism, Communalism, and the Yeoman Freeholder: The American Revolution Considered as a Social Accident," in Kurtz and Hutson, *Essays on the American Revoultion,* pp. 256-288.

75. John M. Murrin, "Review Essay," *History and Theory* 2 (1972): 226-275.

4. Colonial Origins of Loyalist Ideology

1. Zimmer, *Jonathan Boucher,* pp. 118-139; Calhoon, *Loyalists in Revolutionary America,* pp. 76-84; McCaughey, *From Loyalist to Founding Father,* pp. 35-47.

2. One exception is a recent article tracing the origins of a more conservative ideology to counter the radical, evangelical, Calvinist ideology of the Great Awakening: Donald F. M. Gerardi, "The King's College Controversy 1753-1756 and the Ideological Roots of Toryism in New York," *Perspectives in American History* 11 (1977-78): 145-196.

3. "The Address of the General Assembly to the Governor," *NYJGA,* May 29, 1767; *EG,* Feb. 4-11, 1772; "Lottery," *NYG,* May 3, 1764; *BEP,* July 29, 1765, Sept. 23, 1765; "Letter to Daniel Howard, Esq., Representative of the Inhabitants of the Town of Bridgewater, Mass.," *BEP,* Sept. 30, 1765; "Town of Norton, Instructions to Their Representative," *BEP,* Nov. 4, 1765; "Instructions of the Freeholders and Other Inhabitants of the Town of Boston to Their Representatives," *BC,* Dec. 28, 1767; "A Law for Assizing All Kinds of Victuals," *NYM,* Aug. 29, 1763, Dec. 3, 1764; Probus, in *NYM,* Nov. 9, 1767.

4. A Tradesman, in *NYJGA,* Dec. 17, 1767; "Weymouth Letter," *BEP,* Oct. 21, 1765.

5. *BEP,* July 30, 1770; Philander, in *NYJGA,* Jan. 7, 1768; see also A Friend to the Distressed, in *NYM,* Jan. 6, 1766; A Friend to the Distressed, in *NYM,* Jan. 27, 1766.

6. Wood, *Creation of the American Republic*, pp. 110–111.

7. "Sermon to Asses," *NYG*, July 5, 1773; see also "The First Book of the American Chronicles of the Times" (1775) in Tyler, *Literary History*, I: 263; *NYJGA*, Aug. 6, 1767.

8. *The Occasionalist* (New York, 1768); A Son of New England, in *RIV*, Jan. 19, 1775.

9. Providence Amicus, in *BEP*, Nov. 2, 1767; "Letters in Answer to the Farmer's," *BEP*, Feb. 27, 1769; *BEP*, March 13, 1769.

10. The Anatomist, in *NYJGA*, suppl., Feb. 23, 1769; Cethegus, in *NYC*, May 15, 1769; A Dutchman, in *NYJGA*, April 12, 1770; "The Dougliad," *NYGWM*, April 9, 1770, April 16, 1770; "A Whip," *NYGWM*, March 13, 1769.

11. *A Political Creed for the Day* (New York, 1768); *BC*, Sept. 10, 1769.

12. *A Better Creed than the Last* (New York, 1767); *The Occasionalist* (New York, 1768); Cleomenes, in *NYJGA*, Feb. 18, 1768.

13. *NYJGA*, suppl., Mar. 4, 1768.

14. *A Toothful of Advice* (New York, 1767); Philanthrop, *A Few Observations on the Conduct of the General Assembly of New York* (New York, 1768); *A Card*; *Jack Hatchaway and Tom Bawling* (New York, 1767).

15. *NYJGA*, Feb. 18, 1768; see also Jack P. Greene, "Search for Identity: An Interpretation of the Meaning of Selected Patterns of Social Response in Eighteenth Century America," *Journal of Social History* 3 (1970), pp. 194–196; "Worcester Letter," *BEP*, June 5, 1769; An Old American, in *BEP*, Oct. 5, 1772.

16. Ellen E. Brennan, *Plural Officeholding in Massachusetts, 1760–80: Its Relation to the Separation of Departments of Government* (Chapel Hill, N.C., 1945); Waters, *Otis Family*, pp. 138–150; Bailyn, *Ordeal*, pp. 50–54; Martin, *Men in Rebellion*, pp. 26–33; Ferguson, "Reason in Madness," pp. 194–214.

17. *BEP*, May 19, 1766; *BNL&NEC*, Apr. 7, 1763; *BEP*, Mar. 31, June 23, 1766; "Epitaph for Jemmy," *BEP* June 15, 1767.

18. Philanthrop, in *BEP*, Jan. 6, 1767; *BEP*, Dec. 21, 1767; Feb. 29, 1768.

19. Butler, in *BEP*, Feb. 29, 1768; *BEP*, Dec. 21, 1767.

20. See also Berkin, *Jonathan Sewall*, pp. 31–34.

21. J., in *BEP*, May 23, 1763.

22. *BEP*, June 3, 1771; see also *BEP*, June 9, 1766.

23. "Letters in Answer to the Farmer's," *BEP*, Feb. 20, 1769.

24. *MGBWNL*, Feb. 11, 1773; Chronus, in *MGBWNL*, Dec. 12, 1771.

25. J., in *BEP*, Mar. 28, 1763; see also *BEP*, May 12, June 23, 1766. Benevolus, in *MGBWNL*, Aug. 8, 1771, explained why Governor Hutchinson was criticized so incessantly: "It is not Mr. *Hutchinson*, Sir, at whom the Shafts of Malevolence are aimed. Had you not quitted your private Station, you would have been unenvied, and enjoyed, in full, the publick Esteem . . . No, Sir, it is the Governor of the Province, whom the shaft is levelled at; several of your Predecessors have met with the same illiberal Treatment, from Men of the same Stamp." Philo Patria, in *MGBWNL*, Dec. 22, 1774, made the same point about criticisms of General Thomas Gage.

26. Philanthrop, in *BEP*, Dec. 1, 1766.

27. A Friend to the Press, in *BEP*, Mar. 9, 1767; J., in *BEP*, Apr. 25, 1763;

"Hingham," *MGBWNL*, Mar. 4, 1773; *BEP*, Mar. 31, 1766; A New England Man, in *MGBWNL*, Dec. 10, 1772; Yeoman, in *MGBWNL*, Dec. 10, 1772.

28. "The Plot," *BEP*, Feb. 2, 1767; see also "Letters in Answer to the Farmer's," *BEP*, Mar. 20, 1769; *BEP*, June 3, 1771; Dec. 21, 1767.

29. A New England Man, in *MGBWNL*, Dec. 10, 1772.

30. A By-Stander, in *BEP*, May 5, 1766.

31. Z. T., in *BEP*, May 15, 1769; see also "Protest against the Resolves," *MGBPB&AD*, Dec. 28, 1772; Philanthrop, in *BEP*, Dec. 15, 1766; *MGBWNL*, Apr. 9, 1772; A Yeoman, in *MGBWNL*, Dec. 10, 1772, denounced "his eminence," Dr. Young, for coercing people to stop taking the *Massachusetts Gazette*; *BC*, Oct. 16, 1769.

32. A True Patriot, in *BEP*, Dec. 21, 1767; see also Manlius, in *BEP*, Dec. 23, 1771.

33. *BEP*, Oct. 12, 1767.

34. Crito, in *MGBWNL*, Mar. 18, 1773; see also N. P., in *BEP*, Feb. 6, 1769.

35. "Letters in Answer to the Farmer's," *BEP*, May 22, 1769.

36. Philander, in *MGBWNL*, July 30, 1767.

37. ABC, in *BEP*, Sept. 20, 1773; *MGBWNL*, Nov. 26, 1772; N.P., in *BEP*, Feb. 6, 1769; M.Y., in *MGBWNL*, Apr. 9, 1772; A New England Man, in *MGBWNL*, Dec 10, 1772.

38. Z. Z., in *BWNL*, Aug. 25, 1768; *EG*, Aug. 23–30, 1768.

39. "Remarks on the Times," *BEP*, Mar. 10, 1766; *BEP*, May 12, 1766; Philander, in *MGBWNL*, July 30, 1767.

40. A friend to Peace and good Order, in *BEP*, Oct. 31, 1768.

41. *BEP*, Dec. 30, 1765; see also "Petersham Letter," *BEP*, Mar. 13, 1769; *BEP*, Nov. 14, 1768.

42. X., in *MGBWNL*, Dec. 24, 1772; see also "Letters in Answer to the Farmer's," *BEP*, Apr. 3, 1769; "A Protest of Some of the Inhabitants of the Town of Plymouth," *BEP*, Dec. 27, 1773, claimed that their opponents' actions had a "tendency to introduce anarchy, confusion and disorder . . . whether the same be proposed by Bodies of Men or by an individual"; Philander, in *MGBWNL*, July 30, 1767, warned that confusion was a way for "one Man to seize all Power into his own Hands"; Philanthrop, in *BEP*, Jan. 6, 1767, Dec. 10, 1770; Sophocles, in *MGBWNL*, Dec. 17, 1772; *BEP*, May 27, 1771; May 11, 1772.

43. Philanthrop, in *BEP*, Jan. 28, 1771; A. Z., in *MGBWNL*, Mar. 5, 1772, also contended that the institution of trial by jury was being perverted; "Letters in Answer to the Farmer's," *BEP*, Apr. 10, 1769, argued that judges should remain independent of control by the assembly, as did "A Letter from a Quaker," *BEP*, Jan. 25, 1773, which also contended that trial by jury was being undermined.

44. *Censor*, Dec. 21, 1771.

45. *Censor*, Dec. 21, Dec. 28, 1771; Jan. 11, 1772; see also "Epitaph for Jemmy," *BEP*, June 15, 1767, criticizing the Massachusetts Act for Compensation because the assembly usurped the royal prerogative power to pardon; ABC, in *BEP*, Sept. 20, 1773, warned that "if the Governor is strip'd of all power to injure the people, it will effectually disable him to do any good . . . each branch of the legislature

should have a check upon the other; and as far as possible be alike free from the un-due influence of the others."

46. Chronus, in *MGBPB&AD,* Jan. 6, 1772; see also Impavidus, in *BEP,* May 27, 1771, who warned of the plot to undermine the prerogative and vest the govern-ment in the people; he alleged that the opponents of the governor "seize every op-portunity to cast a mist over the Eyes of the People, to harrass and perplex the legislative part of the Constitution to effect certain purposes, to glut the insatiable thirst of democratical power. To vest the supreme authority in the hands of the peo-ple, and in fine to subjugate mankind to a state of Slavery." Later in the same article Impavidus dealt with criticisms of the governor's power to veto councillors by ask-ing rhetorically: "What is the Prerogative to be considered in Government as a mere blank? Is the Constitution to be totally democratical?" The *Censor's* description of the steps by which the Patriots subverted the constitution of Massachusetts was ex-actly the same as that presented by Daniel Leonard in 1775; see for instance, Leonard, *Mass.,* Dec. 26, 1774, p. 158.

47. "A Letter from a Quaker," *BEP,* Jan. 25, 1773; see also "Letters in Answer to the Farmer's," *BEP,* May 15,1769; Observator, in *MGBWNL,* Feb. 25, 1773; A Yeoman, in *MGBWNL,* Dec. 17, 1772.

48. "Letters in Answer to the Farmer's," *BEP,* Feb. 13, 1769.

49. Liber, in *BC,* Feb. 22, 1770; see also *BC,* Oct. 30, 1769; *BC,* Oct. 23, 1769, attacked the "well disposed" who "dare to arrogate to themselves such a supreme command over the bread of others, earned from the sweat of the brow, as of their own mere motion, to stop up the channel from whence it flowed." See also A Bostonian, in *BC,* Feb. 5, Feb. 12, 1770; Martyr, in *BC,* Feb. 5, 1770.

50. *BC,* Oct. 30, 1769. See also *BC,* Oct. 16, 1769, protesting against the at-tempts of the "well disposed" "to stop the circulation of a certain paper through the country."

51. Theophilus Lillie, *BC,* Jan. 15, 1770. Lillie signed the "Loyal Address from the Gentlemen and Principal Inhabitants of Boston to Governor Gage on His Depar-ture for England, Oct. 6, 1775"; see Stark, *Loyalists of Massachusetts,* p. 132. Another Loyalist who made a similar protest against the coercive nonimportation scheme and was indicted by a grand jury for "publicly speaking against the country and the clergy" was Colborn Barrell, *BC,* Dec. 11, 1769. John Taylor, a merchant and Loyalist, also protested against the activities of the committees. See *MGBWNL,* Nov. 17, 1769, for Colborn Barrell's letter, and *MGBWNL,* Jan. 11, 1770 for letters by Taylor and Lillie. Barrell and Taylor signed the "Address to the Late Gov. Hutch-inson," *MHS* 18 (1870): 392–393.

52. Martyr, in *BC,* Jan. 15, 1770; Feb. 5, 1770.

53. See, for instance, Plain Truth, in *NYGWM,* June 20, 1768; "A Whip," *NYGWM,* Nov. 14, 1768; Jan. 16, Mar. 13, 1769. See also Bridenbaugh, *Mitre and Sceptre;* Bonomi, *Factious People,* pp. 248–251; Frederick V. Mills, *Bishops by Ballot: An Eighteenth Century Ecclesiastical Revolution* (New York, 1978), pt. I.

54. "A Whip," *NYGWM,* Apr. 4, 1768.

55. "A Whip," *NYGWM,* Apr. 25, July 25, Aug. 22, 1768.

56. Ibid., Apr. 11, Apr. 25, 1768.

57. The Anatomist, in *NYJGA*, Nov. 3, Nov. 17, 1768; suppl., Feb. 23, 1769; "A Whip," *NYGWM*, Apr. 25, June 13, 1768.

58. The Anatomist, in *NYJGA*, Nov. 17, 1768.

59. "A Whip," *NYGWM*, May 16, Aug. 22, 1768; The Anatomist, in *NYJGA*, Nov. 17, 1768.

60. "A Whip," *NYGWM*, Apr. 11, Apr. 4, 1768.

61. "A Whip," *NYGWM*, Apr. 4, May 16, 1768.

62. "A Whip," *NYGWM*, Aug. 8, 1768; The Anatomist, in *NYJGA*, Dec. 29, 1768; "A Whip," *NYGWM*, Apr. 4, 1768; The Anatomist, *NYJGA*, Jan. 12, 1769.

63. "A Whip," June 27, Apr. 11, Sept. 12, Aug. 1, 1768; The Anatomist, in *NYJGA*, Dec. 23, 1768, believed the "late illiberal attacks" on the church "scandalize our common Christianity . . . leads to divisions and malice," as opposed to "Charity and brotherly good will to the church"; "A Whip," *NYGWM*, July 4, 1768; The Anatomist, in *NYJGA*, Feb. 23, 1769, suppl., claimed that the Anglican church was the "main bulwark of the Reformation"; in *NYJGA*, Dec. 23, 1768 he described the Anglican Church as a "church so long honoured among true Protestants."

64. "A Whip," *NYGWM*, Nov. 14, 1768.

65. Ibid., Sept. 5, 1768; see also Aug. 15, 1768: "The well-being of Religion is productive of well-being to the state, and consequently to every individual. Can those men then be your friends, who are, and ever have been, endeavouring to prejudice the cause of Christianity and to bring its ministers into disgrace?"

66. Ibid., Nov. 14, 1768.

67. Ibid., Aug. 22, Aug. 29, Oct. 24, 1768; The Anatomist, in *NYJGA*, Dec. 16, 1768, claimed that in attacking the church, the Centinel was attacking the "frame of [the] English government," since the two were so closely interwoven. The Anatomist, in *NYJGA*, Nov. 17, 1768, asserted that the aim of the Centinel was to "prejudice and enflame the minds of their followers, not only against their episcopal brethren in America but . . . to alienate their affections from the constitution of the mother country."

68. "A Whip," *NYGWM*, Oct. 24, Aug. 29, 1768.

69. "A Whip," *NYGWM*, Mar. 13, 1769.

70. Ibid., Apr. 11, June 13, 1768.

71. "A Whip," *NYGWM*, Aug. 1, 1768; The Anatomist, in *NYJGA*, Dec. 16, 1768.

72. "A Whip," *NYGWM*, May 23, 1768.

73. The Anatomist, in *NYJGA*, Nov. 17, 1768.

74. "A Whip," *NYGWM*, Apr. 4, Aug. 1, 1768; The Anatomist, in *NYJGA*, Dec. 16, 1768.

75. "A Whip," *NYGWM*, Apr. 25, 1768; The Anatomist, in *NYJGA*, Nov. 17, 1768.

76. "The Dougliad," *NYGWM*, Apr. 23, 1770. For accounts of this controversy, see Becker, *History of Political Parties*, pp. 78-81; Bonomi, *Factious People*, pp. 267-275; Champagne, *Alexander McDougall*, pp. 17-26.

77. "The Dougliad," *NYGWM,* Apr. 9, June 25, Apr. 9, June 4, 1770.

78. Ibid., Apr. 9, 1770.

79. Ibid., Apr. 23, 1770.

80. Ibid., May 28, 1770.

81. Ibid., Apr. 23, June 25, 1770.

82. Ibid., May 21, Apr. 23, 1770.

83. Ibid., Apr. 16, Apr. 23, June 25, 1770.

84. Leonard, *Mass.,* Feb. 13, 1775, p. 195; Feb. 6, 1775, p. 189; Seabury, *A View,* p. 116; Leonard, *Mass.,* Dec. 26, 1774, p. 153.

85. Leonard, *Mass.,* Jan. 2, 1775, p. 163; Seabury, *A View,* pp. 123-124; Leonard, *Mass.,* Dec. 26, 1774, pp. 151-158, 155-156; Seabury, *A View,* p. 145.

86. "The Dougliad," *NYGWM,* Apr. 30, 1770; May 14, 1770; see also Chronus, in *MGBWNL,* Feb. 13, 1772.

87. Seabury, *Congress Canvassed,* p. 83; see also A Farmer, *Letter to the Inhabitants of the City and Colony of New York* (New York, 1773); *Advices from Philadelphia* (New York, 1774); Wilkins, *Short Advice,* pp. 10-11; A Citizen, *To John M. S. . . . ,* (New York, 1774.)

88. ABC, in *BEP,* Sept. 20, 1773.

89. "The Dougliad," *NYGWM,* Apr. 23, 1770.

90. Leonard, *Mass.,* Jan. 2, 1775, p. 166; see also Poplicola, *The cause . . .*

91. Tyrants, in *BEP,* Dec. 10, 1770.

92. "Great is the Truth and it will prevail," Leonard, *Mass.,* Dec. 26, 1774, p. 158.

5. British Roots of Loyalist Ideology

1. Peter Gay, *The Enlightenment: An Interpretation*: I, *The Rise of Modern Paganism* (New York, 1966); Bernard Bailyn, "Political Experience and Enlightenment Ideas in Eighteenth-Century America," *AHR* 67 (1962): 339-351; Greene, "An Uneasy Connection," pp. 47-56; Henry F. May, *The Enlightenment in America* (New York, 1976).

2. Bailyn, *Ideological Origins;* Bailyn, "The Central Themes of the American Revolution: An Interpretation," in Kurtz and Hutson, *Essays on The American Revolution,* pp. 3-31; Stanley N. Katz, "Origins of American Constitutional Thought," *Perspectives in American History* 3 (1969): 474-490.

3. Caroline Robbins, *The Eighteenth-Century Commonwealthmen: Studies in the Transmission, Development and Circumstances of English Liberal Thought from the Restoration of Charles II until the War with the Thirteen Colonies* (Cambridge, Mass., 1961); Maier, *From Resistance to Revolution;* Morton White, *The Philosophy of the American Revolution* (New York, 1978).

4. Jack P. Greene, "Paine, America and the Modernization of Political Consciousness," *Political Science Quarterly* 93 (1978): 73-92.

5. Wills, *Inventing America;* see also Ronald Hamowy, "Jefferson and the Scottish Enlightenment: A Critique of Garry Wills' *Inventing America: Jefferson's Declaration of Independence,*" *WMQ,* 3rd ser., 36 (1979): 503-523.

6. L. F. S. Upton, "The Dilemma of the Loyalist Pamphleteers," *Studies in Burke and His Time* 18 (1977): 71–85.

7. Maier, *From Resistance to Revolution,* pp. 162–169.

8. For a superb explanation of this point, see Jeffrey M. Nelson, "Ideology in Search of a Context: Eighteenth-Century British Political Thought and the Loyalists of the American Revolution," *The Historical Journal* 20 (1977): 741–749.

9. Mary Beth Norton, "The Loyalists' critique of the Revolution," in *The Development of a Revolutionary Mentality,* Library of Congress Symposia on the American Revolution I (Washington, 1972), pp. 127–148; Benton, *Whig-Loyalism.*

10. John Dunn, "The Politics of Locke in England and America in the Eighteenth Century," in *John Locke: Problems and Perspectives: A Collection of New Essays,* ed. John W. Yolton (Cambridge, 1967), pp. 45–80.

11. Locke's works were included in private libraries; see E. Millicent Sowerby, *Catalogue of the Library of Thomas Jefferson,* 4 vols. (Washington, 1952); *A Catalogue of John Mein's Circulating Library at the London Book Store* (Boston, 1765). Loyalist references to Locke include Hutchinson, "Dialogue"; Ferling, *Loyalist Mind,* pp. 69, 72; Poplicola, *No subject . . .* ; Van Schaack, "Journal," Jan. 1776, in *Life of Peter Van Schaack,* p. 55; Inglis, *True Interest,* pp. 41–55.

12. John Locke, *Two Treatises of Government: A Critical Edition with an Introduction and Apparatus Criticus by Peter Laslett,* ed. Peter Laslett (Cambridge, 1964).

13. Corinne C. Weston, "The Theory of Mixed Monarchy under Charles I and After," *English Historical Review* 75 (1960): 426–443; M. J. C. Vile, *Constitutionalism and the Separation of Powers* (Oxford, 1967), pp. 23–39.

14. James Harrington, *The Commonwealth of Oceana* (Morley's Universal Library, 1656); Locke, *Two Treatises of Government,* XII, XIII.

15. Locke, *Two Treatises of Government,* XIX, p. 212.

16. Hutchinson, "Dialogue," pp. 390–394.

17. Ibid., pp. 391–397.

18. "The Controversy Between Britain and Her Colonies Reviewed," *BC,* Apr. 13–July 10, 1769; May 18, 1769.

19. J. H. Plumb, *The Growth of Political Stability in England, 1675–1725* (London, 1967); Isaac Kramnick, *Bolingbroke and His Circle: The Politics of Nostalgia in the Age of Walpole* (Cambridge, Mass., 1968); Foord, *His Majesties' Opposition.*

20. Bernard Bailyn, "The Origins of American Politics," *Perspectives in American History* 1 (1967): 18–20.

21. J. G. A. Pocock, "Machiavelli, Harrington and English Political Ideologies in the Eighteenth Century," *WMQ,* 3rd ser., 22 (1965): 549–583; Foord, *His Majesties' Opposition,* pp. 79–80; Ian R. Christie, *Wilkes, Wyvill and Reform* (London, 1962), pp. 25–67; Baron George Lyttelton, *Considerations Upon the Present State of Our Affairs at Home and Abroad in a Letter to a Member of Parliament from a Friend in the Country* (London, 1739); William Pulteney, *An Humble Address to the Knights, Citizens, and Burgesses Elected to Represent the Commons of Great Britain in the Ensuing Parliament, by a Freeholder* (London, 1734); *The Conduct of his Grace the Duke of Ar——le [Argyle] for the Last Four Years Review'd Together with His Grace's Speech* (London, 1740); H. Hume, *A Serious Exhortation to the Electors of Great Britain* (London, 1740).

22. Baron John Hervey, *Observations on the Writings of the Craftsman* (London, 1730), pp. 15–16; W. Arnall, *The Free Briton Extraordinary; or a Short Review of British Affairs in Answer to a Pamphlet Intitled, A Short View with Remarks on the Treaty of Seville & c* (London, 1730), p. 29; *The Important Question Discussed or, a Serious and Impartial Enquiry into the True Interest of England with Respect to the Continent* (London, 1746), p. 3; *The Abuse of Standing Parliaments and the Great Advantage of Frequent Elections in a Letter to a Noble Lord* (London, 1750), p. 31.

23. *Faction Detected, by the Evidence of Facts Containing An Impartial View of Parties at Home and Affairs Abroad* (London, 1743), p. 5; *The Present Necessity of Distinguishing Publick Spirit from Party* (London, 1736), p. 4; Thomas Gordon, *The Conspirators, or, the Case of Cataline* (London, 1721), p. v.

24. William Pulteney, *Some Considerations on the National Debts, the Sinking Fund and the State of Publick Credit; In a Letter to a Friend in the Country* (London, 1729), p. 4; *Salus Populi Suprema Lex; Shew'd in the Behaviour of British Parliaments toward Parricides & c.* (London, 1721), p. 5; *An Examination of the Principles and an Enquiry into the Conduct of the Two B— —rs, In Regard to the Establishment of their Power and their Prosecution of the War, Until the Signing of the Preliminaries in a Letter to a Member of Parliament* (London, 1749).

25. *Second Political Dialogues Between the Celebrated Statues of Pasquin and Marforio at Rome* (London, 1737); *National Unanimity Recommended: or, the Necessity of a Constitutional Resistance to the Sinister Designs of False Brethren* (London, 1742); W. Thornton, *The Counterpoise, Being Thoughts on a Militia and a Standing Army* (London, 1753); N. Amherst, *An Answer to a Late Pamphlet Intitled, Observations on the Writings of the Craftsman* (London, 1731).

26. William Pulteney, *A Short View of the State of Affairs with Relation to Great Britain for Four Years Past; with Some Remarks on the Treaty lately Published and a Pamphlet Intitled Observations upon it ...* (London, 1730); Benjamin Hoadly, *An Inquiry into the Reasons of the Conduct of Great Britain with Relation to the Present State of Affairs in Europe* (London, 1727); Ian R. Christie, *Myth and Reality in Late Eighteenth Century British Politics* (London, 1970), intro.

27. Robert Walpole, *Some Considerations Concerning the Publick Funds; The Publick Revenues and the Annual Supplies Granted by Parliament* (London, 1735), p. 6; *The Important Question Discussed or a Serious and Impartial Enquiry into the True Interest of England with Respect to the Continent* (London, 1746); Baron John Hervey, *Observations on the Writings of the Craftsman* (London, 1730), p. 26; *A Series of Wisdom and Policy Manifested in a Review of our Foreign Negotiations and Transactions for Several Years Past* (London, 1735), pp. 5–6; *An Appeal to the Landholders Concerning the Reasonableness and General Benefit of an Excise upon Tobacco and Wine* (London, 1733), pp. 4–7; *Some Observations on the Present State of Affairs in a Letter to a Member of the House of Commons* (London, 1731).

28. *Considerations on the Present State of Affairs in Europe, and Particularly with Regard to the Number of Forces in the Pay of Great Britain*, 2nd ed. (London, 1730), p. 52; *An Enquiry into the Danger of Multiplying Incapacities on the Gentlemen of England to Sit in Parliament Occasioned by the Late Writings in Favour of a Placebill: In a Letter to a Member of Parliament* (London, 1739).

29. *A Letter to Mr. P. on the Occasion of his Late Letter in Answer to the Remarks &*

c. (London, 1731); *Sedition and Defamation Display'd: In a Letter to the Author of the Craftsman* (London, 1731); *A Letter to a Member of Parliament Concerning the Present State of Affairs at Home and Abroad* (London, 1740); *A Letter to the Oxford Tories: By an Englishman* (London, 1750).

30. *The Case of Opposition Stated Between the Craftsman and the People Occasioned by His Paper of Dec. the 4th, 1731* (London, 1731); Nestor, *A Letter from a Member of Parliament to the Freeholders in His County, on the Present State of the Nation* (London, 1731); *Remarks on Foggs Journal of February 10, 1733. Exciting the People to an Assassination* (London, 1733).

31. Bailyn, *Ideological Origins,* pp. 34–54.

32. Gerardi, "King's College Controversy," p. 172.

33. " 'Thoughts on the Origin and Nature of Government, Occasioned by the Disputes Between Great Britain and Her American Colonies,' from *Gentleman's Magazine,*" *BC,* June 29, 1769.

34. Bailyn, *Ordeal,* pp. 76–78.

35. *BC,* June 29, 1769; it was the last part of the pamphlet which was excerpted.

36. "A Letter in Vindication of the Earl of Bute, Occasioned by His Resignation," *BEP,* July 11, 1763. Other defenses of Bute were in *BEP,* July 18, 1763; *Gentleman's Magazine* reprint in *BEP,* Oct. 3, 1763; "Foresight," *BEP,* Sept. 29, 1766. For other court or ministerial articles, see "Sir Wm. Draper's Defence of Lord Granby in Answer to the Author of the Review of the Present Administration," *BC,* June 1, 1769; "Sir Wm. Draper's Reply to Junius in Defence of Himself," *BC,* June 22, 1769; *Lloyd's Evening Post* reprint, in *BC,* Nov. 27, 1769; *Public Advertiser* reprint, in *MGBPB&AD,* Jan. 15, 1770; Modestus, in *MGBPB&AD,* Mar. 12, 1770; *General Evening Post* reprint, in *MGBNL,* Feb. 15, 1770; Modestus, in *NYGWM,* Feb. 26, 1770; *London Chronicle* reprint, in *NYGWM,* Dec. 16, 1771; *Public Ledger* reprint, in *NYGWM,* Jan. 13, 1772; Portius, in *NYJGA,* Mar. 1, 1770; *Liverpool Mercury* reprint, in *NYC,* July 20, 1769; *London Chronicle* reprint, in *NYC,* Aug. 31, 1769; *London Evening Post* reprint, in *NYC,* Sept. 7, 1769; *London Chronicle* reprint, in *NYC,* Oct. 5, 1769.

37. Keith Feiling, *A History of England: From the Coming of the English to 1918* (Toronto, 1966), pp. 700–705; Richard Pares, *King George III and the Politicians* (London, 1970), pp. 99–109; Maier, *From Resistance to Revolution,* pp. 56, 71.

38. "Letter in Vindication of the Earl of Bute."

39. Ibid.

40. Maier, *From Resistance to Revolution,* pp. 162–169.

41. *London Chronicle* reprint, in *NYGWM,* Dec. 16, 1771.

42. "Sir Wm. Draper's Defence."

43. Portius, in *NYJGA,* Mar. 1, 1770.

44. "Letter in Vindication of the Earl of Bute." See also *BEP,* July 18, 1763.

45. *London Advertiser* reprint, in MGBPB&AD, Jan. 15, 1770.

46. *London Chronicle* reprint, in NYC, Oct. 5, 1769; see also, Modestus, in MGBPB&AD, Mar. 12, 1770; *Gentleman's Magazine* reprint, in BEP, Oct. 3, 1763, for a similar view of Junius' motives.

47. "Letter in Vindication of the Earl of Bute."

48. *Morning Chronicle* reprint, in *MGBPB&AD,* Nov. 4, 1771.

49. *General Evening Post* reprint, in *MGBNL,* Feb. 15, 1770; Portius, in *NYJGA,* Mar. 1, 1770; *BEP,* Oct. 10, 1763.

50. *BEP,* Oct. 10, 1763.

51. *Public Advertiser* reprint, in *MGBPB&AD,* Jan. 15, 1770; see also Modestus, in *MGBPB&AD,* Mar. 12, 1770.

52. *General Evening Post* reprint, in *MGBNL,* Feb. 15, 1770.

53. "Sir Wm. Draper's Defence." The wording in this quote was strikingly similar to that used in Leonard, *Mass.,* Mar. 6, 1775, p. 209, which described the Patriots as "bankrupts in fortune, business and fame."

54. *London Chronicle* reprint, in *NYC,* Oct. 5, 1769.

55. Modestus, in *MGBPB&AD,* Mar. 12, 1770.

56. *General Evening Post* reprint, in *MGBNL,* Feb. 15, 1770.

57. Portius, in *NYJGA,* Mar. 1, 1770; *MGBNL,* Feb. 15, 1770.

58. "A Serious Expostulation," *NYC,* Aug. 31, 1769.

59. Robbins, *Eighteenth-Century Commonwealthmen;* Bailyn, "Origins of American Politics," pp. 34–36; Wood, *Creation of the American Republic,* pp. 15–26.

60. MacPherson, *Political Theory of Possessive Individualism,* pp. 3–4, 270; see also Appleby, "Social Origins."

61. Robbins, *Eighteenth-Century Commonwealthmen,* p. 5.

62. Robbins, *Eighteenth-Century Commonwealthmen,* pp. 7–8.

63. Wood, *Creation of the American Republic,* pp. 15–36.

64. Ibid.

65. John Trenchard and Thomas Gordon, *Cato's Letters or Essays on Liberty, Civil and Religious, and Other Important Subjects,* 2 vols. (New York, 1969); James Burgh, *Britain's Remembrancer,* 4th ed. (London, 1747).

66. *Cato's Letters,* II, Dec. 30, 1721, p. 59; Apr. 15, 1721, p. 64; I, Feb. 11, 1720, p. 16; *Britain's Remembrancer,* p. 8.

67. *Britain's Remembrancer,* pp. 30–38.

68. *Cato's Letters,* I, Sat. Feb. 11, 1720, p. 16.

69. Isaac Kramnick, ed., *Bolingbroke: Political Writings* (New York, 1970), p. viii.

70. Viscount Bolingbroke, "The Idea of a Patriot King," in *The Works of Lord Bolingbroke,* II (4 vols., Philadelphia, 1841).

71. Bolingbroke, "A Letter on the Spirit of Patriotism" (1735–1738), in Kramnick, *Bolingbroke,* p. 33.

72. Ibid., pp. 33–37.

73. Bolingbroke, "A Dissertation Upon Parties. To the Right Honourable Sir Robert Walpole," in *Works,* II: 112–115.

74. Bolingbroke, "Remarks on the History of England, Written in 1730" (Letter II), in *Works,* I: 306.

75. Bolingbroke, "Letter on the Spirit," p. 37.

76. Bolingbroke, "Remarks on the History," p. 305.

77. Bolingbroke, "Dissertation upon Parties," p. 7.

78. Bolingbroke, "The Occasional Writer Number II" (1726-27), in *Works*, I: 212.

79. For an analysis of the Patriots' use of Bolingbroke's ideas, see William D. Liddle, "A Patriot King or None: Lord Bolingbroke and the American Renunciation of George III," *JAH* 65 (1979): 951-970; Wills, *Inventing America*, p. 173, states that Bolingbroke was a favorite of Thomas Jefferson; Patterson, *Political Parties*, pp. 20-21, claims that Bolingbroke was "as widely read in America as the radicals." For libraries containing Bolingbroke's writings, see Sowerby, *Library of Thomas Jefferson*, pp. 3, 129-140; "The Bowdoin Library," *Proceedings of the Massachusetts Historical Society* 51 (1917-18), p. 365; *A Catalogue of Mein's Circulating Library*; an advertisement for "Lord Bolingbroke's Whole Works," sold at James Rivington's, was in *The New-York Gazette and Weekly Post Boy*, Nov. 5, 1761. Monitor X [Provost William Smith], in *NYJGA*, May 26, 1768, quoted Bolingbroke to support the view that man was made for society; see also *BEP*, Dec. 1, 1766; "Letters in Answer to the Farmer's," *BEP*, Mar. 20, 1769; Berkin, *Jonathan Sewall*, p. 132.

80. Baron de Montesquieu, *The Spirit of the Laws*, trans. Thomas Nugent, 2 vols. (London, 1878); M. J. C. Vile, *Constitutionalism and the Separation of Powers* (Oxford, 1967). For references to Montesquieu, see Sowerby, *Library of Thomas Jefferson*, pp. 3, 22; Inglis, *True Interest*, pp. 21-25; *MGBWNL*, Oct. 22, 1772, included a proposal for reprinting *L'Esprit des Lois*; Poplicola, *No subject . . .* ; J. in *BEP*, May 23, 1763; A Protestant, in *BC*, Dec. 11, 1769; "The Dougliad," *NYGWM*, Apr. 23, 1770.

81. Vile, *Constitutionalism*, p. 88, p. 90.

82. Vile, *Constitutionalism*, pp. 28-31.

83. J., in *BEP*, May 23, 1763.

84. Polpicola, *No subject . . .* ; Montesquieu, *Spirit of the Laws*, bk. xi, p. 161; see also, J., in *BEP*, May 23, 1763; "The Dougliad," *NYGWM*, Apr. 23, 1770.

85. J. G. A. Pocock, *The Ancient Constitution and the Feudal Law: A Study of English Historical Thought in the Seventeenth Century* (Cambridge, 1957), pp. 242-243.

86. James T. Boulton, *The Language of Politics in the Age of Wilkes and Burke* (Toronto, 1963), p. 112.

87. Ibid., pp. 114-115.

88. Ibid., pp. 106-112.

89. Sir William Blackstone, *Commentaries on the Laws of England in Four Books*, ed. St. George Tucker, 4 vols., (Philadelphia, 1803); see Sowerby, *Library of Thomas Jefferson*, pp. 2, 319. Advertisements for Blackstone's *Commentaries* were in *BEP*, July 2, 1764; *MGBPB&AD*, Nov. 8-15, 1773; *NYGWM*, Aug. 5, 1771; *NYG*, Apr. 8, 1771, had a large advertisement for an American printing of the *Commentaries*. Blackstone was quoted or cited in the following works: A Constitutionalist, in *EG*, Aug. 4-11, 1772; *NYG*, Apr. 8, 1771; Chandler, *Friendly Address*, p. 17; Leonard, *Mass.*, Feb. 6, 1775, p. 188; Chronus, in *MGBPB&AD*, Jan. 6, 1772; Censor, Dec. 28, 1771, Jan. 25, 1772; Ferling, *Loyalist Mind*, p. 69; Zimmer, *Jonathan Boucher*, p. 127.

90. Blackstone, *Commentaries*, I: intro., 6.

91. Ibid., II: 443.

92. Ibid., II: 142.

93. Ibid., I: 123.

94. Ibid., II: 43.

95. Ibid., I: 124–125.

96. Ibid.

97. Robbins, *Eighteenth-Century Commonwealthmen*, p. 46; Henry Neville, *Plato Redivivus or a Dialogue Concerning Government in Two English Republican Tracts*, ed. Caroline Robbins (Cambridge, 1969); Blackstone, *Commentaries*, II: 27.

98. Blackstone, *Commentaries*, I: 124–125.

99. Ibid., pp. 161–162.

100. Ernest Barker, *Essays on Government* (Oxford, 1945), p. 103.

101. Blackstone, *Commentaries*, II: 50–52; an even better explanation of this view of the balanced constitution was provided by Bolingbroke, *Works*, II: 99–101.

102. Chronus, in *MGBPB&AD*, Jan. 6, 1772; according to Barker, *Essays on Government*, p. 102, it was "often through Blackstone's eyes that the colonists saw the Montesquieu theory."

103. Blackstone, *Commentaries*, II: 48.

104. Ibid., p. 443.

105. Ibid., p. 159.

106. Ibid., pp. 140–143.

6. The Loyalists' Anglo-American Vision

1. Poplicola, in *RIV*, Nov. 18, 1773.

2. See, for example, Greene, "Uneasy Connection."

3. See Egnal, "Economic Development of the Thirteen Continental Colonies;" Egnal and Ernst, "Economic Interpretation of the American Revolution;" Bernard Bailyn, *The New England Merchants in the Seventeenth Century* (New York, 1955); Harrington, *New York Merchants on the Eve*; I. K. Steele, "Moat Theories and the English Atlantic 1675–1740," in Canadian Historical Association, *Historical Papers* (1978): 18–33.

4. Greene, "Uneasy Connection," pp. 32–80; Greene, "Political Mimesis: A Consideration of the Historical and Cultural Roots of Legislative Behavior in the British Colonies in the Eighteenth Century," *AHR* 75 (1969): 337–360.

5. Kenneth A. Lockridge, *A New England Town, the First Hundred Years*: *Dedham, Massachusetts, 1636–1736* (New York, 1970); Allan Kulikoff, "The Progress of Inequality in Revolutionary Boston," *WMQ*, 3rd ser., 28 (1971) : 375–412.

6. See, for example, Max Savelle, "Nationalism and Other Loyalities in the American Revolution," *AHR* 68 (1962): 901–924.

7. Adams, *Works of John Adams*, III: 461–462, quoted in Tyler, *Literary History*, I, 97.

8. Otis, *Rights of the British Colonies*, p. 25; see also "Answer of the House of Representatives to the Speech of the Governor, of Sixth January . . . January 26, 1773," in Hosmer, *Life Of Thomas Hutchinson*, pp. 380–396.

9. Isaac Skillman, *The Alarm or The Boston Plea* (Boston, 1773) (emphasis added).

10. "Dedication of the Book of Poems," *MGBNL*, May 5, 1763.

11. A British Bostonian, *Alarm IV: The Pernicious Effects* (New York, 1773); see also Jonathan Mayhew, *The Snare Broken* (Boston, 1766), in Davidson, *Propaganda*, p. 134; Philip Livingston, *To the Inhabitants of the City and County of New York* (New York, 1775).

12. R. L. Merritt, *Symbols of American Community, 1735–1775* (New Haven, Conn., 1966); Merritt, "Symbolic Division of North America, 1752–75," *Canadian Review of Studies in Nationalism* 6 (1979): 193–217.

13. R. W. Van Alstyne, *The Rising American Empire* (Oxford, 1960); for another study of the convergence of a distintive American outlook, see Robert M. Weir, "Who Shall Rule at Home: The American Revolution as a Crisis of Legitimacy for the Colonial Elite," *Journal of Interdisciplinary History* 6 (1976): 679–700.

14. William Livingston, "The American Whig" (1768), quoted in Richard Koebner, *Empire* (Cambridge, 1961), pp. 171–172.

15. "A Whip," *NYGWM*, May 16, 1768.

16. Ibid.

17. See Henry Barry, *The General Attacked by a Subaltern* (New York, 1775), pp. 9, 11; Chandler, *Friendly Address*, p. 7; Chandler, *American Querist*, p. 6; Inglis, *True Interest*, pp. vii, 17; Smith, *Historical Memoirs*, June 9, 1776, pp. 271–272; Smith, "Thoughts upon the Dispute," p. 112; J. M. Bumsted, "Loyalists and Nationalists: An Essay on the Problem of Definitions," *Canadian Review of Studies in Nationalism*, 6 (1979): 218–232.

18. Seabury, *A View*, p. 110.

19. Chandler, *What Think Ye*, p. 48.

20. Van Schaack, "Journal," Jan. 1776, in *Life of Peter Van Schaack*, p. 55.

21. Poplicola, *No subject . . .*

22. Chronus, in *MGBPB&AD,* Jan. 6, 1772; see also Leonard, *Mass.,* Jan. 23, 1775, pp. 179–180; Potter and Calhoon, "Character and Coherence of the Loyalist Press," pp. 250–258.

23. Rusticus, in *NYGWM*, Jan. 16, 1775; "An Account Between Britain and Her Colonies Candidly Stated, "*NYGWM*, June 6, 1774; Inglis, *True Interest*, pp. 48–50.

24. Freeholder in the County of Worcester, in *MGBWNL*, Feb. 2, 1775.

25. Poplicola, in *RIV*, Nov. 18, 1773; Potter and Calhoon, "Character and Coherence of the Loyalist Press," pp. 250–258.

26. A Plain Dealer, in *NYJGA*, July 21, 1774; a writer in *NYJGA*, Feb. 23, 1775, asserted that his ancestors fled to America in search of liberty; see also Liberus, in *BEP*, Mar. 23, 1767; *Boston Gazette* reprint, in *NYJGA*, Sept. 10, 1767.

27. Otis, *Rights of the British Colonies*, p. 25.

28. Adams, *Works of John Adams*, III, 452, quoted in Tyler, *Literary History*, I: 95–96.

29. Jonathan Mayhew, "The Snare Broken," in Davidson, *Propaganda*, p. 134; A British Bostonian, *Alarm IV: The Pernicious Effects.*

30. "Answer of the Council to the Speech of Governor Hutchinson of Jan. 6," Jan. 25, 1773, in Hosmer, *Life of Thomas Hutchinson*, p. 377.

31. *Pennsylvania Gazette*, Mar. 6, 1776, in Davidson, *Propaganda*, pp. 158–159; see also *BEP*, Nov. 3, 1766.

32. Wilkins, "Speech," *RIV*, Apr. 6, 1775; see also Henry Barry, *The Advantages Which America Derives* (Boston, 1775), p. 4.

33. Inglis, *True Interest*, pp. 39–40; see also Seabury, *A View*, p. 111.

34. Leonard, *Mass.*, Jan. 23, 1775, pp. 178–179.

35. *Censor*, Jan. 25, 1772; see also, "To the Publick," *MGBWNL,* Mar. 5, 1772.

36. Seabury, *Free Thoughts*, p. 55; *BEP* reprint, in *RIV*, Sept. 8, 1774.

37. Inglis, *True Interest*, p. 41; Chandler, *American Querist,* p. 16.

38. Oxenbridge Thatcher, *The Sentiments of a British American* (Boston, 1774), in Tyler, *Literary History*, I: 54; see also *Boston Gazette*, Feb. 24, 1766, in Davidson, *Propaganda*, p. 159.

39. Chandler, *American Querist*, p. 26; Leonard, *Mass.*, Jan. 30, 1775, p. 184; Rusticus, in *NYGWM*, Jan. 16, 1775; Inglis, *True Interest*, pp. 48–49.

40. Leonard, *Mass.,* Jan. 30, 1775, p. 184, p. 186; see also "Letters in Answer to the Farmer's," *BEP,* June 5, 1769; Ferling, *Loyalist Mind*, p. 16; Americanus, in *NYJGA*, Oct. 30, 1766.

41. Chandler, *Friendly Address*, p. 26.

42. Chandler, *Strictures on the Friendly Address*, p. 14.

43. Seabury, *A View*, p. 117.

44. Phileirene, Apr. 6, 1775, in *Am. Arch.,* 4th ser., 2: 287.

45. "Form of an Association in Cortlandt's Manor," *RIV*, Feb. 16, 1775; see also Rusticus, in *NYGWM*, Jan. 16, 1775; Calhoon, *Loyalists in Revolutionary America*, p. 167.

46. "A Whip," *NYGWM*, May 16, 1768.

47. *Boston Gazette*, Sept. 29, 1760.

48. "A Few Thoughts on the Method of Improving," *NYM*, Aug. 27, 1764.

49. Samuel Dunbar, *The Presence of God with His People, Their Only Safety and Happiness* (Boston, 1760), p. 19, quoted in J. D. Livermore, "*Carthaga Deleta Est*: New England's Response to the Fall of New France, 1758–1761," unpublished paper, Queen's University, Kingston, Ont., 1971.

50. "Speech of James Otis at a Meeting to Elect Town Officers," *BEP*, Mar. 21, 1763; "Dedication of the Book of Poems," *MGBWNL,* May 5, 1763; "A Few Thoughts," *NYM*, Aug. 27, 1764.

51. William Adams, *A Discourse Delivered at New London* (New London, Conn., 1761), p. 8; see also Akers, "Religion and the American Revolution," pp. 486–487.

52. "Dedication of the Book of Poems;" *MGBNL*, May 5, 1763; *NYG*, Sept. 23, Sept. 9, Sept. 23, 1754; Dunbar, *Presence of God*, p. 6; "Speech of James Otis," *BEP*, Mar. 21, 1763; Samuel Cooper, *A Sermon Preached before His Excellency Thomas Pownall, Esq. . . . Upon the Occasion of the Success of His Majesty's Arms in the Reduction of Quebec* (Boston, 1758), pp. 47–48. Similar ideas were expressed about the 1745 Louisbourg expedition; see Shortt, "Conflict and Identity in Massachusetts," pp. 165–185; and George A. Rawlyk, *Nova Scotia's Massachusetts: A Study of Nova Scotia-Massachusetts Relations, 1630 to 1784* (Montreal, 1973), pp. 172–175; see also Nathan

V. Hatch, *The Sacred Cause of Liberty: Republican Thought and the Millenium in Revolutionary New England* (New Haven, Conn., 1977), chap. 1.

53. "Form of an Association in Cortlandt's Manor," *RIV*, Feb. 16, 1775; Phileirene, in *MGBWNL*, Jan. 26, 1775; Phileirene, in *Am. Arch.*, 4th ser., 2: 286-287; see also Ferling, "American Revolution and American Security."

54. Inglis, *True Interest*, pp. 47-49; Wilkins, "Speech," *RIV*, Apr. 6, 1775.

55. See, for example, Bailyn, *Ideological Origins*, pp. 94-159.

56. Inglis, *True Interest*, p. 70.

57. Chronus, in *MGBPB&AD*, Dec. 2, 1771; see also Philanthrop, in *BEP*, Jan. 14, 1771; A New York Freeholder, in *NYGWM*, Sept. 12, 1774; Crito, in *MGBWNL*, Mar. 18, 1773; The Querist, in *MGBWNL*, Nov. 24, 1774; Andrew Tremulus, in *BEP*, Jan. 25, 1773; Seabury, *A View*, p. 121; "Letters in Answer to the Farmer's," *BEP*, Feb. 13, 1769; Leonard, *Mass.*, Jan. 9, 1775, pp. 169-170.

58. "Dutchess County Address," *RIV*, Feb. 9, 1775; "An Address to the Inhabitants of Cortlandt's Manor," *RIV*, Feb. 16, 1775.

59. "Form of an Association in Cortlandt's Manor," *RIV*, Feb. 16, 1775; see also Chandler, *Friendly Address*, p. 3; Potter and Calhoon, *"Character and Coherence of the Loyalist Press,"* pp. 251-252.

60. Inglis, *True Interest*, p. 15, p. 31; Leonard, *Mass.*, Jan. 9, 1775, p. 172; Plain English, in *RIV*, Mar. 9, 1775; "Letters in Answer to the Farmer's," *BEP*, Mar. 6, 1769; Adair and Schutz, *Oliver's Origin*, p. 24; Seabury, *Congress Canvassed*, p. 98.

61. Inglis, *True Interest*, pp. 16-18.

62. Ibid., pp. 52-53, 17-18; see also Leonard, *Mass.*, Jan. 9, 1775, pp. 169-170; Chronus, in *MGBPB&AD*, Jan. 6, 1772; *Censor*, Nov. 30, Dec. 14, Dec. 28, 1771, June 25, 1772; ABC, in *BEP*, Sept. 20, 1773; Crito, in *MGBWNL*, Mar. 18, 1773; "A Letter from a Quaker," *BEP*, Jan. 25, 1773; Chandler, *Friendly Address*, p. 3; Philanthrop, in *BEP*, Jan. 28, 1771; Seabury, *A View*, p. 110; John Derry, *English Politics and the American Revolution* (New York, 1976), pp. 1-38.

63. Hutchinson, "Speech of the Governor," Feb. 16, 1773, in Hosmer, *Life of Thomas Hutchinson*, p. 404.

64. Seabury, *A View*, p. 111; see also "Letters in Answer to the Farmer's," *BEP*, Feb. 13, 1769; *BEP*, Mar. 6, 1769; Chandler, *What Think Ye*, pp. 43-44.

65. Greene, "Uneasy Connection," pp. 32-80.

66. Greene, "Political Mimesis," pp. 337-360.

67. Greene, "Uneasy Connection," p. 50.

68. Carl Berger, *The Sense of Power: Studies in the Ideas of Canadian Imperialism 1867-1914* (Toronto, 1970) discusses the concept of imperial unity and the status associated with being a member of the British Empire.

69. Seabury, *Congress Canvassed*, p. 73.

70. Chandler, *American Querist*, pp. 22-23; Chandler, *Friendly Address*, p. 8; see also ABC, in *BEP*, Jan. 25, 1773; A Lover of Justice, in *MGBPB&AD*, Apr. 25 – May 2, 1774; Van Schaack, "Journal," Jan. 1776, in *Life of Peter Van Schaack*, p. 57.

71. "Resolves of the Town Meeting, Hampstead, Queen's County," *RIV*, Apr. 6, 1775.

72. Chronus, in *MGBPB&AD*, Jan. 6, 1772; see also "Letters in Answer to the Farmer's," *BEP*, Feb. 13, 1769.

73. Inglis, *True Interest*, p. 41.

74. Leonard, *Mass.*, Jan. 2, 1775, p. 167.

75. Inglis, *True Interest*, pp. 47–49.

76. Wilkins, "Speech," *RIV*, Apr. 6, 1775; see also "Speech of Cadwallader Colden to the New York General Assembly," *RIV*, Jan. 19, 1775.

77. Phileirene, in *MGBWNL*, Jan. 26, 1775.

78. Poplicola, in *RIV*, Dec. 2, 1773; see also Chandler, *What Think Ye*, p. 18; Seabury, *Congress Canvassed*, p. 71; A Merchant of New York, in *RIV*, Aug. 18, 1774; Edwin G. Burrows and Michael Wallace, "The American Revolution: The Ideology and Psychology of National Liberation," *Perspectives in American History* 6 (1972): 167–306.

79. "An Address to the Inhabitants of Cortlandt's Manor," *RIV*, Feb. 16, 1775; see also, Wilkins, "Speech," *RIV*, Apr. 6, 1775.

80. Z. A., "On Peace," *BPB*, Sept. 26, 1763; see also Librus, in *BEP*, Mar. 23, 1767; Americanus, in *NYJGA*, Oct. 30, 1766.

81. "The Portrait of an Imposter," *RIV*, Feb. 16, 1775.

82. *RIV*, Feb. 23, 1775; see also Colden, "Speech," *RIV*, Jan. 19, 1775; in "Tribute to Governor Tryon," *RIV*, Apr. 7, 1774, the governor was described as the "Father of the fatherless."

83. Bailyn, *New England Merchants*; Harrington, *New York Merchants*.

84. E. J. Hobsbawn, *Industry and Empire: The Pelican Economic History of Britain* (Suffolk, Eng., 1974), 3, pp. 34–55; Egnal, "Economic Development of the Thirteen Colonies"; Egnal and Ernst, "Economic Interpretation of the American Revolution"; Michael G. Kammen, *Empire and Interest: The American Colonies and the Politics of Mercantilism* (New York, 1970), pp. 73, 93. For another view of the role of economic factors in the Revolution, see Joseph D. Reid, Jr., "Economic Burden: Spark to the American Revolution?" *Journal of Economic History* 38 (1978): 81–100.

85. Egnal and Ernst, "Economic Interpretation of the American Revolution," p. 17; Harrington, *New York Merchants*, p. 173.

86. Benjamin Davis, in *NYGWM*, Aug. 11, 1771; Walter Franklin, in *NYGWM*, June 30, 1772; Benjamin Booth, in *NYGWM*, Aug. 29, 1768; John Laboyteaux, in *RIV*, Oct. 13, 1774; Greg Cunningham & Co., in *RIV*, Oct. 13, 1774; Richard Smith, in *MGBWNL*, Nov. 5, 1767; John Laboyteaux, in *RIV*, Oct. 13, 1774; Thomas Persall, in *NYJGA*, Mar. 5, 1772; Samuel Broome & Co., in *NYGWM*, Mar. 16, 1772; Samuel Hake, in *NYGWM*, Oct. 31, 1768; George Ball, in *NYGWM*, Aug. 28, 1770; Abel & Byvanck, in *NYGWM*, Aug. 28, 1770; Henry Remsen, in *NYGWM*, May 16, 1768; Benjamin Davis, in *NYGWM*, Apr. 25, 1768; Samuel Deall, in *NYGWM*, Aug. 19, 1771.

87. John Hutt, in *RIV*, Sept. 16, 1773; John Lewis, in *NYM*, Aug. 22, 1768; Whitehouse & Reeve, in *RIV*, Oct. 13, 1774; James Yeoman, in *NYGWM*, Aug. 27, 1770. The New York newspapers abounded with such advertisements in the 1760s and 1770s. Massachusetts, perhaps because there were fewer immigrants, did not have nearly as many; see, however, Samuel Dickinfield, *BPB*, Aug. 22, 1763,

who advertised himself as a wallpaperer from London. William Tonge, in *RIV*, Oct. 13, 1774.

88. Joseph Albert Ernst, "The Currency Act Repeal Movement: A Study of Imperial Politics and Revolutionary Crisis, 1764–1767," *WMQ*, 3rd ser., 25 (1968): 177–211; Ernst, *Money and Politics in America.*

89. This argument was made by northern merchants in their opposition to the Sugar Act's restrictions on the foreign West Indies trade; see for instance, "An Essay on the Trade of the Northern Colonies," *NYM*, Feb. 6, 1764; *Considerations upon the Act of Parliament whereby a Duty is Laid of Six Pence Sterling per Gallon on Molasses, and Five Shillings per Hundred on Sugar of Foreign Growth, Imported into Any of the British Colonies* (Boston, 1764); *The Memorial of the Merchants of the City of New York in America to the Honourable, the Knights, Citizens and Burgesses in Parliament Assembled* (New York, April 20, 1764); "New York Merchants' Petition to the House of Commons against the Sugar Act," *BEP*, May 11, 1767. See also Harrington, *New York Merchants*, pp. 164–172; Henretta, *Evolution of American Society*, pp. 45–49.

90. For instance, in the trade contractions following the Seven Years' War, when British merchants called in their debts three prominent Boston merchants— John Scollay, Joseph Scott, and Nathanial Wheelwright—went bankrupt; see Harrington, *New York Merchants*, p. 318; Ernst, *Money and Politics in America*, p. 350.

91. James Abeel, in *NYGWM*, Feb. 5, 1770; Dennis McCready, ibid.; Rickman and Browne, in *NYGWM*, June 15, 1772.

92. Henry Bass, in *MGBWNL*, Nov. 30, 1769.

93. *NYG*, May 3, 1764.

94. Philo Patriae, in *MG*, suppl., Nov. 19, 1767.

95. See, for instance, "New York Letter," *MG*, July 31, 1766; *MG*, Sept. 6, 1764; "*Boston Gazette* Letter," *NYJGA*, Nov. 19, 1767; *NYM*, Dec. 2, 1765; "Instructions of Freeholders and Other Inhabitants of the Town of Boston to Their Representatives," *BC*, Dec. 28, 1767; The Unmasker, in *MGBWNL*, Jan. 5, 1769.

96. *MG*, Sept. 6, 1764; see also "New York Letter," *MG*, July 31, 1766; Cethegus, in *NYC*, May 8, 1769.

97. John Keating, in *NYGWM*, July 18, 1768; William Shaffer, in ibid., Feb. 12, 1772; see also, *BPB*, Nov. 16, 1767; *MG*, Sept. 6, 1764; The Unmasker, in *MGWNL*, Jan. 5, 1769; Agricola, in *NYGWM*, Feb. 1, 1768; *NYJGA*, Oct. 30, 1766; *Boston Gazette and Country Journal* reprint, in *NYJGA*, Nov. 5, 1767.

98. This particular slogan was the headline in *BPB*, Nov. 2, 1767.

99. *BEP*, July 11, 1774.

100. T., in *BEP*, Sept. 15, 1766.

101. "House of Representatives Resolves," *BEP*, Feb. 29, 1768; see also Morgan, "Puritan Ethic," pp. 3–18.

102. Linen Draper, "The Commercial Conduct of the Province of New York considered," *MGBWNL*, Dec. 4, 1767. Similar lengthy treatments of the same subject include Philo Patriae, in *MG*, suppl., Nov. 19, 1767; *MG*, suppl., Sept. 13, 1764, included articles advocating retrenchment and the protection of native manufacturers from other colonies; a lengthy article in favor of linen manufacturing appeared in *NYJGA*, Dec. 24, 1767; *The Commercial Conduct of the Province of New*

York Considered and the True Interest of That Colony Attempted to be Shown in a Letter to the Society of Arts, Agriculture and Oeconomy (New York, 1767).

103. Appleby, *Economic Thought and Ideology*, p. 123; see also, William Appleman Williams, "The Age of Mercantilism: An Interpretation of the American Political Economy, 1763 to 1828," *WMQ*, 3rd ser., 15 (1958): 419–437; Egnal and Ernst, "Economic Interpretation of the American Revolution."

104. *Considerations Upon the Act of Parliament;* "New York Merchants' Petition," *BEP*, May 11, 1767; see also "Reasons of the Honourable Brigadier-General [Timothy] Ruggles, *BC*, Mar. 7, 1768; *BEP*, Feb., 29, 1768; Oct. 15, 1764; "The Petition of the Merchants in the City of New York Addressed to the House of Commons," *NYJGA*, Apr. 23, 1767; *Reasons Against the Renewal of the Sugar Act* (Boston, 1764).

105. *Considerations Upon the Act of Parliament;* "New York Merchants' Petition," *BEP*, May 11, 1767; see also Americanus, in *NYJGA*, Oct. 30, 1766.

106. The Impartialist, in *MGBWNL*, Dec. 22, 1768; see also ibid., Feb., 16, 1769; *BEP*, Jan. 2, 1764, Nov. 21, 1763.

107. The Impartialist, in *MGBWNL*, Dec. 22, 1768; see also ibid., Feb. 16, 1769.

108. "A Few Thoughts," *NYM*, Aug. 27, 1764; see also *Considerations Upon the Act of Parliament*, pp. 3–4, 6.

109. Z. T., in *BEP*, Feb. 6, July 3, 1769; "Letters in Answer to the Farmer's," *BEP*, June 5, 1769; Americanus, in *BC*, Feb. 12, 1770; John Herbert, in *BEP*, Mar. 13, 1769.

110. "A Few Thoughts," *NYM*, Aug. 27, 1764.

111. "To the Publick," *MGBWNL*, Dec. 19, 1771.

112. See William D. Liddle, "Virtue and Liberty: An Inquiry into the Role of the Agrarian Myth in the Rhetoric of The American Revolutionary Era," *South Atlantic Quarterly* 77 (1978): 15–38.

113. Seabury, *Free Thoughts*, p. 44.

114. Ibid., p. 47.

115. Seabury, *Congress Canvassed*, p. 71.

116. Brutus, in *MGBWNL*, Aug. 4, 1774.

117. Phileirene, Apr. 1775, in *Am. Arch.*, 4th ser., 2: 289; see also Poplicola, *Every good citizen . . . ;* Leonard, *Mass.*, Jan. 2, 1775, pp. 159–160; Seabury, *Free Thoughts*, p. 55; Inglis, *True Interest*, pp. 47–49. Two British articles published in New York stressed the importance of commerce to national wealth and power: *Public Ledger* reprint, in *NYJGA*, Apr. 27, 1769; Rationalis, in *NYM*, Jan. 20, 1766.

118. See Ralph Lerner, "Commerce and Character: The Anglo-American as New-Model Man," *WMQ*, 3rd ser., 36 (1979): 3–26; Drew R. McCoy, "Benjamin Franklin's Vision of a Republican Political Economy," *WMQ*, 3rd ser., 35 (1978): 605–628.

119. Leonard, *Mass.*, Mar. 20, 1775, pp. 215–216.

120. "An Address to the Inhabitants of Cortlandt's Manor," *RIV*, Feb. 16, 1775; Ferling, *Loyalist Mind*, p. 13.

121. Lerner, "Commerce and Character," p. 14.

122. Inglis, *True Interest,* pp. 47–49; Seabury, *A View,* pp. 122, 135; Smith, "Thoughts Upon the Dispute," p. 118; Phileirene, in *MGBWNL,* Jan. 26, 1775; Leonard, *Mass.,* Mar. 20, 1775, pp. 213–215; Timothy Ruggles, in *BEP,* Feb. 29, 1768; *BC,* Mar. 7, 1768; Potter and Calhoon, "Character and Coherence of The Loyalist Press," pp. 250–258.

123. Poplicola, in *RIV,* Nov. 18, 1773.

124. Appleby, *Economic Thought and Ideology,* p. 277.

125. Inglis, *True Interest,* p. 40; see also "A Plan to Perpetuate the Union between Great Britain and America to the Latest Period of Time," *BEP,* July 26, 1773; Leonard, *Mass.,* Mar. 20, 1775, p. 213; Phileirene, Apr. 1775, in *Am. Arch.,* 4th ser., 2: p. 287.

126. Wilkins, "Speech," *RIV,* Apr. 6, 1775.

7. Loyalist Ideology and the First Continental Congress

1. Chandler, *American Querist,* p. 5.

2. Leonard, *Mass.,* Dec. 12, 1774, pp. 144–145; also, Oliver, "An Address"; Phileirene, in *MGBWNL,* Jan. 26, 1775.

3. Seabury, *Free Thoughts,* p. 49.

4. Seabury, *Free Thoughts,* pp. 46–50; also Phileirene, in *MGBWNL,* Feb. 9, 1775.

5. Seabury, *A View,* p. 140; Leonard, *Mass.,* Dec. 19, 1774, p. 150.

6. Democritus, *Remarks Upon the Resolves of the New Committee* (New York, 1774); see also Plain Heart, in *MGBWNL,* Feb. 16, 1775; Chandler, *What Think Ye,* p. 14; Seabury, *Free Thoughts,* p. 46.

7. Wilkins, "Speech," *RIV,* Apr. 6, 1775; see also Adair and Schutz, *Oliver's Origin,* p. 74; Chandler, *American Querist,* p. 20; Leonard, *Mass.,* Dec. 12, 1774, p. 145; Oliver, "An Address."

8. Oliver, "An Address"; Phileirene, in *MGBWNL,* Jan. 26, 1775; A Friend to New England, in *MGBPB&AD,* Jan. 16–23, 1775; Seabury, *A View,* pp. 140–141.

9. See Maier, *From Resistance to Revolution,* pp. 161–197.

10. Leonard, *Mass.,* Dec. 12, 1774, p. 143.

11. Ibid., Jan. 23, 1775, p. 183; Jan. 9, 1775, p. 169.

12. Oliver, "An Address"; see also Leonard, *Mass.,* Dec. 12, 1774, p. 145; X, in *MGBWNL,* June 16, 1774; *MGBWNL,* June 23, 1774.

13. Major Benjamin Floyd and a great number of others, in *RIV,* Apr. 6, 1775; "Extract of a Letter from London," *RIV,* Feb. 16, 1775; "Declaration of the Grand Jury," *RIV,* Apr. 6, 1775; "Colonel Guy Johnson to New York Congress," July 8, 1775, in *Am. Arch.,* 4th ser., 2: 1669; A New York Freeholder, in *NYGWM,* Oct. 10, 1774; Seabury, *Congress Canvassed,* p. 75; M, in *RIV,* Dec. 1, 1774; America's Real Friend, in *RIV,* Feb. 16, 1775; Chandler, *Friendly Address,* pp. 23–24.

14. Chandler, *Friendly Address,* pp. 49, 53; see also Bellisarius, in *RIV,* Mar. 9, 1775.

15. Seabury, *An Alarm,* p. 160; see also *Congress Canvassed,* p. 88; Inglis, *True Interest,* pp. vi, vii; Chandler, *Friendly Address,* p. 24; Lieutenant Governor

Cadwallader Colden, "Answer to the New York Association," May 13, 1775, in *The American Revolution: New York as a Case Study,* ed. Larry R. Gerlach (Belmont, Calif., 1972), pp. 75–76.

16. John Adams, *Novanglus,* in Leonard, *Mass.,* Feb. 6, 1775, p. 28.

17. Leonard, *Mass.,* Dec. 12, 1774, p. 145; see also Phileirene, in *MGBWNL,* Jan. 26, 1775; X.W., in *MGBWNL,* Jan. 5, 1775.

18. Leonard, *Mass.,* Jan. 2, 1775, p. 166.

19. *To the Freeholders, Freemen and Inhabitants of the City of New York; and Particularly to Our Steady Friends and Associates the Children, and Negroes of the Said City* (New York, 1774).

20. Agrippa, in *RIV,* Mar. 30, 1775.

21. A Freeman, in *RIV,* July 21, 1774; "To the Principal Gentlemen and Merchants of New York," *RIV,* Sept. 29, 1774; "Queen's County, Long Island, Letters," *RIV,* Jan. 19, 1775; Agrippa, in *RIV,* Mar. 30, 1775; America's Real Friend, in *RIV,* Feb. 16, 1775; Philo-Libertas, in *RIV,* Oct. 20, 1774; R.L., Jamaica, Long Island, in *RIV,* Dec. 22, 1774.

22. See, for instance, "Lancaster Instructions to their Representative, Asa Whitecomb," *MGBWNL,* May 26, 1774; "Braintree Instructions to Ebenezer Thayer," *MGBWNL,* June 2, 1774; K.D., in *MGBWNL,* June 16, 1774; Brown, *Revolutionary Politics in Massachusetts,* pp. 178–210; "Protest against the Solemn League and Covenant [Boston]," *MHS* 10–13 (1871–1873): 46–47.

23. See, for instance, "Address of the Gentlemen Who Were Driven from Their Habitants in the Country to the Town of Boston, To His Excellency Thomas Gage, Esq. (76 signatures)," in *Am. Arch.,* 4th ser., 3: 970–979; "Address Presented to His Excellency Governor Gage, June 11, 1774 on His Arrival at Salem (48 signatures)," in Stark, *Massachusetts Loyalists,* p. 131; "The Loyal Address from the Gentlemen and Principal Inhabitants of Boston to Governor Gage on His Departure for England, October 6, 1775 (97 signatures)," ibid., p. 132; "The Loyal Address to Governor Gage on His Departure, October 14, 1775, of Those Gentlemen who were driven from Their Habitations in the Country to the Town of Boston," ibid., p. 132; see also "Letter from Falmouth Casco Bay to Governor Hutchinson," Feb. 10, 1774, in *Am. Arch.,* 4th ser., 3: 675–676; Loyalist Association, in *MGBWNL,* Dec. 29, 1774; "A Protest of Some of the Inhabitants of the Town of Plymouth against Town Resolves," *BEP,* Dec. 27, 1773; "Marshfield Town Meeting," *MGBPB&AD,* Jan. 31–Feb. 7, 1774; article from *Boston Weekly News-Letter,* June 30, 1774, in Brown, *Revolutionary Politics in Massachusetts,* pp. 206–207; "Addressers to Governor Thomas Hutchinson," *BEP,* May 30, 1774; "Protest by Forty-Three Voters and Freeholders, June 20, 1774, at Worcester Town Meeting," in Davis, *Confiscation of John Chandler's Estate,* pp. 252–253.

24. "White Plains, Westchester County Meeting, I. Wilkins, S. Seabury (312 signatures)," *RIV,* Apr. 20, 1775; "Subscribers, Freeholders and Inhabitants of Rye in Westchester Country (82 signatures)," *RIV,* Oct. 13, 1774; *RIV,* Jan. 12, 1775; "A Number in Ulster (Resolution)," *RIV,* Jan. 26, 1775; "Newton, Queen's County, Long Island, (57 signaures)," *RIV,* Jan. 19, 1775; Loyalist Association, in *RIV,* Feb. 9, 1775; "Dutchess County Address," *RIV,* Feb. 9, 1775; "Form of an

Association in Cortlandt's Manor," *RIV,* Feb. 16, 1775; "Remarks about Danbury Town Meeting," *RIV,* Feb. 23, 1775; One of the Associations in Dutchess County, in *RIV,* Mar. 30, 1775; Major Benjamin Floyd and a great number of others, in *RIV,* Apr. 6, 1775; "Declaration of Grand Jury," *RIV,* Apr. 6, 1775; "Resolves of the Town Meeting, Hampstead, Queen's County," *RIV,* Apr. 6, 1775; "Borough of Westchester," *RIV,* Apr. 6, 1775; "Reading Association (150 signatures)," *RIV,* Apr. 20, 1775; "Protest of the Freeholders of the Seven Precincts in Dutchess County, New York, Apr. 1775," in *Am. Arch.,* 4th ser., 2: 304.

25. Charles Inglis to the Rev. Richard Hind, secretary of SPG, Oct. 31, 1776, in Lydekker, *Life and Letters of Charles Inglis,* p. 159.

26. Oliver, "An Address"; "Form of an Association in Cortlandt's Manor," *RIV,* Feb. 16, 1775; "Extract of a Letter from London," *RIV,* Feb. 16, 1775; Inglis, *True Interest,* p. 30; "An Account Between Britain and Her Colonies Candidly Stated," *NYGWM,* June 6, 1774; Rusticus, in *NYGWM,* Jan. 16, 1775; Phileirene, in *MGBWNL,* Jan. 26, 1775; *RIV,* July 13, 1775.

27. Wilkins, "Speech," *RIV,* Apr. 6, 1775; see also A Merchant of New York, in *RIV,* Aug. 18, 1774, who stated that a parent could not "kneel" to a child, "human nature revolts from such an idea."

28. Van Schaack, "Journal," Jan. 1776, in *Life of Peter Van Schaack,* p. 56; see also Z.F., in *MGBPB&AD,* Aug. 15–22, 1774; "A Tory Grafted on Whig Principles," *MGBPB&AD,* Jan. 23–30, 1775; C., in *MGBWNL,* Feb. 16, 1775; Plain Heart, in *MGBWNL,* Feb. 16, 1775.

29. Even William Smith, Jr., of New York, who delayed his ultimate decision to remain loyal until after the Declaration of Independence, devoted all of his efforts toward reconciliation. See, for example, Smith to Philip Schuyler, 16 May, 1775, in Smith, *Historical Memoirs,* p. 223; Smith to General Haldimand, Oct. 6, 1775, ibid., p. 241, wrote, "The Weal of the Whole Empire is my Aim."

30. Leonard, *Mass.,* Mar. 20, 1775, p. 217; see also A Yeoman of Suffolk County, in *RIV,* Feb. 16, 1775.

31. Phileirene, in *MGBWNL,* Mar. 9, 1775; Conciliator, in *MGBPB&AD,* Feb. 6–13, 1775; Leonard, *Mass.,* Feb. 27, 1775, p. 202; Mar. 20, 1775, p. 217; A Non Consumer, in *MGBWNL,* Aug. 25, 1774; C., in *MGBWNL,* Feb. 16, 1775; Plain Heart, in *MGBWNL,* Feb. 16, 1775.

32. *At a Meeting of the True Sons of Liberty in the City of New York* (New York, 1774).

33. "Extract of a Letter from a Gentleman in London to His Correspondent in Boston," *MGBWNL,* May 26, 1774; Leonard, *Mass.,* Jan. 2, 1775, pp. 160–163; Phileirene, April 1775, in *Am. Arch.,* 4th ser., 2: 325; Z., in *BEP,* Oct. 25, 1773; "Tradesmen's Protest," *BEP,* Nov. 15, 1773.

34. The Querist, in *MGBWNL,* Nov. 24, 1774; "A Tory Grafted on Whig Principles," *MGBPB&AD,* Jan. 23–30, 1775; A New York Freeholder, in *NYGWM,* Sept. 26, 1774; Seabury, *Free Thoughts,* p. 48.

35. Poplicola, *The cause . . .* ; Seabury, *Congress Canvassed,* p. 93; "Declaration of Grand Jury," *RIV,* Apr. 6, 1775.

36. Seabury, *Free Thoughts,* p. 48; Chandler, *American Querist,* p. 25; Wilkins,

"Speech," *RIV*, Apr. 6, 1775; Oliver, "An Address."

37. "Declaration of Grand Jury," *RIV*, Apr. 6, 1775; A New York Freeholder, in *NYGWM*, Sept. 26, 1774; Phileirene, in *Am. Arch.*, 4th ser., 2: 325; "A Protest of Some of the Inhabitants of the Town of Plymouth against the Town Resolves," *BEP*, Dec. 27, 1773; Grotius, *Pills for the Delegates or the Chairman Chastised* (New York, 1775); "Marshfield Town Meeting," *MGBPB&AD*, Jan. 31-Feb. 7, 1774; Wilkins, "Speech," *RIV*, Apr. 6, 1775.

38. A New York Freeholder, in *NYGWM*, Sept. 26, 1774; "Rev. William Clarke, rector of St. Paul's Church, Dedham, to William Fisher, Aug. 6, 1774," in Crary, *Price of Loyalty*, pp. 20, 26; Phileirene, in *Am. Arch.*, 4th ser., 2: 325; Grotius, *Pills for the Delegates.*

39. See Bushman, "Massachusetts Farmers in the Revolution," pp. 77-124, 104-109 for an analysis of the Massachusetts Patriot view of the significance of the 1688-89 Revolution; Bushman argued that the events of that time "perpetrated" anxieties about the security of land titles and about the greed of placemen.

40. Van Schaack, "Journal," Jan. 1776, in *Life of Peter Van Schaack*, p. 55.

41. Wilkins, "Speech," *RIV*, Apr. 6, 1775; see also Poplicola, in *RIV*, Nov. 18, 1773; Inglis, *True Interest*, p. 17; Plain English, in *RIV*, Mar. 9, 1775; Seabury, *A View*, p. 110; Leonard, *Mass.*, Jan. 9, 1775, p. 170.

42. Chandler, *American Querist*, p. 6.

43. Seabury, *A View*, pp. 111-112; see also "An Address to the Inhabitants of Cortlandt's Manor," *RIV*, Feb. 16, 1775; A Lover of Justice, in *MGBPB&AD*, Apr. 25-May 2, 1774; Leonard, *Mass.*, Jan. 9, 1775, p. 170.

44. Leonard, *Mass.*, Jan. 23, 1775, p. 180; see also *BEP* reprint, in *RIV*, Sept. 8, 1774; Seabury, *A View*, p. 116; T., in *BC*, Mar. 30, 1769; A Lover of Justice, in *MGBPB&AD*, Apr. 25-May 2, 1774; Thomas Hutchinson, "Speech of the Governor to the Two Houses, Jan. 6, 1773," in Hosmer, *Life of Thomas Hutchinson*, p. 364.

45. Seabury, *Congress Canvassed*, p. 97; Wilkins, "Speech," *RIV*, Apr. 6, 1775; Leonard, *Mass.*, Jan. 30, 1775, pp. 184-185.

46. "Extract of a Letter from London," *RIV*, Feb. 16, 1775; see also Inglis, *True Interest*, p. 50; Seabury, *A View*, pp. 111-112.

47. Leonard, *Mass.*, Feb. 20, 1775, p. 198.

48. Seabury, *Congress Canvassed*, p. 97.

49. Chandler, *American Querist*, p. 26.

50. Van Schaack, "Journal," Jan. 1776, in *Life of Peter Van Schaack*, p. 57.

51. "Form of an Association in Cortlandt's Manor," *RIV*, Feb. 16, 1775.

52. Leonard, *Mass.*, Dec. 26, 1774, p. 158.

53. Ibid., Jan. 9, 1775, pp. 171-172.

54. Hutchinson, *Diary and Letters*, London, July 14, 1774, pp. 188-189.

55. See, for instance, Chandler, *What Think Ye*; Seabury, *Congress Canvassed*; Grotius, "To the Honourable Peyton Randolph, Esq.," *MGBPB&AD*, Jan. 23-30, 1775; Grotius, *Pills for the Delegates*; Bob Jingles Esq., *The Association and Co*; A Freeholder of Essex, in *RIV*, Jan. 5, 1775.

56. Wilkins, *Short Advice*, p. 10.

57. Leonard, *Mass.*, Mar. 27, 1775, p. 220; see also Chandler, *What Think Ye,* pp. 25, 40; Seabury, *Congress Canvassed,* p. 73; Phileirene, April 1775, in *Am. Arch.,* 4th ser., 2: 325; *A Dialogue Between a Southern Delegate and his Spouse* (New York, 1774).

58. Benjamin W. Labaree, "The Idea of American Independence: The British View," *Proceedings of Massachusetts Historical Society* 82 (1970): 3-20; Ammerman, *In the Common Cause,* pp. 13-15.

59. Ammerman, *In the Common Cause,* pp. 53-88; Rakove, "Decision for American Independence"; Rakove, *Beginnings of National Politics,* pp. 21-62.

60. Bailyn, *Ordeal,* pp. 62-63.

61. Ibid., pp. 64-65.

62. Ibid., p. 279.

63. Ibid., pp. 274-310.

64. Rakove, "Decision for American Independence," pp. 233-234; Ammerman, *In the Common Cause,* pp. 73-87.

65. Rakove, "Decision for American Independence"; Ammerman, *In the Common Cause,* pp. 134-135.

66. Frederick V. Mills, "Anglican Expansion in Colonial America, 1761-1775," *Historical Magazine of the Protestant Episcopal Church* 39 (1970): 315-324; see also Bruce E. Steiner, "New England Anglicanism: A Genteel Faith?" *WMQ,* 3rd ser., 27 (1970): 136-144.

67. Bernard Bailyn and John Clive, "England's Cultural Provinces: Scotland and America," *WMQ,* 3rd ser., 25 (1968): 177-211.

68. See, for instance, Smith, *Historical Memoirs,* Oct. 13, 1766, p. 35; Smith wrote that British merchants advised the governor of New York that the New York merchants Henry White, Hugh Wallace, and James McEvers be appointed to the New York Council. Upton, *Loyal Whig,* p. 58, pointed out that William Livingston and John Morin Scott had no influence in Britain and that the British government opposed their appointments to the Council.

69. Bradley Chapin, *The American Law of Treason: Revolutionary and Early National Origins* (Seattle, 1964), pp. 6-9.

70. James A. Henretta, *"Salutary Neglect": Colonial Administration under the Duke of Newcastle* (Princeton, 1972); Jack P. Greene, "The Plunge of Lemmings: A Consideration of Recent Writings on British Politics and The American Revolution," *South Atlantic Quarterly* 67 (1968): 141-175; Ian R. Christie, *Crisis of Empire: Great Britain and the American Colonies, 1754-83* (London, 1966); Christie, *Myth and Reality;* Michael Kammen, *A Rope of Sand: The Colonial Agents, British Politics and the American Revolution* (Ithaca, N.Y., 1968); John Shy, *Toward Lexington: The Role of the British Army in the Coming of the American Revolution* (Princeton, 1962); Jack M. Soisin, *Agents and Merchants: British Colonial Policy and the Origins of the American Revolution, 1763-1775* (Lincoln, Neb., 1965); Greene, "Uneasy Connection"; Greene, "A Posture of Hostility: A Reconsideration of Some Aspects of the Origins of the American Revolution," *American Antiquarian Society Proceedings,* 87 (1977): 27-68.

71. See Chapter 8.

72. See Pares, *King George III and the Politicians;* Foord, *His Majesties' Opposition;* John Brewer, *Party Ideology and Popular Politics at the Accession of George III* (New York, 1976); Greene, "Plunge of Lemmings."

73. Greene, "Plunge of Lemmings"; Labaree, "Idea of American Independence," pp. 6–8; Koebner, *Empire.*

74. Ammerman, *In the Common Cause,* pp. 35–50.

75. See Kammen, "American Revolution as a *Crise de Conscience,*" pp. 144–155; Bruce Bliven, Jr., *Under the Guns: New York, 1775–1776* (New York, 1972), p. 50.

76. "The Pausing American Loyalist" (1776), in Tyler, *Literary History,* II: 54–55.

77. Rhys Isaac, "Preachers and Patriots: Popular Culture and the Revolution in Virginia," in Young, *American Revolution: Explorations in the History of American Radicalism,* pp. 125–156.

78. Plain Heart, in *MGBWNL,* Feb. 16, 1775; Anti-Licentiousness, in *RIV,* Apr. 20, 1775; Z. T., in *BEP,* May 15, 1769, quoted in Potter and Calhoon, "Character and Coherence of the Loyalist Press," pp. 239–240.

79. See Chapter 8.

80. Phileirene, in *MGBWNL,* Mar. 30, 1775; Jan. 26, 1775.

81. Phileirene, in *MGBWNL,* Jan. 26, 1775.

82. Rakove, "Decision for American Independence," p. 222–224; Ammerman, *In the Common Cause,* pp. 150–151.

83. Rakove, "Decision for American Independence," p. 224.

84. *Dialogue Between a Southern Delegate and His Spouse.*

8. The Loyalist Alternative

1. Phileirene, in *MGBWNL,* Feb. 9, 1775; Wilkins, *Short Advice,* p. 15.

2. Chronus, in *MGBPB&AD,* Dec. 2, 1771; *At a Meeting of the True Sons of Liberty in the City of New York, July 27, 1774* (New York, 1774).

3. Seabury, *Free Thoughts,* p. 66; Freeman, in *MGBWNL,* Aug. 4, 1774; Brutus, in *MGBWNL,* July 28, 1774, County of Ulster, in *RIV,* Jan. 26, 1775; see also Jonathan Boucher, *A Letter from a Virginian to the Members of Congress* (New York, 1774), p. 24; Ferling, *Loyalist Mind,* p. 123.

4. *RIV,* Apr. 20, 1775.

5. "Newton, Queen's County, Long Island," *RIV,* Jan. 19, 1775; "Danbury Town Meeting," *RIV,* Feb. 23, 1775; "Resolves of Town Meeting, Hampstead, Queen's County," *RIV,* Apr. 6, 1775.

6. *RIV,* Apr. 13, 1775.

7. County of Ulster, in *RIV,* Mar. 2, 1775.

8. *RIV,* Feb. 9, *RIV,* Mar. 2, 1775; Loyalist Association, in *MGBWNL,* Dec. 29, 1774; Kenneth Scott, "Tory Associators of Portsmouth," *WMQ,* 3rd ser., 17 (1960): 507–515.

9. Wilkins, "Speech," *RIV,* Apr. 6, 1775; Rusticus, in *NYGWM,* Jan. 16, 1775; Smith, "Thoughts upon the Dispute," p. 112; Seabury, *Congress Canvassed,*

p. 76; see also Benton, *Whig-Loyalism;* Ferling, *Loyalist Mind,* p. 19; Zimmer, *Jonathan Boucher,* p. 61. Boucher was very critical of the 1763 Proclamation and the Stamp Act.

10. Smith, "Thoughts upon the Dispute," pp. 112, 114; see also Rusticus, in *NYGWM,* Jan. 16, 1775, who complained about the "ignorance or Inattention of a weak or corrupt ministry."

11. Adair and Schutz, *Oliver's Origin,* p. 56; Leonard, *Mass.,* Dec. 26, 1774, p. 155; see also Sir Francis Bernard, *The Bernard-Barrington Correspondence and Illustrative Matter, 1760–1770 Drawn from the Papers of Sir Francis Bernard,* ed. Edward Channing and A. C. Coolidge (Cambridge, Mass., 1912), July 30, 1768, p. 170: "The indifference which has been shown in England to the Checking the Demagogues of America for so long a time has at length so effectually discouraged the friends of government, that they have been gradually falling off, till at length the cause is become desperate."

12. "Plan of Reconciliation," *RIV,* Nov. 2, 1775.

13. Conciliator, in *MGBPB&AD,* Feb. 6–13, 1775; Phileirene, April 1775, in *Am. Arch.,* 4th ser., 2: 325.

14. Seabury, *A View,* pp. 122–123; see also Inglis, *True Interest,* p. 39; Chandler, *What Think Ye,* p. 7; Wilkins, "Speech," *RIV,* Apr. 6, 1775.

15. Henretta, *"Salutary Neglect."*

16. Wilkins, "Speech," *RIV,* Apr. 6, 1775.

17. Jack P. Greene, "Martin Bladen's Blueprint for a Colonial Union," *WMQ,* 3rd ser., 17 (1960): 516.

18. Ibid., p. 530.

19. Koebner, *Empire,* pp. 101–104.

20. Ibid., pp. 106–107.

21. Koebner, *Empire,* pp. 105–118; see also Gerald Stourzh, *Benjamin Franklin and American Foreign Policy* (Chicago, 1954), pp. 33–83; for an earlier American proposal, see Louis B. Wright, ed., *An Essay Upon the Government of the English Plantations on the Continent of America* (San Marino, Calif., 1954), pp. 20–54, cited in Ferling, *Loyalist Mind,* p. 89.

22. Koebner, *Empire,* pp. 61–104; Roy N. Lokken, "Sir William Keith's Theory of the British Empire," *Historian* 25 (1963): 403–418.

23. Francis Bernard, *Principles of Law and Polity Applied to the Government of the British Colonies in America, Written in the Year 1764,* Public Archives of Canada, pamphlet collection; Koebner, *Empire,* pp. 131–140; Morgan, *Stamp Act Crisis,* pp. 7–20.

24. William Knox, *The Present State of the Nation, Particularly with Respect to Trade and Fisheries: Addressed to the King and Both Houses of Parliament* (London, 1768); see also Jack P. Greene, "William Knox's Explanation for the American Revolution," *WMQ,* 3rd ser., 30 (1973): 293–306; Leland J. Bellot, *William Knox: The Life and Thought of an Eighteenth Century Imperialist* (Austin, Tex., 1977).

25. *Barrington-Bernard Correspondence,* Jan. 28, 1768, p. 138.

26. G. H. Gutteridge, "Thomas Pownall's *The Administration of the Colonies, The Six Editions,*" *WMQ,* 3rd ser., 26 (1969): 33, 31–46; Koebner, *Empire,* pp. 175–178; John A. Schutz, *Thomas Pownall: British Defender of American Liberty: A*

Study of Anglo-American Relations in the Eighteenth Century (Glendale, Calif., 1951), pp. 183–194.

27. *Public Ledger* reprint, in *BEP,* Dec. 31, 1764; Jan. 7, 1765; *London Gazetteer* reprint, in *BEP,* Feb. 10, 1766.

28. "Letter from England . . . to Ministry," *BEP,* Dec. 30, 1765; *BC,* Jan. 20, 1769; *London Daily Advertiser* reprint, in *NYM,* Nov. 25, 1765; "Extract from a Member of Parliament in England to a Friend in America," *NYM,* Aug. 5, 1765.

29. *BC,* Jan. 30, 1769.

30. Candidus, in *BEP,* Nov. 21, 1768.

31. Britannicus, in *MG,* Feb. 7, 1765; A.B., in *MG,* Feb. 7, 1765; *BEP,* Feb. 11, 1765; *BEP,* Apr. 28, 1766.

32. Americanus, in *NYJGA,* Oct. 30, 1766; Americanus was the pseudonym used by Galloway, and the ideas in the article resembled Galloway's.

33. *Pennsylvania Gazette* reprint, in *EG,* Aug. 16–23, 1768.

34. Amor Patriae, in *MGBWNL,* Jan. 19, 1769.

35. Smith, "Thoughts upon the Dispute," pp. 114–115.

36. Ibid., pp. 115–116.

37. Chandler, *What Think Ye,* p. 7; Leonard, *Mass.,* Feb. 27, 1775, p. 202; A New York Freeholder, in *NYGWM,* Sept. 26, 1774; Chandler, *Friendly Address,* p. 47; see also "A Plan of Reconciliation," *RIV,* Nov. 2, 1775; Inglis, *True Interest,* pp. 34, 39, 62; *To the Inhabitants of the British Colonies in America* (New York, 1774); "An Account between Britain and Her Colonies Candidly Stated," *NYGWM,* June 6, 1774; Phileirene, in *MGBWNL,* Feb. 9, 1775; Wilkins, "Speech," *RIV,* Apr. 6, 1775; A New York Freeholder, in *NYGWM,* Sept. 19, 1774.

38. Inglis, *True Interest,* p. viii; Seabury, *A View,* p. 126; Wilkins, "Speech," *RIV,* Apr. 6, 1775; "A Plan of Reconciliation," *RIV,* Nov. 2, 1775; see also A Friend to Great Britain, in *MGBWNL,* Jan. 7, 1773; *To the Inhabitants of the British Colonies in America.* "A Plan to Perpetuate the Union Between Britain and America to the Latest Period of Time," *BEP,* July 26, 1773, was one of the few plans which envisaged a union under the king rather than Parliament.

39. Julian P. Boyd, *Anglo-American Union: Joseph Galloway's Plans to Preserve the British Empire, 1774–1787* (Philadelphia, 1941), p. 114; Ferling, *Loyalist Mind,* pp.81–100.

40. "The following Plan of Legislation, Proposed for the Consideration of Both Houses of Parliament; for Establishing a Permanent and Solid Foundation for a Just, Constitutional Union Between Great Britain and Her Colonies," *RIV,* Aug. 4, 1774; *MGBPB&AD,* Aug. 8–15, 1774. The similarity in language and phraseology can be seen where the British author wrote that because of the defects of "their colonial constitutions, many disorders have crept in, subversive of peace and good order . . . and the rights of the commerce of this kingdom." Smith, p. 116, had written that because of "The Diversity of Their Colony Constitutions, many Disorders have crept in, . . . dangerous . . . and detrimental to . . . British Creditors . . . Peace and Good Order." Other British proposals in the 1770s advocating Anglo-American union were also published in the colonies; see, for instance, Rev. Dr. Josiah Tucker, Dean of Gloucester, "A Plan for Settling the Dis-

putes Between Great Britain and the Colonies," *BEP,* Aug. 1, 1774; "A Fresh Proposal of Dean Tucker's for Governing the Colonies," *RIV,* Sept. 15, 1774; *London Chronicle* reprint, in *NYGWM,* May 30, 1774. See also "Earl of Dartmouth to Lieutenant Governor [Cadwallader] Colden, Jan. 7, 1775," in *Am. Arch.,* 4th ser., 2: 1101, where Dartmouth wrote that the plan of constitutional union presented at the Continental Congress by Joseph Galloway was just and attainable. *A Plan for Conciliating the Jarring Political Interests of Great Britain and Her North American Colonies and for Promoting a General Re-Union Throughout the Whole of the British Empire* (London, 1775), advocated the creation of the Supreme Council of Colonies and Commerce, comprising a limited number of British delegates chosen from the House of Lords, House of Commons, and the Privy Council, and American delegates chosen by ballot by members of the assemblies.

41. Morgan, *Stamp Act Crisis,* p. 106.

42. Zimmer, *Jonathan Boucher,* p. 153.

43. Greene, "Uneasy Connection," pp. 40–61.

44. Ibid.; see also Van Alstyne, *Rising American Empire.*

45. Greene, "Uneasy Connection."

46. Inglis, *True Interest,* p. 35; see also Wilkins, "Speech," *RIV,* Apr. 6, 1775; A Friend to Great Britain, in *MGBWNL,* Jan. 7, 1773.

47. Chandler, *Friendly Address,* p. 4.

48. Smith, "Thoughts upon the Dispute," p. 118.

49. Leonard, *Mass.,* Jan. 9, 1775, pp. 172–173; Inglis, *True Interest,* p. 71.

50. Bailyn, *Origins of American Politics,* pp. 66–80; Lucas, "Note on the Structure of Politics."

51. Greene, "Uneasy Connection," pp. 42–43.

52. Greene, "Martin Bladen's Blueprint," p. 520.

53. *Select Letters on the Trade and Government of America, and the Principles of Law and Polity, Applied to the American Colonies* (London, 1764), quoted in Morgan, *Stamp Act Crisis,* p. 14; see also Koebner, *Empire,* pp. 136–143; Schutz, *Thomas Pownall,* pp. 186–187; Pownall worried about the excessive power of the assemblies and the weakness of the governors.

54. The "Dougliad," *NYGWM,* Apr. 23, 1770.

55. "Epitaph for Jemmy," *BEP,* June 15, 1767; "Letters in Answer to the Farmer's Letters," *BEP,* Apr. 10, 1769; see also ABC, in *BEP,* Sept. 20, 1773; Morgan, *Stamp Act Crisis,* p. 18–19.

56. Morgan, *Stamp Act Crisis,* pp. 16–17.

57. *MGBNL,* May 31, 1764.

58. Smith, "Thoughts upon the Dispute," p. 115.

59. Joseph Galloway, "Two Plans of Union: Set forth in a Letter from Joseph Galloway to Lord George Germain, March 18, 1779," in Boyd, *Anglo-American Union,* pp. 117, 121; see also Calhoon, *Loyalists in Revolutionary America,* p. 83.

60. *Censor,* Dec. 21, Dec. 7, Nov. 30, 1771; Chronus, in *MGBPB&AD,* Jan. 6, 1772; Leonard, *Mass.,* Dec. 26, 1774, p. 158.

61. *Censor,* Nov. 30, 1771; Jan. 4, 1772; Adair and Schutz, *Oliver's Origin,* pp.

108, 30, 113; Sewall advocated an independent council and judiciary as in England: see Phileirene, in *MGBWNL,* Mar. 9, 1775.

62. Leonard, *Mass.,* Jan. 9, 1775, pp. 171–172; Feb. 13, 1775, pp. 192–194; see also The Querist, in *MGBWNL,* Nov. 24, 1774, who supported the changes in the Massachusetts government contained in the Coercive Acts.

63. *Censor,* Nov. 30, 1771; Jan. 4, 1772.

64. Paine, *Common Sense,* pp. 9–12.

65. *Censor,* Dec. 7, 1771.

66. Philanthrop, in *BEP,* Jan. 14, 1771; see also Inglis, *True Interest,* p. 70; Crito, in *MGBWNL,* Mar. 18, 1773; Seabury, *A View,* p. 111; The Querist, in *MGBWNL,* Nov. 24, 1774; Zimmer, *Jonathan Boucher,* p. 277.

INDEX

A.B.C., 70

Act of Settlement, 88

Adams, John, 39; on *Massachusettensis,* 4; on man's nature, 40; on colonial history, 112; on British Empire, 109; on America, 136

Adams, Samuel, 23, 24, 71

addresses: Loyalist, 11, 137, 149, 155; Patriot, 143, 155

Administration of the Colonies (Pownall), 161-162

agrarian myth, 128

America: social and economic changes in, 51, 180; as part of New World, 110; colonization of, 112-113; defense of, 113-114; Loyalist views of, 130, 135-136, 141-142, 171-172; American views of, 160-161, 163; British views of, 160-161, 163

Americanus, 163. *See also* Galloway, Joseph

"American Whig," 74-77

anarchy: warnings of, 15, 16, 25, 71-72, 79, 80-82; and Loyalist view of Revolution, 25-28, 179; continental, 34-36, 130; and passion, 45; and factionalism, 50; and Loyalist ideology, 54-55, 64-65; Loyalist and Patriot views of, 59-60; and political disputes, 62-63, 65, 74; and mixed government, 86; and court party ideology, 90, 91, 94; Blackstone on, 103; and Parliamentary sovereignty, 142, 143

Anatomist, the, 75-77

Anglican church: in New York, 2, 74-77; and Loyalist spokesmen, 3, 9, 10, 188n39; defense of, 3, 74-77; and Loyalist history of Revolution, 21; and Book of Common Prayer, 33; political disputes involving, 162, 174; as trans-Atlantic institution, 144, 145-146; and Loyalist appeal, 149. *See also* church; Protestantism; religion

Anglo-American crisis, *see* British-American crisis

Anti-Licentiousness, 22

Appleby, Joyce, 130

aristocracy, 86, 175

army: British, 31, 37, 141-142, 148; standing, 90

Ashfield, Mass., 12-13

assembly: New York, 77-78, 79; and colonial reform, 173, 175; and balanced constitution, 177

Association, the: and Loyalist appeal, 7; Loyalist views of, 29, 143, 148, 156; and Patriot tyranny, 37-38; and Patriot appeal, 150

associations, Loyalist, 4, 11, 137, 155-156

Bailey, Jacob, 9

balance-of-trade theory, 126

Baptists, 12-13

Baron, Richard, 95

Barrell, Colburn, 203n51

Bernard, Francis, 174; defense of, 4, 66-70, 157-158; on imperial reform, 161, 162; and colonial reform, 173

bill of rights, 57; of 1689, 88, 177

Blackstone, Sir William, 10, 85, 86, 101-106

Bladen, Martin, 159, 160, 173, 175

Bolingbroke, Viscount (Henry St. John),